CW01664002

Plantsmen on Plants

Helleborus orientalis hybrids

PLANTSMEN ON PLANTS

An Anthology in Memory of

Barbara White

Compiled and Edited by

Richard Bird

HARDY PLANT SOCIETY

First published 1990

ISBN 0901687 04 9

© Hardy Plant Society
Garden Cottage
214 Ruxley Lane
West Ewell
Surrey KT17 9EU

Photo credits:
Black and white from the Harry Smith Collection
Colour by Richard Bird

Printed by Satellite Press, Huntingdon

Contents

Coloured illustrations

Introduction

by Richard Bird

MISS White was the Secretary of the Hardy Plant Society from 1963 until her death in 1987. It was through her hard work and enthusiasm that the Society kept alive in difficult times and then began to build up its strength towards the force it is today. We all have a great deal for which to be grateful to her. Even those recent Members, who possibly have never heard of Miss White, are benefiting from the years of hard work and generosity she put into the Society. Shortly before her final illness, the then Chairman discovered by chance her age and was horrified at the amount of work she was putting in, which would have eclipsed that of a person thirty years her junior.

It is to the memory of this indefatigable person that this volume is dedicated

As a lasting tribute, here are presented articles from the Society's bulletin, covering the years from its inception until the year of Miss White's death. The selection has been difficult as there have been hundreds of worthy pieces written over the years, but I have tried to select those that will stand the test of being read over again, that inform and entertain. Many of the authors have gone on to become very familiar names and I hope many readers will delight in reading some of their writings that they have not seen before.

It is essential that the reader bears in mind that these articles were written over the last thirty-five years and that many things have changed in the intervening years. Plants that are now popular were not necessarily known, plants that were then popular have disappeared. At the beginning of this period it was still considered legitimate to collect plants from the wild and comments relating to this practice must be read with this in mind. I have resisted the temptation to rewrite parts of some of the articles in light of modern knowledge and experience; essentially they are the same as they first appeared with the exception of the updating of many of the botanical names to those with which we are more familiar today. In some cases this has been impractical to do without rewriting parts of the articles and this I have been reluctant to do. The date of each article is given at its conclusion and, while reading, should be borne in mind.

The order of the articles gave cause for thought. The possibility of placing them in rough groups, according to the subject and treatment, was abandoned to the notion of keeping them in chronological order. This gives the anthology a sense of continuity, but at the same time adds an element of excitement of not knowing what the next chapter will be about. With luck this makes it an ideal book for dipping into; perhaps for keeping beside the bed.

Miss White was a person to shun publicity, but I am sure that she would delight in the publication of this book in her name, in the anticipation of pleasure and information it will give to many of her fellow gardeners.

Miss Barbara White

by Noël J. Prockter

BARBARA White was born at Brockley in South East London on May 17th 1907 and died on April 9th 1987. Had she been spared for another five weeks she would have been eighty. Her parents left London in 1939 on account of the Second World War, and it was then that they moved to Emmer Green, Caversham, Reading. Her father was Head of the Engineering Department at Goldsmiths College, London and it was not surprising that Barbara White, who researched on seaweed, received a B.Sc. at Kings College, London.

Through her death the Hardy Plant Society has lost a stalwart and painstaking Secretary. It did not matter whether it was a new Member, home or abroad, or one who had been a Member for a long time, they all had the same friendly treatment.

We must thank Miss R. B. Pole, who was chairman from 1961 to 1971, for securing Barbara White as Honorary Secretary, the *News Letter* No. 6, July 1963 stated '. . . your committee has elected Miss Barbara White . . . to be acting Secretary until the next Annual General Meeting.' Therefore on March 10th 1964 Miss B. White was elected Honorary Secretary, a position she held up to the time of her death — which means she had steered the Hardy Plant Society both successfully and faithfully for twenty-three years.

In 1946, when she lived in her flat in London, she became a personal assistant to Dr Francis Avery Jones C.B.E., who was knighted for his medical research work in 1970. Sir Francis tells me that in the twenty-four years Barbara White worked for him in the Gastroenterological Research Department at the Central Middlesex Hospital, she kept records and looked after the library and helped overseas students with the same meticulous care and attention she later gave the Hardy Plant Society. I know this only too well as she was Honorary Secretary in my thirteen years as Chairman (1971-1984). When I became Chairman the membership was 543, by 1983 we had 2001 members, as I said in my Chairman's Annual Report 1982: 'Our thanks are due to our conscientious and loyal Hon. Secretary, Miss Barbara White . . . During Miss White's time the Society has held its 10th anniversary in 1967 and its 25th, its Silver Jubilee, in 1981.'

Miss Pole and Miss White did much to bring the H.P.S. in front of the public by staging stands at the Royal Horticultural Society, London, and also at Southport, Kent, Surrey and Sussex. Another way of interesting Members as well as attracting new ones was the opening of private gardens, in England, Scotland and Wales.

In June 1964, there were requests for a 'Seed Exchange'. I quote: 'If you are interested, please let the Hon. Secretary know . . . ' and in the past twenty years the Seed Exchange has grown to a major activity of the Society and seed comes from many Members in this country and abroad.

It must not be overlooked that Barbara White put in a great deal of work on the Society's various activities such as outings and exhibitions, of which the latter were always superbly arranged. The Royal Horticultural Society's July Hardy Flower Competitions have helped to create interest in hardy herbacious perennials, and Barbara White was always there.

The Society, both as a whole and as individual Members, owe her a great debt of gratitude and will truly miss her.

Originally published in 1987. Volume 9, number 1.

Advance of the Lupin

by A. G. L. Hellyer

IT is now six years since George Russell died and a good many more since he ceased to take a very active part in lupin breeding. What has happened since to the plant, for which he did so much, that Russell and lupin are now names indissolubly linked?

It must be admitted that he laid the foundations so well that no further spectacular advance was to be expected. But that does not mean that all the intensive breeding of lupins which has been carried on since his death has been wasted. Advances have been made in certain directions, new combinations of colour have appeared and the vigour of the race has been maintained. That, in itself, is a very important matter with a rather short-lived perennial such as the lupin, for in time the old varieties, however good they may be, must weaken, and some will do this more quickly than others.

All the same, some of the original Russell varieties still hold their own with all comers. This is true of 'Mrs Micklethwaite', a lupin that has been with us a number of years and is still as good as ever. If there is a better in its particular shade of salmon I have not seen it.

That magnificent yellow variety, 'Tom Reeves', is also no newcomer, but it is unsurpassed of its type; indeed, I know one good judge who considers it the best lupin ever raised.

'Lady Diana Abdy' is still one of the best blue and white lupins, though it has been with us for a generation and has had the later competition of such excellent varieties as 'Bluejacket' and 'Sailorboy'.

'George Russell' in clear-pink and 'City of York' which is red suffused with orange, are also old familiar names in the lupin world, but names which are unlikely to be superseded for a good many years to come.

One profitable line of development has been in the further extension of the lupin colour range already so magnificently endowed by George Russell himself. 'Charmaine' is an example, a lupin which starts as a fine terra-cotta red, the colour deepening as the flowers expand and finally fade. It is a grand variety in every way.

'Heatherglow' is aptly named for it brings the typical dulled red-purple of wild heather into the lupin. It is not, perhaps, everyone's choice, as I feel sure 'Charmaine' would be, but it is a welcome change for those who like something a bit different. The same is true of 'Wheatsheaf', which puts a flush of pink into a clear-yellow base.

In some cases the newer lupins repeat the charms of older varieties, but with improvements in detail. That, I think, is true of 'Rita', which is much like the old 'Beryl Viscountess Cowdray', but has a better constitution and will certainly be easier to keep for a number of years. It is a curious thing that these rich-red lupins have always had a tendency to be rather less robust (or perhaps it is that they are rather more subject to winter damp) than the rest, which, of course, gives one of the clues to successful lupin cultivation—good drainage, If I were asked to name a second essential it would be freedom from lime.

Two wonderful orange lupins are 'F. C. Puddle' and 'Guardsman', the first with deeper colour in the standards than in the keel petals, the second almost the same shade throughout.

The violet-purple 'Thundercloud' is the best in this colour, though I still feel that there is room for a Russell lupin with the depth and intensity of the old pre-Russell variety 'Happiness'. As a contrast to such deep shades, nothing could be better than the light-yellow 'Canary Bird' or cream 'Alicia Parrett'. Both are excellent, trouble-free garden plants.

I also have a particular affection for 'Gaiety Girl', a lively combination of cerise and cream. It is a most cheerful plant to have in the garden. And as, ever since the days of that great pre-Russell lupin 'Pink Pearls', I have felt that clear, self-pink is the loveliest of all lupin colours, I would add to my collection 'Betty Astell' as a companion to 'George Russell' already recommended. Its only fault is that it is not as strong-growing as some.

Originally published in 1957. Volume 1, number 1

Foliage Plants

by Margery Fish

A GOOD garden, to my way of thinking, is one that never has its off moments. Flowers come and go, and it needs skilful planning to prevent dull patches at various times in the season.

One way to keep the garden looking furnished and attractive all the time is to use a certain number of foliage plants which are large and solid enough to give a feeling of maturity and restfulness, and enhance the beauty of the flowers planted among them. With a good backbone of foliage it doesn't matter so much if there is a bad season and some plants are thin on the ground, or if things come out at the wrong time so that carefully planned sequences of colour go awry.

One of these 'backbone' plants is *Euphorbia characias wulfenii*. Its blue-green foliage is good all the year round, and given room to

Euphorbia characias wulfenii

spread it makes a bold symmetrical plant. It is quite adaptable and looks just as good planted in a corner or against a wall. I believe May is the conventional time for its flowering but it seems to vary in different places. With me, the great trusses of love-bird-green flowers come very early in the year but I have seen them as late as June.

Rue is another of my standbys. Any rue is good in the garden, but for the bluest foliage the one to choose is 'Jackman's Blue'. It makes a compact, bushy plant, about 2½ to 3 ft (75–100cm) tall, and has small yellow flowers in late June. The variegated form has much cream in the foliage and tends to grow upright rather than rounded.

Othonnopsis (Hertia) cheirifolia is rather low and spreading and does best in a hot, dry position. It has fleshy glaucous leaves which look just the same winter and summer, and golden daisy flowers early in the year.

It is hardly necessary to mention bergenia because I think we have all come to realize its usefulness in garden planning. Many flowers that look rather flimsy grown in the ordinary way take on a new beauty if planted with bergenia in front of them, and there is nothing better for giving strength and solidity to difficult beds, for clothing odd corners or bordering a path.

Marrubium incanum makes a nice hummock of woolly-grey-green which is an irresistible foil for nearly every kind of flower. The flowers are not worth worrying about and when the flower spikes get to the untidy stage of falling apart I cut them off so that the side shoots can have a chance.

Sages are evergreen and colourful and will make mounds of massive proportions in quite a short time. I think my favourite is the golden variegated version, *Salvia officinalis* 'Icterina'. It doesn't flower and it really doesn't need to because it brings as much sunshine into the border as a clump of golden flowers. The common green sage is a wonderful foil for roses, purple sage associates well with soft blue flowers, and I grow pink flowers near the purple form that is splashed with white and cherry.

Silver foliage is perhaps the most useful and there are several hardy plants from which to choose. In Somerset I find *Cineraria maritima* and *Centaurea gymnocarpa* will weather most winters, *Senecio* 'Blue Diamond' is all right if not too exposed, and *Senecio leuchostachys* is quite happy against a south wall, but in other parts of the country it is safer to take a few cuttings each year, or grow the cineraria from seed. The best artemisia for a vast swirl of feathery silver is *A. absinthium*, and it is quite hardy. When it begins to look untidy it can be trimmed back drastically and very soon a good crop of new growth will cover the plant and carry it through the winter. *Artemisia pontica* has pewter-coloured ferny foliage and is compact in growth, but loses its foliage in winter.

Santolina chamaecyparissus (S. incana) is ever-grey, hard wearing and dependable. In narrow beds the smaller version *S. incana nana* makes a neat mound, and does well in a wall, too. The lighter, more feathery *S. pinnata neapolitana* is taller and looser. In a neat garden I would plant it in a corner or against a wall. Some people do not like the rich yellow of typical santolina flowers and remove them ruthlessly. I too prefer pale colours and am lucky to have found several santolinas with sulphur flowers. The green leaved *S. rosmarinifolia (S. viridis)* makes a big cushion of bright green foliage, with flowers the greenish-yellow of lemons, which tone well with the green.

Whenever I have a problem corner to fill I use variegated apple-mint, *Mentha suaveolens* 'Variegata'. Softest grey-green generously dappled with white, it fits in anywhere. I have seen variegated figwort, *Scrophularia nodosa* 'Variegata', in several gardens this year. It is a most handsome plant when well grown and seems to do better with a little shade.

Originally published in 1957. Volume 1, number 2

Hardy Perennials for Dry Shade

by Will Ingwersen

MENTION of shade and shade-loving plants is apt to conjure visions of cool, damp places, in which ferns and candelabra primulas will riot. Very often the exact reverse is the case, and shade, especially when it is cast by tall and vigorous trees, implies a very considerable aridity of soil. Not only does the canopy of leafy branches keep off much of the rain which would otherwise fall on the ground, but the thirsty and far-spreading tree roots sup all the available moisture from the soil. Such positions as these are too often left bare and unclothed, or planted with quite unsuitable subjects which, finding conditions little to their liking, wilt, pine and finally succumb.

It is possible, by selection of plants which will grow in very dry soil and do not object to being overhung by branches, to create a rather special type of garden beneath trees. The number of plants appropriate to such a shade garden is not large, but is greater than is generally supposed.

It is only right to say, before describing a few of the plants which I have proved will thrive in such conditions, that some further limitations are imposed by the type of trees beneath which the plants are to grow. It is difficult, for example, to colonise plants beneath any type of coniferous tree, and, of deciduous trees, beeches are notoriously inhospitable to plant life. Even here, however, the difficulties are far from being insuperable, and certain plants can be induced to carpet the ground among acid decaying pine needles, or in the dense shade of far-flung beech tree branches carrying millions of horizontally arranged leaves.

A certain amount of preparation is advisable before attempting to establish plants in the dry shade of trees, but caution is advisable before embarking upon any too ambitious scheme involving hard work and possibly not inconsiderable expense. It is of little use to dig over the whole area, attempting at the same time to free it of tree roots, and then to add rich soil in which to establish the colonist. To do so would, of course, assist the new plants to establish more

Somerset County Council, but apart from this his chief recreation was his visits to Paris for the French Exhibitions.

If any plant is more closely associated with the name of Kelway than any other it is the paeony, for when my great grandfather became interested in it there were very few varieties, but under him, followed by his son William, and later again my father, another James Kelway, the firm raised scores of new paeonies for which it became justly famous. Their Paeony Valley in June is one of the loveliest sights it is possible to see and should be visited by all paeony lovers. Though a County Councillor, a magistrate and at one time a leading figure in local politics, most of the life of James Kelway II was given up to the raising of hardy plants. His greatest love was undoubtedly the paeony as we read in his book *Garden Paeonies* published in 1954 after his death.

He was responsible too for the introduction into this country of *Acidanthera bicolor murieliae*. The first corms were sent to him at Langport by Captain Erskine, British representative at Gore, in Abyssinia, in 1925, and I well remember them being flowered in the garden of our home. My father was anxious for this new scented flower to be called 'Erskini', but the discoverer wished it named after his wife, and they dubbed it *Gladiolus murieliae*. Though given an Award of Merit by the British Gladiolus Society in 1932 it was later decided by the botanists that though akin to the genus gladiolus it was a new variety of *Acidanthera bicolor*.

Some years after the death of his grandfather in 1891 James Kelway II had begun to develop the wholesale seed trade of the business and was himself in Hungary inspecting hundreds of acres of the firm's garden peas grown there when the first World War was declared. Like every other horticultural business Kelways suffered great hardship from two wars, when their stocks of hardy plants had to be drastically reduced and essential crops grown instead. Before the last war the firm became a limited company under the directorship of Mr Owen Lloyd, who from 1940 to 1947 worked arduously for the Somerset Agricultural Committee, and it is really surprising that the firm was able to get through the years 1940–44 and this was only done by cutting down labour very drastically and concentrating on farm crops. In 1951 Kelways celebrated its centenary and to their specialities of paeonies, gladioli, pyrethrums and delphiumins added that of irises.

Originally published in 1958. Volume 1, number 5

rapidly, but it is questionable if they would get really settled in before their sheltering host had discovered the banquet so temptingly close to its avid feeding roots.

A certain stealth should be employed, and plants introduced with as little disturbance of the ground as possible, doing no more than to take out a hole adequate to contain the roots without cramping, and adding a few handfuls of better soil just to start them off. Watering too, should be reduced to the minimum necessary to keep the newcomers alive until their own roots start to forage for themselves. Generous applications of water given too frequently would only encourage an influx of tree roots. For these reasons it is probably wisest to put in the plants at a time when deciduous trees are leafless and more or less at rest, and root activity is at a minimum.

A race of plants which I have found to be particularly well adapted to growing in dry shade is the hardy geranium. It is, in any case a rather neglected family, and, although some of them are such avid sun lovers that it would be shameful to condemn them to a more or less sunless existance, there are others which will not only grow, but flower freely for months on end beneath trees. *Geranium endressii* is an excellent example. The lobed leaves are almost evergreen and the plant forms a bushy mass some 12–18 in (30–45cm) in height. The cup-shaped, inch-wide flowers of the typical plant are rose-red in colour but there are several named garden forms with which to provide variety. One, raised by that great gardener, A. T. Johnson, in his garden in Wales, and bearing his name, bears flowers of light silvery pink. *G.e.* 'Rose Clair' has rather larger flowers, of warm salmon-rose.

Geranium macrorrhizum, with aromatic foliage and pink flowers, is a good coloniser for dry shade, and is surpassed in beauty by a variety collected many years ago by my father, and now grown as 'Ingwersen's Variety', which carries very large flowers of clear light rose-pink on 15 in (38cm) stems. There is also a good albino, and all three dwell contentedly and prettily together. *G. sylvaticum* always seeks the shade in nature and will find a position such as we are attempting to clothe very much to its taste. It is a little taller than the preceding kinds with deeply cut, handsome leaves and showers of rather small pink flowers. This too, has a white flowered form of peculiar charm, the white flowers developing from soft pink buds.

The mourning widow geranium, *G. phaeum*, does not dazzle the passerby with flaunted beauty, but never fails to charm those who pause to examine its flowers, with curiously reflexed petals of

Dicentra spectabilis

deepest purple. The less common variety *G.p. lividum* has flowers of a lighter shade, and more luminous. *G. viscosissimum*, another shade lover, is less easy to place for the flowers are a shade of purple-red which is not pleasing to everyone. It is not a colour which I personally like very much, but I find it so much softened in fairly dense shade that I lose my objection to it when it is so situated. The individual flowers are large, and are carried on stems up to 18 in (4.5cm) high.

Alchemilla mollis will endure any amount of drought and will grow and flourish in shade. Its large, handsomely lobed leaves and great heads of small straw-yellow flowers make a brave display for many weeks. A good companion for this is *Dicentra spectabilis*, whose arching sprays of white and scarlet flowers are so striking in early summer. All kinds of acanthuses too, may be employed to clothe our dry shade, which they will do very magnificently with their beautiful foliage—foliage which has inspired designers of pottery and furniture and architects right down the ages.

I could continue for pages yet, but space forbids that I do more than mention these few more names which may be sought as occupants of dry shade: *Stipa pennata, Buphthalmum salicifolium*, and most of the species of *Lamium*.

Originally published in 1957. Volume 1, number 3

Amos Perry

by Frances Perry

THE late Amos Perry came of a long line of nurserymen for his father, grandfather and great-grandfather before him were all growers of hardy plants. The family came from Exeter and seem to have long made the name Amos peculiarly their own, for it has carried on (usually through the eldest son) right through the years.

Amos Perry's father, Amos Isaac Perry, was intended for a change of vocation and for a time became a schoolmaster in the West Country. But he too hankered to grow plants and after a series of changes came in the mid-19th century to Tottenham, where eventually he became a partner in the famous firm of T. S. Ware.

The Amos Perry of this biography however was born at Tottenham on August 8th, 1869, and right from early boyhood knew that horticulture was to be his vocation. A love of flowers seems to have been an inherent trait which he must satisfy and he used to say that he never felt the slightest urge to adopt any other calling. Consequently, after leaving Tottenham Grammar School, his father had him apprenticed—he was not yet partner to T. S. Ware of Hale Farm Nursery. At that time this was one of the largest general nurseries in the country and stretched for some miles along the marshes adjoining the River Lea at Tottenham. Many famous nurserymen served their apprenticeship at Ware's, including the late T. Reuthe of Keston, and the Dutch B. Ruys of Dedemsvaart and Van Santen.

Here Amos Perry worked through the several sections, until training completed he became foreman of the bulb department. Here it was that the joys and fascination of growing miscellaneous rare bulbs first revealed themselves and he never lost the urge for growing them all through his long life.

About this time he regularly attended Covent Garden market and there met the great carnation specialist George Beckwith. On the latter's inducement he decided to leave Ware's and start in business on his own account as a carnation grower. This was about 1889. Eventually his father joined him and in 1890 the two secured four acres of land at Winchmore Hill and procured from Beckwith 1500 large forced plants of border carnations, old plants 5–6 ft (1.5–1.8m) high in some cases but packed with layers. This was the start. It is interesting to note that the consignment included plants of 'Mrs Frank Watts' (named after the wife of one of the pioneer growers in the Scilly Isles), a variety which was in great demand and at that time considered to be the best white carnation ever introduced.

It was the Perry's intention to grow carnations for the wholesale trade, but meantime they were gradually acquiring a collection of miscellaneous bulbs and eventually the latter claimed prior interest. In later life Amos Perry seems to have turned entirely against carnations. Several times at Chelsea or the R.H.S. Hall I was given carnations but he would not travel home with them. They had to come with someone else or in the van later. He wouldn't be seen with such rubbish.

Early collections of bulbs came from such men as the late Max Leichtlin of Baden Baden, Louis Van Houtte of Ghent, De Graaff of Holland and Dr Regel of St Petersburg, a famous gardener then in control of the finest collection of plants in Europe.

About this period also they received a large consignment of plants from the Chilean Andes, collected by a French political refugee. Many were seen for the first time in Britain. They included *Tecophilea cyanocrocus* and its variety *T.c. leichtlinii, Placea ornata* and various stenomessons.

In 1890 Amos Perry first met George Yeld. This grand old man of hemerocallis fame was even then interested in the genus and his enthusiasm sparked a flame which the younger man was never to lose. The two remained friends and correspondents for years, and in 1922 Yeld selected a *H. thunbergii cypriana* seedling from the thousands then flowering at the Enfield Nurseries (to which they moved in 1903). This was named 'George Yeld' and is still a popular variety.

But other hardy plants also claimed interest. I have never met a man—or woman—with such a keen eye for a plant. During his years as a nurseryman no fewer than 173 plants* submitted to the Royal Horticultural Society received an Award of Merit. These were not always raised by himself it is true, but they were, however,

*A number which does not take into account First Class Certificates and other awards from Societies at home and abroad.

introduced or reintroduced or discovered by him.

His tastes were catholic. Waterplants, hardy ferns, perennials, rock plants, bulbs and chrysanthemums; he was interested in them all. His enthusiasms were lively and infectious. As one interest palled another took its place—rubellum chrysanthemums, tropical fish, underwater oxygenators, lilies, insectivorous plants. He had a great capacity for work and would read far into the night. Saturdays and Sundays he was still amongst his beloved plants; even holidays were taken far from haunts of man. Into the Arctic wastes, Lapland and Russia he went looking for plants. At 3 a.m. one day, starting a trip across a Lappish lake the boatman wearily said, 'We had one other Englishman here once—he also was mad—his name was Kingdom-Ward'.

Yet the end justified the work. And amongst some of the better known plants which originated in the Enfield Nurseries are *Linum* 'June Perfield' (1934); *Erigeron* 'Amos Perry' (1910); *Achillea ptarmica* 'Perry's White' (1912); *Coreopsis grandiflora* 'Perry's Var.' (1920); *Anthemis tinctoria* 'Perry's Var.' (1929) and 'Roger Perry' (1937); *Monarda* 'Mrs Perry' (1929); *Catananche caerulea major* (1935) also *C. caerulea alba; Chrysanthemum rubellum* 'Clara Curtis' (1938); *Hemerocallis* 'Margaret Perry' (1920) and 'Pink Lady', (1940); *Iris hybrida* 'Margot Holmes' (1927); *I. sibirica* 'Perry's Blue' (1916) and 'Marcus Perry' (1930); *Papaver* 'Mrs Perry' (1906), 'Perry's White' (1912), 'Lord Lambourne' (1920) and 'Marcus Perry' (1942).

In his professional life he was a member of the following standing R.H.S. committees. Floral B, Cory Cup Committee, Iris Committee, Lily Committee and Alpine Committee. He was awarded the V.M.H., also the Veitch Memorial Medal and was Founder Patron of the Guild of Trade Horticulturalist.

His home life too was a happy one. He married twice and had eight children and during the last years of his life retired to Thorpe le Soken in Essex. Here to the very end he preserved his interest in hardy plants. He died on August 21st 1953.

Originally published in 1958. Volume 1, number 4

The Genus Liatris

by Will Ingwersen

THE genus *Liatris* belongs to the natural order *Compositae*, which is the largest family of flowering plants and contains more than 800 genera and more than 13,000 species, ranging from herbs to shrubs and even trees and widely distributed throughout the temperate, tropical and arctic regions of the world. *Liatris* itself is a small genus of about 16 species, all perennial herbs, confined in their natural distribution to North America. Not all the known species are in cultivation in this country, but those which are, and at least some of the species not generally met with outside botanical gardens, are easily grown hardy plants for the flower border, flourishing in any moderately good, well drained soil and open, sunny positions. For the interest of apiarists they are all said to be good bee-plants. The origin of the generic name seems to be unknown, and they are designated, apart from their botanical names, by several attractive names, such as 'Kansas gayfeather', 'blazing star' and 'button snake-root'.

Their erect spikes of closely packed flowerheads strike an unusual note in the border during late summer and autumn, and most of them have the unusual characteristic of developing the topmost flowers before those lower down on the spike open. The flowers last well in water when cut, and they may also be dried with considerable success and used for winter decorations. Those marked with an asterisk * in the alphabetical list which follows below are the ones most likely to be found in nurserymen's catalogues.

The basal leaves are narrow, almost strap-shaped, dark green in colour and form a loose rosette arrangement close to the ground. The flower stems are also clothed with leaves, which may be alternate or scattered in their arrangement, and taper and become narrower as they ascend the stems. Propagation is easily effected by division, preferably in the spring, or by sowing seeds in the case of the species. Named garden varieties, which are few in number, are either sterile or do not produce offspring true to type and must be increased vegetatively.

*L. callilepis**. I am unable to discover a reference to the meaning of this specific epithet, but from my distressingly scanty knowledge of Greek I should imagine it might be translated into 'beautiful scale', in which case it might well refer to the involucral scales which are noticeable features in the inflorescences of the liatris species. This is one of the earliest to flower, usually blossoming from July to September, and bearing the spikes of bright carmine flowers on stems which vary in height according to soil and growing conditions from 1½ to almost 3 ft (0.45–1m).

L. cylindracea. This species was first introduced to this country from eastern North America in 1811, but remains almost unknown in gardens. There may be a good reason for this as it does not appear to be a particularly attractive plant, the flower heads being small, and not very generously produced. The colour is pink and the stature dwarf, the stems seldom exceeding a foot in height. It flowers in September.

L. elegans (elegant). This was introduced in 1787 from the south east United States, and would appear to be a species well worth growing. It is a tall growing plant, attaining as much as 4 ft (1.2m) under favourable conditions, with flower spikes which may be more than a foot in length. The flowers are purple, and borne in late summer and autumn.

L. graminifolia (grass-leaved). This came from eastern North America in 1838. The leaves are narrow and sharply pointed and the rich purple flowers are carried in dense spikes on 2–3 ft (60–90cm) stems, usually in early September. Two varieties of this species have been described, one *L. g. dubia* and the other *L. g. pilosa*, but neither appears to be in cultivation.

L. pumila is a name which may be met by those making a collection of liatris species, but it is only a synonym for a dwarf form of *L. spicata*.

*L. pycnostachya** (densely-spiked). This is one of the best known species and has been confused in gardens with *L. callilepis*. It adds yet another to the list of vernacular names and is sometimes referred to as 'cat-tail gay-feather'. It was introduced from the central United States as long ago as 1732. It flowers from August to October in favourable seasons and the crowded purple flowers are carried on erect stems often four feet tall. If grown in wet, cold soil the roots are apt to rot during the winter.

*L. scariosa** (dry, shrivelled). This was introduced from Canada and the USA in 1739. A tall growing species with cyclamen-purple flowers in late summer, it is best grown in the variety *L. s. magnifica* (synonym 'September Glory') the flower spike being very full and richly coloured. There is also a variety named *L. s. alba* (synonym 'White Spire') which is a striking and handsome plant. These do best in rather dry soil and the tall stems usually need support.

*L. spicata** (spike-like). This is from the eastern and southern United States. The stems seldom exceed two feet in height and it is a species which will grow well in moist soil and is earlier flowering than some others. The reddish-purple flowers are very striking, and there is a variety *L. s. alba* with pure white flowers, and another, *L. s. montana* (synonym *L. pumila*), which is even more dwarf than the type and has stems only a foot in height.

L. squarrosa, (overlapping leaves). A species introduced from the eastern United States in 1732. The stems are tall, reaching between two and three feet (60–100cm) in height, and the closely-packed flowers of bright purple are quite showy, although the plant is not often encountered in gardens. There is a recorded variety, *L. s. intermedia*, with which I am not acquainted, rather shorter in stature, with narrower leaves and rose-purple flowers.

Out of alphabetical order comes *L.* 'Kobold', which is supposed to be a hybrid between *L. spicata* and *L. callilepis*. It is intermediate in appearance between the two species with fine, fully formed flower spikes. The plant which may be encountered under the name of *L.* 'Gnome' is probably synonymous with this.

Originally published in 1958. Volume 1, number 4

Three Generations of Kelways

by Christine Kelway

THE late James Kelway, who died in 1952 at the age of 81, came of a line of plantsmen, for his father and his grandfather before him had devoted their long lives to the study and raising of hardy plants. In 1851 my great grandfather James Kelway, founded the firm of Kelways at Langport in Somerset where it still is, and his name very soon became associated with the cutlivation of the gladiolus. Indeed he was the pioneer in this country for raising and exhibiting the large-flowered (gandavensis) gladiolus and was referred to in the press of those days as 'The King of Gladiolus Culture, who has spent nearly seventy years in bringing them to their present state of perfection'.

I have beside me, as I write, an article he read to the Royal Horticultural Society in 1890, which differs little from the advice we are given to-day on their cultivation. He should certainly have known what he talked about, for at that time nearly forty acres at Langport were given up to growing of gladioli, and a familiar sight to be seen walking among them was the sturdy and heavily-bearded figure of this great flower lover. To this speciality he soon added the improvement of the delphinium, the paeony, and the pyrethrum, and Kelways established a reputation as growers of new varieties of these hardy plants and exhibited them with great success at the Royal Horticultural, Crystal Palace, and Alexandra Palace Exhibitions.

When he had taken the pyrethrum in hand it had been rather an insignificant flower but before long the most attractive new kinds were being exhibited at the shows, and the rich blood-crimson 'James Kelway' is still one of the very best singles we have. With delphiniums he was equally successful and by 1897 an acre of the most beautiful new varieties was being grown in a field bordering the main road at Langport which excited great interest among passers-by.

When at the turn of the century Kelways first flowered corms of *Gladiolus primulinus* ('The Maid of the Mist'), sent to them in 1904

Paeonia 'Kelway's Glorious'

by Sir Francis Fox from the Victoria Falls on the Zambesi, it was clear that there were great possibilities in hybridising these light, graceful flowers of soft butter yellow with those of the highly coloured but more massive blooms of the popular large-flowered gladioli. William Kelway, son of the founder, who had taken over management of the firm in 1899, was fortunately as devoted to the task of raising new varieties of plants as his father had been, and immediately set about raising an entirely new race of gladioli, exhibiting them both in this country and on the Continent with the greatest success.

His success was due to a great love of flowers and an equal capacity for hard work, since even towards the end of a long life (he died at the age of 96), he rose at six each morning and when weather permitted would be out in the nurseries marking and appraising his beloved flowers. In those days hours of work were from 6 a.m. to 6 p.m. less half an hour for breakfast and an hour for dinner for six days in the week, and he was usually the first on the spot in the mornings and the last to leave at night. He was a member of the

Plants I Long To Have

by Margery Fish

SOME of the plants I long for may not even exist. I have never met anyone who has seen the double form of *Vinca minor alba*, and yet I feel there must be such a plant, perhaps growing in some old garden. I thought it would be the kind of plant the late Mr Bowles would cherish but I could not find it among the many vincas growing in the garden at Myddleton House. Since my visit there a friend of his tells me that she knows he did not possess it in 1940, which was the last time she saw him. He told her than that he felt it must be growing somewhere and that he hoped to find it to complete his collection. According to reference books there are two more periwinkles that we don't see to-day, a double form of a pink vinca, and a single brick red, but I do not think they are as likely to be in existence as the double white.

Is there a variegated bergenia, I wonder? Again, I have never seen one, nor do I know anyone who has, but I feel it may well exist somewhere. The late Clifford Whitley had a magnificent collection of variegated plants at the Paignton Zoo, but bergenia was not among them.

What has happened to the sky-blue double primrose raised by Hugh Buxton and known as 'Buxton Blue'? It was always scarce but I hope it has not disappeared completely. A few years ago the story came to me that quite a number of sky-blue double primroses had been sold in Dorchester market, but I was never able to track down anyone who had bought them or the source from which they came. For weeks after that I haunted the market and scoured the district to find growers of double primroses, but never found anything that pointed to a clue.

Has anyone a double green primrose, I wonder? A few people grow the form in which the double flowers are composed of sepals, but the one I am looking for is a true double flower. The single green primrose sometimes has an extra petal or two when first it opens but it soon reverts to its single state and my hopes are dashed again.

Originally published in 1958. Volume 1, number 5

Aster ericoides

by P. W. Barret

ASTER *ericoides* or heath-like asters almost seem to be the Cinderella of the genus in the past thirty years. At the shows, choice and emphasis is almost entirely confined to the *A. novi-belgii* with a few *A. amellus*. If the new varieties on show (or in the trials at Wisley) are carefully examined, the only plants of merit would necessarily appear to need a red or purplish colour, and ever larger flower heads, not to mention the duplicating of many names of the oldest kinds. A few *ericoides* always can be found in the trials at Wisley, but are they ever seen at Vincent Square or at any other shows?

To my mind they have many merits, especially when compared with the newer *A. novi-belgii.* They rarely suffer from verticillium wilt, which has become such a scourge in my own collection, and they do not readily get powdery mildew fungus in dry summers. The only one that seems to get the wilt is unfortunately the tallest and a good rosy-mauve colour—'Hon. Vicary Gibbs'. Also they do not literally sit down in despair in rough wet weather which with me is such a common feature with the modern *novi-belgii*, unless staked or otherwise protected from wind. They have a habit of twisting their stems and going almost flat, and when the rough period is over, only the last few inches of the tip grow vertically, and many stems lie in a tangled mass. The *ericoides* group with their stiffer woody, even wiry, stems, are so much more resilient, and resume almost naturally, a vertical position from the rootstock upwards, thus not impairing their ultimate autumn display.

The flower heads seldom exceed ¾ in (2cm) in diameter, but the lack of size is amply made up by the enormous paniculate sprays of clouds of dainty, tiny flowers. The small, rigid and narrow linear leaves add to the neat and pleasing appearance, and when planted in close groups of about 20 strongly growing stems they appear to be a delicate shade of yellow-green, topped with white, pink, blue, or the very yellow flowers of 'Brimstone' or 'Golden Fleece', with small white ray florets and the more prominent yellow disc.

I have managed to gather together nearly all the varieties still in cultivation, and *in my own mind,* divide them into three classes, which in each case exhibit general characteristics of growth. The flowers are much the same in all of them but height and leaf differ.

In the first class I group those of 3 ft (1m) and over with rather stumpy leaves, hardly correctly described as linear. The 'Hon. Vicary Gibbs' is the tallest with flower heads a rosy-mauve, and the foliage a darker green. Very similar in growth are 'Amy', 'May' and 'Twilight', all having lighter green leaves, and respectively silvery mauve, white with a slight pink tinge and white with a mauve tinge blooms. The leaves of the last named also have a purplish shading. Another very similar trio are 'Maidenhood', 'Golden Rain' and 'Golden Fleece', the foliage of all three having a yellow green colour. The flower heads are white, creamy white and white again, but the ray florets of the last named curve backwards. 'Mrs Arthur G. N. Launder' has purplish green leaves and pale bluish mauve flowers. Finally, in this class 'Ringdove' and 'Enchantress', of a similar green foliage, have rosy-lavender and blush pink blooms.

The second class have similar foliage to the first, but are less than 3 ft (1m) in height. 'Brimstone' has small white ray florets with a yellow disc, the whole only being ⅜ in (1cm) in diameter, and with feathery pale green foliage. 'Esther', not more than 2 ft (60cm) tall has delicate pale pink flowers, the only one of the whole species which is decidedly pink. Together with 'Blue Star' these are my two favourites, and I think few will disagree when they see these in the mass. The latter is taller, reaching 3 ft (1m) and has pale blue flowers about ⅜in (1cm) in diameter. 'Mrs A. E. Underdown' is another short one which I never stake and her pale lavender flowers are the first to open at the end of August. 'Delight' has clouds of flat tiny white flowers.

The third class only differs in its more linear leaves and its stiff woody stems. 'White Heather' is the most delicate with its sprays of tiny white flowers. 'Perfection' and 'Star Shower' have a shade larger flowers of pure white, the latter blooming about a week earlier, and they are all about 3½ ft (1.1m) high.

Another variety still in commerce is 'Chieftain', which I had from a reliable source, but its basal leaves are heart shaped and I think it is more likely to be a *cordifolius* . . . It usually reaches about 4 ft (1.2m) and has flowers of a light bluish mauve.

The foregoing in no way is intended to deprecate the *novi-belgii* asters, which have a colour range almost complete except for yellow. Their time of flowering is much more spread out from early August to 'Blue Gown' in mid-October, but I can say from experience that the *ericoides* will be a joy in season, not sprinkled with many disappointments every year.

Originally published in 1959. Volume 2, number 1

Gardening in Wind and Sand

by S. E. Lytle

I HAVE the misfortune, or perhaps shall we say, good fortune, to garden on the coastal strip between Liverpool and Southport. The soil (we call it that out of courtesy), is practically one hundred per cent wind blown sand, devoid of almost anything in the way of humus. Unless some artificial shelter has been erected, the salt laden wind blows in from the sea, cutting down everything in its path.

In conditions like these, it is remarkable that anything grows, but we can produce some quite satisfying results and plants that are quite difficult in what one would think better conditions, grow vigorously with us.

Shelter, moisture and food are the problems, so let us deal with these independently.

Shelter we can make in two ways, by fencing—an expensive and not too permanent method, and by planting screens of trees and shrubs. Sycamores and silver poplar appear to be the hardiest trees to plant, for, much as we dislike them, nothing else can be put in when fairly large to give shelter within a reasonable time. The willow, where the soil contains some moisture, is also successful. Among shrubs, *Euonymus japonicus* with its leathery evergreen leaves, *Olearia haastii*, the New Zealand daisy bush, and *Senecio laxifolius* with silvery leaves and yellow daisy-like flowers, are all successful evergreens, while tamarisk with its feathery leaves, and sea buckthorn (*Hippophae rhamnoides*) smothered with its orange berries, seem to delight in the most bleak and open situation. Among conifers, the Austrian pine and Weymouth pine, can hold their own with the elements, but one must only plant two-year old seedlings about 10–12 in (25–30cm) high for success. The mortality among larger plants put in, is almost one hundred per cent. *Juniperus sabina* 'Tamariscifolia' and *Juniperus chinensis* will, if given some slight protection, grow quite well. *Cupressus macrocarpa* is the only one of the family to attempt the struggle for existence, and here again small pot-grown plants 1½–2 ft (45–60cm) are quite big enough to plant.

Our soil began clean enough to make concrete, with each year it becomes darker with the addition of organic matter. I find that spent hops in the raw state from the brewery is the best form of material to apply, although leaves, peat and any form of organic waste will serve the purpose.

Our practice is to apply a 2 in (5cm) layer of the manure to the surface where it acts as a mulch and conserves moisture. In fact the less digging our light soil gets, the better, for if loosened the subsoil water cannot rise to the surface. It is this store of water, two or three feet below the surface which enables us to have such success in the cultivation of some of the more difficult plants. If we want to grow primulas, astilbes, Japanese iris, or other moisture lovers, all we need to do is to dig out the top foot or so of our bed, and there we have a ready-made bog garden.

Height is the most important thing to watch. Tall growing herbaceous plants that flop over in the first gale no matter how well staked, are out. We look for something which grows about 1½–2 ft (45–60cm) gives plenty of colour and hardly needs staking at all. In this category I would place the following hardy plants. Although only a coloured form of the common milfoil or yarrow, *Achillea*

Crambe cordifolia

millefolium 'Cerise Queen' fills all the requirements. Its bright cerise flowers appear on wiry stems from June until late autumn.

All erigerons succeed with us. The new hybrid forms like 'Charity', 'Frivolity', 'Serenity', with their large daisy-like heads in mauve, pink and lilac shades are seldom if ever out of bloom. One of the first plants to flower is *Euphorbia polychroma*, a delightful little spurge, it forms a rounded bush covered with sulphur yellow flowers and bracts, which as they age, become green, but never appear untidy.

The annual evening primrose grows in profusion on our sand dunes so it is not surprising that *Oenothera* 'Fireworks' and 'Yellow River' succeed. Their more or less prostrate stems can be allowed to ramble along the ground and are covered with yellow and orange flowers throughout the season.

Although only a variegated form of the wild figwort, *Scrophularia auriculata* 'Variegata' is an outstanding plant in any garden. Its large handsome leaves about 6 in (15cm) long are mottled and striped with creams, making it a 'must' for floral decoration.

Crambe cordifolia is a giant suitable only for an isolated position, but being a form of sea kale it thrives in the sandy coastal soil. Stout stems bear clusters of white starry flowers, for all the world like a giant gypsophila.

Provided we build up our soil with organic matter and look to the shelter, there is really no hardy plant that we cannot grow, and when it comes to digging, we can work our soil with ease after a violent thunderstorm.

Originally published in 1959. Volume 2, number 1

Plant Breeding with Hardiness in Mind

by Geoffrey Smith

IT is human nature to climb difficult mountains, it is human nature to attempt to colonize the moon. I suppose it is the same type of impulse which encourages gardeners to attempt to grow the plants classed for general purposes as 'borderline'. I do not subscribe to the growing of plants with nothing else to recommend them except that they are difficult but there are serveral very lovely specimens which I should enjoy growing here but which are a gamble in our climate. Before attempting to grow one of these borderline types I read any information to be found on the subject, especially notes made in the field. This should give some indication as to soil, aspect and water requirements needed if the selected plant is to succeed.

Soil is of as much importance in most cases as climate. The two types of soil in the garden here give a very clear indication of this. I can grow agapanthus on the light alluvial soil in the valley, but the plants are quite impossible on the heavy wet clay at the top of the hill. On the other hand the two species of grevillea which grow in the garden are promptly killed the first winter if planted in the valley, but grow very well indeed if planted in the heavy clay, well laced with peat on top of the hill.

In most cases a wet heavy clay, with a tendency to waterlog in winter is utterly useless for growing any of the borderline plants unless the question of drainage is dealt with. In the case of the grevillia, stones were put down to lead the water away and the bed was raised some 12 ins (30cm) above the normal level. The clay being slow to warm up in spring prevents the plants moving into premature growth and being caught by the east winds which are the real killers in this part of the world. Aspect, of course, must also be carefully considered.

Water requirement is usually fairly obvious and again an example of this essential can be found in the Iridaceae. *Iris kaempferi* I grow under woodland conditions, in a bed which has a constant supply of water from an underground spring. The rhizomatus iris, of course, requires a position in freely drained soil in full sun.

Having dealt with the questions of soil and aspect, comes the consideration of whether to raise the subject to be grown from seed or to buy in plants, hold them in pots for a while and then plant out when sufficiently acclimatized. In every case with borderline plants, where possible, I think it is better to try from seed. For several years I tried bought in bulbs of *Lilium japonicum* in the garden here, while waiting for seedlings to mature sufficiently to be planted out. In every instance they flowered once and never appeared again. The seedlings were planted three years ago and have flowered each year since with only moderate losses.

Coming into the realm of the hybrid, the field is much more vast. Frequently in a genus, can be found species with every qualification for inclusion in the garden except the most important; the ability to withstand the vagaries of our inland winters. I speak now of the average conditions existing over the greater part of the country and not of the more favoured coastal areas. These doubtfully hardy or bud tender species can be induced by careful crossing and selection to bestow the virtues which make them desirable onto a different species without possibly the floral attributes but with the required hardiness. A great deal of work is being done by many expert gardeners, improving existing varieties and introducing new ones. Often I wonder if in the chase for bigger and brighter coloured flowers, we lose the taste we should traditionally have for character, grace and perfection of shape and colouring.

All who love gardening and plants can find interest in trying to breed and fix a new colour or sometimes even a new bigeneric race. Carrying the idea further an added interest can be given to a walk round a garden or into the country if a careful watch is kept for an unusually large calluna or a white flowered form of the common heather, to name only two of many possibilities. Before embarking on the rather turbulent sea of plant breeding, it is well to understand certain points. For instance if an attempt is going to be made to raise a large quantity of *Primula denticulata*, a careful selection must be made over the proposed seed parents. Notes must be made on vigour, flower colour, resistance to disease, and seed only saved from plants reaching a certain standard.

Sometimes quite by chance due to some complication in cell division a single plant will produce a colour break which warrants it being afforded special treatment. However, in most cases this is too slow and must be quickened up a little by introducing 'new blood' into what was previously a pure breeding line. I usually make the cross both ways if possible, pollen of A to B and from B to A, especially with lilium. Mutations can be and are being induced within a species by the use of ultra violet rays, and other types of radiation, but this is very much a job for the 'backroom boys' and scientifically minded horticulturalists. Having made the cross successfully a 'true breeding line' with the desired characters fixed can be produced by continual self pollination.

The primula must, I think, be one of the most satisfactory genera for experimental work. The species readily cross within the various sub-sections and the resulting seedlings quickly reach flowering size and the results can be noted and selections made.

Before any work can be done the breeding system of the plant must be studied, and the technique modified to meet the demands of that plant. Quite often the species from which the cross is to be made do not flower at the same time. Again I am thinking of the primula and lilium with which I have been working here. Pollen of a early flowering species can be preserved in a viable condition for several weeks if stored in a sealed tube on paper with a little granulated Calcii Chloride in the bottom. In this way a much greater range of variability is produced from which selection can be made. Decide which characters are required, select for parents the plants most likely to give those characters, then select only those progeny which fulfil the said requirements, but which also have the ability and vigour to survive in our climate and resist the many diseases which are likely to afflict them.

In the very young garden here at Harlow, we are through necessity only on the threshold of the realm of plant breeding. It will be many years before the ground we have can be said to be fully planted. Propagation is in the main limited to what I term 'bread and butter' stuff, but still there is time and room for a little experiment and breeding. I look forward with interest to seeing some agapanthus seedlings flower, next year. Primulas, of course, we have been crossing for some time. As the garden grows so must the scope for trial both with our own plant children and the progeny of other gardeners. The field is immense and unlike some of the more exact sciences, our experiments can give only pleasure.

Originally published in 1960. Volume 2, number 44.

Geoffrey Smith was Superintendent of the Northern Horticultural Society Garden at Harlow Car at the time of this article.

Out of Sight, Out of Mind!

by Will Ingwersen

A GREAT many hardy perennial plants spend their resting period below ground, leaving no visible sign of their presence on the surface. The result of this, I am afraid, is that they are sometimes injured, or even destroyed during winter operations in the flower borders. In the case of plants which make a vigorous mat of fibrous roots there is little danger of serious damage being done to them as one is very soon made aware of their presence when using tools near them. Others, which may have little more than a tap root, may be cut to pieces with a spade, or pierced through and through by the prongs of a fork.

It may seem an elementary precaution to mark sleeping plants so that they can be avoided, but it is surprising how seldom this is done and many is the treasured plant which has 'turned up missing' in the spring, not because it has perished through natural causes, but simply because it has been seriously injured when the border was being forked over in the autumn, or when manure was being dug in, or during replanting operations.

Such accidental damage is not the only reason for careful marking of dormant plants. I have known enthusiastic, but not very knowledgeable, gardeners to uproot and convey to the bonfire roots of incarvillea and anchusa, filled with the warm glow inspired by the hard labour and satisfaction of having (as they thought), excavated a nasty colony of docks, or other pernicious tap-rooting weed.

I am much opposed to the habit of deep digging in established flower borders in any case. Even if it is carefully done by a skilled worker it is almost impossible to avoid some damage to roots or the crowns of plants. Any necessary cleaning and soil loosening can be done by carefully using a light border-fork, or some sort of small hand cultivator or hoe.

The marking of plants which will be dormant for long periods must be done whilst they can still be seen. A large and possibly unsightly stake is not necessary. Short bamboo canes pushed into the soil near the plant are all that is necessary for individual plants. Groups of several can be marked by outlining the colony with short markers.

It should be remembered too, that the nearer to the spring the cleaning operations are carried out in the border, the more vulnerable are the resting plants, for growth will have commenced which may not yet be visible on the surface and a plant may receive a serious check if these first, vigorous shoots are injured. Much harm can also be done by careless feet, and one must tread as gently as Agag. It is extraordinarily and fatally easy, with apparently ample space to tread, to step on promising young growths and injure them beyond repair. In my own garden I scarcely dare attempt any serious cleaning or weeding until late in the spring. Plants are put in so thickly that it is virtually impossible to insert a tool without hitting something.

An exhaustive list of plants which die down completely during the winter is obviously neither possible or desirable in the space of this short article, but I append below a list of a few which I have observed to be particularly vulnerable and which should always be carefully marked before they disappear completely beneath the soil. Aconitums, adenophoras, adonis, agapanthus, alliums, alstroemeria, anchusa, antholyza, aquilegia, asphodelus, catananche, cimicifuga, delphinium, dicentra, dodecatheon, eremurus, euphorbias (the herbaceous species), helianthus, hosta, incarvillea, *Lobelia cardinalis* (if left in the open garden), paeonies, platycodon, *Ranunculus aconitifolius*, roscoeas, smilacina, stylophorum, trollius, veratrum.

Originally published in 1960. Volume 2, number 4

Lobelias

by G. W. Robinson

IN the older floras lobelias were included in *Campanulaceae*, but in recent years they have been raised to family rank as *Lobeliaceae.* The genus commemorates the name of Matthias de L'Obel, botanist to James I, and in his day one of the leaders of horticulture. He established a Physic Garden at Hackney which was maintained until his death in 1616. There are some 250 species in this genus and their geographical distribution is interesting. On the American continent they range from Chile and Argentina in the south to Kamtschatka and in Africa from the Cape to the tropics. Both New Zealand and Australia have representatives and two are natives of Britain. They are also extremely diverse from the dwarf growing *L. erinus* to the giant forms of tropical Africa which can reach many feet in height.

Of the scarlet flowered herbaceous species the hardiest is undoubtedly *L. cardinalis*, a native of the United States and Canada. The true plant however is rarely seen outside Botanic Gardens though introduced in 1626. The species is glabrous and has dark green to purple foliage oblong lanceolate in shape and 3–4 in (7.5–10cm) in length, with denticulate margins. In flower it is usually from 2 to 4 ft (0.6–1.2m) in height and brilliant crimson scarlet. It does not flower until late July and August. There is a figure of the plant in the *Bot. Mag.* t. 320. The closely allied *L. splendens* hails from Texas and is less hardy. In this plant the foliage and stems are glabrous and usually red and the flowers scarlet. In *Bot. Reg.* t. 60 it is described as the shining lobelia. *L. fulgens*, on the contrary, has downy and more lanceolate foliage and both leaves and stems are red or reddish, the flowers again being scarlet. Introduced in 1809 it is a native of Mexico and the flowering period is earlier, from May onwards. It is considerably less hardy and must be protected in winter.

Blues and whites are provided by *L. syphilitica* also North American in origin and introduced in 1665. It is reasonably hardy with us. There is also a dwarf form *L. syphilitica nana* which is a

Lobelia syphilitica

useful rock garden plant. The inter-crossing of these species has, over a long period of time, given rise to a considerable range of garden varieties in an extensive range of colour from white through pink to scarlet and purple. Many of them are vigorous erect growing plants which for sheer colour are unequalled. Three varieties with both red foliage and scarlet to vermillion flowers are 'Huntsman', 'The Bishop' and that old favourite 'Queen Victoria'. In purple, 'Purple Emperor' is one of the best, and *L. vedrariensis* is a vigorous grower with purple to violet flowers. This received the Award of Merit of the R.H.S. when showed in August 1959. A surprising number of these hybrids have received Awards of Merit even First Class Certificates but have now dropped out of cultivation. All these cultivars should be regarded as doubtfully hardy and be protected in winter. They dislike our wet conditions and damp may prove more deadly than cold. In districts with severe winters they are best in protected cold frames; in milder areas they can be laid in ashes at the base of a warm wall until April when they can again be planted out. If propagation is necessary the old plants can be divided in early March and the small plants grown on in cold frames until it is safe to plant out.

Two other species are in cultivation *L. tupa* from Chile and *L. laxiflora* from Mexico. *L. tupa* is a Chilean plant which in its native habitat may reach so much as 10–12 ft (3–3.6m) in height the inflorescences being at least 2 ft (60cm) long and the individual flowers 2 in (5cm). Here in Britain it may reach 5–6 ft (1.5–1.8m) with large woolly leaves rather like a verbascum. It requires a warm and sunny corner and benefits from a little protection in winter at least in cold districts. It has been in cultivation since 1824 and there is a figure of the plant in *Bot. Mag.* t. 2550. It also received the R.H.S. Award of Merit in 1927. Closely allied and from the same country is *L. polyphylla* with dark chocolate coloured or maroon flowers. I do not think this is now in cultivation.

Though it is in cultivation the Mexican *L. laxiflora* is not reliably hardy. It seems to like a light warm soil and sunny situation and given these will go on for some years. I have however tried and lost it repeatedly. It is on the border line between a perennial herb and a sub shrub, reaching 2–3 ft (60–90cm) in height and with loose inflorescences of red and yellow flowers about 1½ in (4cm) in length. It was figured in *Bot. Mag.* 5. 3600 as *L. cavanillesii*.

Although not hardy, but very interesting are the giants of the family, the Central African species. While some of these have been introduced and raised in Britain we have had little success with them. One species can be flowered under glass *L. gibberoa*. This will reach 10–12 ft (3–3.6m) with a compact inflorescence of white flowers. It has been recorded as reaching a height of 29 ft (8.8m) on Mount Elgon at 9,000 ft. These gigantic plants are described and figured in the *Journal* of the Royal Horticultural Society 1938. By way of contrast one of the British species the water lobelia, *L. dortmanna*, grows in shallow lakes and tarns in Wales, the Lake District and in Scotland and Ireland. The flowers are pale lilac in colour and the plant a perennial, spreading by stolons and forming a green carpet on the floor of the pond or lake.

Originally published in 1960. Volume 2, number 6

Some Notes on Lupins

by Mary Gallup

EVERYONE knows and admires the modern lupins with their magnificent spikes in such a wonderful range of colours. In a good up-to-date variety the keels and bells which compose the florets are so large and well formed that they completely hide the stem—how different from the rather gappy spikes of indifferent blue produced by some of its forbears.

It is interesting to take a glance at the history of this race of garden plants. There are in existence about 70 known species including hardy annuals, perennials and not quite so hardy shrubby evergreens. The first to be introduced to this country in 1596 were *L. albus* from the Levant, the yellow *L. luteus* from Sicily and *L. varius* blue and white, from southern Europe. All through the 18th and 19th centuries other species were brought home from America, including the yellow tree lupin *L. arboreus*. Perhaps the most important introductions were *L. polyphyllus* and *L. p. albus* from California in 1826, and about 80 years later the pink *L. moerheimi*. Upon this material the hybridists worked and to what good purpose is to be seen in the endless beautiful varieties exhibited at the flower shows of to-day. George Russell will be remembered for the work he did by the strain which bears his name. Downer was another great grower and the work is still being carried on by many other present-day nurserymen.

None of the lupins are indigenous to Britain, but occasionally garden escapes, particularly of the yellow tree lupin, arc found in waste places and the blue perennial *L. nootkatensis* (a native of Nootka Sound) has become naturalized in parts of Scotland, usually growing on shingle by the riverside. It is worth noting the conditions under which they grow wild, *i.e.*, silt and gravel by the water. Good drainage and abundant moisture is what they choose. Lupins prefer an acid soil so probably a deep well-drained sandy loam with a pH below 7 is ideal.

It is only necessary to dig up a healthy plant and see the extent of the root system to realize the depth they need and how much they

Lupinus Russell hybrids

appreciate a friable rooting medium. Small nodules will be noticed on the roots; these contain nitrifying bacteria which are extremely beneficial. Lupins are hungry by nature (the name is derived from 'lupus' a wolf) but owing to the nodule forming bacteria they share with many legumes the advantage of being able to utilize nitrogen from the air. To encourage this it is important to stimulate a vigorous root system, and to this end the ground in preparation should be deeply cultivated and manured with an organic phosphatic fertilizer. Bone meal 2 or 3 oz. per sq. yard may be worked into the ground before planting or given as a dressing in autumn or spring. Potash is valuable to general health and is conveniently given in the form of wood ash or ½ oz. of sulphate of potash in spring. Some growers advise a liquid seaweed fertilizer to be given in April or early May.

Summer mulching is a great help in conserving moisture which is so very essential. Spent hops, leaf mould or even lawn mowings can be used; lupins resent farmyard manure coming into direct contact with their roots but it would be safe used as a mulch if well rotted.

Nowadays, when plants seem more and more prone to diseases and pests it is refreshing to find that the lupin produces no major troubles of this kind. Bud dropping is a fault which occasionally appears but since there is no cure it is better to destroy the plant as the tendency might be transmitted to its progeny.

Lupins are not among the longest lived perennials; this may be because of some annual ancestry in the many crossings which have gone to produce modern varieties but may also be accounted for by the quantity of large seed pods they produce which if left to ripen must exhaust the plant. Apart from the unsightliness of dead flower heads it is time well spent to remove all but the pods actually needed for seed saving. Three pods from several plants of exceptionally good colour would produce a splendid bed of seedlings and though none could be relied on to come true the majority would be as good as their parents and one or two might be better.

When raising lupins from seed a more even germination will be obtained if the seeds are soaked for twenty-four hours or chipped before sowing. Seedlings raised in frames in April or May and planted out by early July will often flower at the end of the summer and show what they are going to be; they can also be sown out of doors in May or June.

When a new variety is first shown there is often a great demand for it. If the grower has only a limited stock his number of cuttings is equally limited and this is the only way of propagating plants true to name. When the demand exceeds the supply, it has to be withdrawn from the catalogues for a time while the stock is built up again. Varieties are not equally prolific in throwing up cutting material and the shyer they are in this respect the more expensive they will be. This is sometimes disappointing for those who were not prepared to pay the very high price fetched by a novelty and then find it withdrawn from the market, but in the long run a variety that in succeeding years has the vigour to become plentiful and reasonably cheap has greater merit as a garden plant and is more worth while to buy.

It is not necessary here to give a long descriptive list of varieties as there are many catalogues for this purpose, but for those who like pastel shades these are a few outstandingly good ones: 'George Russell', pink; 'Gladys Cooper', smoky blue; 'Lady Gay', pale yellow. 'Freedom' is a very pleasing shade of blue and white; 'Betty Astell', clear pink. Strong colours are provided by 'Masterpiece', deep purple; 'Festival', intense orange, and 'Beryl Viscountess Cowdray', red.

Form as well as colour is important in flower grouping and the spikes of the lupins are an invaluable feature in the mixed border. If space can be found for a whole bed to be given up to them in varieties of colours the result when in bloom could be described as the place where the rainbow ends.

Originally published in 1960. Volume 2, number 6

The Charm of Pink

by Alice M. Coats and Kay N. Sanecki

EVERY gardener has his or her special weakness, and mine is for unnaturally-pink flowers—that is, pink forms of flowers that are normally of some other colour. Such forms are fairly common among blue-flowering plants—larkspur, lupin, forget-me-not and Canterbury bell spring instantly to mind; but in these cases the colour is nearly always what the Scots call 'blae', a pink with a hint of lavender about it, which to me is not so attractive. (The exception is the hybrid delphinium 'Pink Sensation', which inherits its colour from its orange-scarlet parent, *D. nudicaule*). Pink forms of white flowers are rather rare, and can be either breath-takingly delicate, as in *Magnolia stellata rosea* and some forms of jasmine, or merely wishy-washy, as in the pink lily-of-the-valley. It is in the families whose flowers are predominantly yellow or orange that the most subtle and exciting shades are to be found.

The pink-trumpeted daffodils are a case in point, resembling in colour the most exquisite shells, picked up still wet and transparent on the sea-shore, before they become lifeless and dry. I cannot understand anybody failing to be charmed by them, and hope that their ethereal dawn shades will not be too rapidly 'improved' by the breeders. The wonderful range of sunset-pinks to be found among the Ligtu Hybrid alstroemerias—from the near-white to near-scarlet, and not a harsh or insipid shade among them—is rapidly becoming familiar to most gardeners, and almost reconciles one to the invasive tactics of their orange cousins. Less well-known, perhaps, is the pink montbretia — rather weedy in habit, but very obliging and floriferous—whose rosy flowers have sweet little cream markings on the lower petals, suggestive of a white moustache on the face of an irate colonel. Unfortunately this charming ornament is only visible on close examination, as the flower does not open widely enough for it to be easily seen.

Among the composites, we have the former rudbeckia, now called *Echinacea purpurea,* of most unusual but effective colouring, whose French-pink (not purple) petals are set off by a cone of warm

Crepis incana

orangey-brown; unfortunately in my garden the pests are even more fond of it than I am. The wild yellow hawkweeds long ago invaded the garden in the shape of their orange representative, grim-the-collier, but few people grow the beautiful pink hawkweed, *Crepis incana*. It is all nonsense that this plant requires alpine-house conditions; I grow it as a front-of-the-border perennial, where it makes cushions 18 in (45cm) across, smothered in July with exquisite shell-pink flowers. The annual *C. rubra* is less good; though pleasant enough, the colour is dull compared to that of *incana*.

And here a word of warning about the description 'salmon-pink' as employed by nurserymen and seedsmen. To me it indicates the colour of prime Scotch salmon, nicely cooked; but others apparently know only the salmon that comes from a tin or the raw fish on a slab, for the adjective may be applied to any colour from orange-tawny to ruby. I was deluded by it many years ago into sowing *Papaver lateritium*, which has no shade of pink in its carrotty countenance, and which I have been weeding up ever since. Salmon-pink oriental poppies can look lovely, especially grown, as I have seen them, with great clumps of anchusa against a grey-and-white chalk wall; and some of the most delectable pink shades are to be found among the newer Iceland poppies. The eschscholzia, also a member of the poppy order, has some attractive pink forms, including an almost edible variety that is cream on the outside and strawberry-pink within.

Many more examples could be given, without counting the multi-coloured races, such as tulips, ranunculus, and zinnias, where pink forms as well as yellow and red are a matter of course. Enough has been said to show that I like to look at my garden through rosy spectacles. Unfortunately I have not been very successful in my attempt to grow the pink day-lily. The plant I obtained sulked for some years, and then produced flowers of a curious greyish shade, very unlike the glowing colour-photograph that induced me to purchase it. But I would still fall a willing prey to any nurseryman who would offer the loveliest flower of my imagination, which I long to see, and which should not be beyond the bounds of possibility—a shell-pink crown imperial.

Alice M. Coats

It was at Wisley at the end of June that I first came across the pink form of chicory, *Cichorium intybus roseum*, growing in the herb border. It was not nearly as robust a plant as the blue chicory which stands in my perennial border, but here on practically solid chalk it is very much at home, and is, in fact, hedgerow weed generally in Buckinghamshire. That may account for the pink form at Wisley seeming to be less rampant, but it was delicate in colour and altogether a delightful plant to find. It set me thinking of 'Pink Sensation' the belladonna type delphinium, which is really a hybrid *D. ruysii* and originated on the famous Moerheim nurseries belonging to Mr Ruys in Holland towards the end of the '30s long after he had abandoned his efforts to produce a pink flowered delphinium seedling. It was a chance seedling, probably with *D. nudicale* as one of its parents accounting for its smallness. It in turn gave rise to 'Rose Beauty' a delphinium of deeper pink with somewhat larger flowers, but variable constitution.

A hybrid such as this is strictly speaking a little different from a named variety that might have pink flowers though one finds usually that where pink flowers are the exception rather than the rule the plant is a hybrid of the type. Veronicas come to mind, a genus universally thought of as blue flowered, but there are varieties of *Veronica spicata* which make most attractive border

Lilium pyrenaicum is a colourful plant for dappled shade

Euphorbia rigida is still attractive after flowering

Centaurea macrocephala is a good plant for the border or for drying

plants and have pink flowers. 'Minuet' is one I like to grow, with clear pink spikes almost fluffy with styles, tapering beautifully above dusty grey foliage. Taller and much deeper pink is 'Pavane' which is also worth growing. 'Erica' is a dull pink, not very pleasing and a deep rose variety is 'Barcarolle'. All flower in July and August and divide easily either in the early autumn or spring. The only other pink flowered veronica I know of is *V. incanca rosea*, less silver leaved than *incana* itself, greyish generally, surface rooting and growing up to a foot and a half in height.

Two pink forms of perennials which are really weedy and anaemic in comparison with their more robust relatives are *Stachys discolor* (syn. *nivea*) and the pink flowered lavender. The stachys is sometimes supplied as *S. byzantina* the beautiful thick felty lamb's ear, but is in fact a much less hairy plant and really only then on the under surfaces of the leaves. The flowers come at the end of June and beginning of July in well-spaced whorls up the stem, as weedy and insignificant as possible against the silver foliage. Like *S. byzantina*, the plant probably has a better value if the flowering spikes are removed, then the mat-like growth is of decorative value and it is in the fortunate position of being able only to display its qualities without any of its weaker points!

Really good border plants, though the criterion seems to be whether or not they can withstand our damp winters are the penstemons, and while *P. campanulatus* 'Evelyn' is probably likely to be the best known pink one at present, great advances are being made both here and in America with the genus. A whole series of tests are being carried out and a range of plants of the *P. barbatus* type are merging with a colour range through the whole compass of mauves, pinks and reds. So we can look forward with practical certainty to more good pink pentstemons.

A useful and showy border plant in June is *Galega* and the mauve varieties are most frequently grown, sometimes the white *G. alba* makes a good companion in clumps for *G. officinalis*, the ordinary goat's rue. The only true clear pink form is *rosea* though *carnea* and *carnea plena* are also good pinks especially when young.

That pink flowered plants exist in many cultivars of herbaceous perennials is not to be disputed. Many of them are varieties which come and go, or something long waited for as in the genus hemerocalis. Verbascum seedlings may include pink, especially if they are of the *V. phoeniceum* form which is wild over great areas of Europe. The well-known 'Pink Domino' rather mauve-pink in colour is considered to be a sport of 'Cotswold Queen', itself a dirty bronze salmon shade. 'Mother of Pearl' is listed as blush pink, but it is a plant I have not seen. Hybrid plants *V. nigrum album* × *V. phoeniceum* are producing a wide range of pink shades now from cream to good deep reds.

In reflecting on scabious one realizes that the biennial form *S. atropurpurea* usually treated as an annual, produces all kinds of reds, pinks and mauves as well as blues and whites but among the perennial species only *S. lucida* produces pink flowers and those late in the summer and not over as long a period as scabious generally are considered to flower. The growth is bushier than with *S. caucasica* varieties, so inevitably border plants, and the flower stems are short in comparison. Similarly among cornflowers, the annual forms produce variations of pink, white and blue, while the perennial forms are not quite so widely varied in colour and the pink is not as common. The dreadful weedy *Centaurea montana* has *carnea* and *rosea* forms but there is nothing as robust as the handsome yellow *C. macrocephala* which dominates all other forms to my mind. *C. dealbata* produces the best pink flowers on 18–25 in (45–60cm) stems for some weeks during July and early August, which contrast prettily with the greyish deeply idented foliage.

Kay N. Sanecki

Originally published in 1960. Volume 2, number 6

Euphorbias

by Margery Fish

THERE is a growing interest in euphorbias, for they are easy to grow and flower over long periods. Many are evergreen and quite a number flower very early in the year, when they are particularly welcome. They thrive in poor soil, and are excellent plants for difficult corners, the arid soil under trees and among stones.

The one that is most often seen in private gardens is the medium sized *Euphorbia epithymoides,* which flowers in spring and makes a neat rounded clump about 18 in (45cm) high of dazzling greenish gold. As in all the euphorbias, it is the bracts and not the minute flowers that give the colour. This euphorbia is usually called *E. polychroma* and, rightly, often appears in plant lists under this name. *E. pilosa major* I believe should be referred to as *E. gregorsonii.* It is a larger edition of *E. epithymoides*, growing to 24–30 in (60–75cm) but (to the unbotanical eye) is practically the same otherwise.

Next, in a popularity that is growing all the time, is *E. characias wulfenii*. There are several euphorbias of the same type, varying slightly in size and the colour of the eye, so that sometimes it is difficult to be absolutely exact. They all make large evergreen plants and flower in February and March. Before they bloom the flower heads bend over to look like a shepherd's crook but though they are quite rigid at this stage they later straighten out to make enormous heads sometimes a foot high. In *E. c. wulfenii* the individual flowers are larger than in the others, and have an orange eye. *E.c.w. sibthorpii* is nearly as large but in this case the eye is brown. There seem to be two forms of *E. characias*, one rather smaller and more compact than the other. Both qualify for the late Mr E. A. Bowles' description of it as the frogs' spawn bush, and both have a very distinct black eye.

Not often grown but very effective in the right place is *E. myrsinites*, which makes a dazzling splash of colour in March and keeps its beauty for many weeks. This prostrate euphorbia is a real sun lover so I plant it to sprawl over a flat stone. Its long, lax stems heavily encrusted with grey green leaves radiate from a central rosette. The flower heads are flat and round with small yellow-

Euphorbia griffithii

bracted florets packed into a frame of foliage, rather like a Victorian posy.

E. rigida is similar but rather bigger and likes to rear its head when it is about to flower, which makes a steep bank a better place on which to grow it than a horizontal stone. But even well placed it does not always last very long, and should be propagated regularly.

I am very fond of the little running euphorbia, *E. cyparissas*, but I know many people find it too invasive for orderly gardens. Country folk call it 'ploughman's mignonette', and it is often found filling the corners of a cottage garden. It is unwise to introduce it to a rock garden or paving but in an open bed it makes a forest of ruffled green flower stems, with heads of small greenish yellow flowers.

E. robbiae is another runner but not a very persistent one. It is named after Mrs Robb, in whose capacious handbag it was brought to England. Its shining evergreen leaves are very dark, and clothe upright stems about 15–18 in (38–45cm) high. The flower heads emerge from the tops of these stems in February, slightly bent to begin with and then straightening out to loose inflorences which persist all through the year.

E. mellifera is supposed not to be completely hardy. I have no trouble in Somerset, but cannot vouch for the rest of the country. It makes a large and handsome bush, with big leaves, which colour in the winter. The flowers are not very conspicuous, but the clustered seed heads are quite distinct.

For a damp position *E. palustris* makes a handsome furnishing. It dies down in the winter to produce in spring handsome stems 30 in (75cm) high, topped with brilliant green-gold heads. *E. androsacinifolia* is rather like it, but has longer stems and less important flower heads. Two other euphorbias that die down in winter are *E. sikkimensis* and *E. griffithii*. Both run slightly when conditions suit them, but they are so attractive that no one would complain. The leaves of *E. sikkimensis* are a brilliant flame colour when first they come through, the soil and the older leaves are deeply tinted with crimson. The flower heads are the usual euphorbia love-bird green. In *E. griffithii* the flower bracts are a brilliant orange. The most brilliant form is known as 'Fireglow', which describes it exactly.

E. amygdaloides, the woodland spurge, is a graceful plant for informal planting and to see a colony growing under trees on a sunlit day is very pleasing. It is a little too natural for ordinary gardens, although the larger, better coloured form, *E. amygdaloides superba*, makes a handsome plant. The variegated *E. amygdaloides* is a collectors' piece, and it originated in Mr Walpole's Irish garden, Mount Usher, and the most beautiful specimens I have ever seen are there. It is not a long-lived plant, and must be kept going with cuttings, and sometimes tends to go back to green. There is also a bronze form of *E. amygdaloides*, rather dwarf as a rule, with new growth that is brilliant in colour.

In *E. coralloides* it is in the autumn that the leaves colour so magnificently. It grows from 12–18 in (30–45cm) and has small fluttering leaves. To get its best autumn effect it should be grown in poor soil in full sun. There is a larger form, with loose branching habit and the same small leaves, which colour well in autumn.

E. hibernica is a British native which has several good forms. It likes to grow in light shade, and is particularly attractive when its young foliage of vivid green is combined with dainty flower heads in lovebird green.

There is no need to describe *E. lathyrus*, the caper spurge, with its seeding habits. No one seems quite certain if it is really disliked by moles, certainly I have never found that it discourages them. If it was not so easy to grow we should cherish this undoubtedly decorative plant, with its evergreen glaucous foliage and graceful flowers and seeds. It is easily removed from the border if it puts itself in the wrong places, and it is straight and sturdy when cut and lasts in water for a long time.

These are but a few members of a genus that includes many hundreds of species, which range from enormous desert shrubs to the greenhouse poinsetta. Most of those we grow in our gardens can be propagated by seed or from cuttings. The milky juice that flows so freely from the cut stems is poisonous, and care is needed when handling cuttings, but the cut can be sealed with a lighted match.

Originally published in 1961. Volume 2, number 7

The Old Double Primrose

by G. E. Emmerson

FEW people now remember the ceremony of the summer bedding out—the deplorable disaster of the intricate pattern of the massed scarlet geraniums, the blue lobelias, the margeurites and the flaming yellow calceolarias (what silly faces calceolarias have, to be sure). That was the summer bedding tradition.

However the spring bedding display (arranged of course in the autumn) was a very pleasing affair and well deserved to survive.

The enchanting double primrose *P.* 'Lilacina Plena' used to make a carpet for the rose tulips. The double primrose, 'Rose du Barri' (that lost treasure) was massed at the feet of the purple tulips. The good old 'Double White' was the partner of the 'Scarlet'. In May, when the flowering was over, the double primroses were dug up, divided, and lined up in a shady bed—much enriched with leaf mould—possibly at the edge of the vegetable garden. In October they were moved back to the position of the spring display. With this treatment they never grew woody knotty roots, and the vine weevil, those tiresome white grubs, orange headed, the larvae of the cockroach, who enjoy many a meal from the roots of all the primula family, could be easily and hard-heartedly dealt with. And so in the days of bedding-out the old double primrose lived and flourished and thrived.

About sixty years ago the 'bedded out' garden, very rightly, fell into complete disfavour. Under the influence, as everybody knows, of William Robinson—'We'll have herbaceous borders', everybody said, 'We'll have rock gardens', they said. 'The double primroses will look lovely on the rock garden' they said—so there they planted them and there they left them. And there they died.

So, let nobody be disheartened by the pessimistic warnings of the foretellers of doom. The old double primrose is a most easy and obliging sort of plant if only it is treated as the plants were treated in the days of bedding out. One should keep to the old tradition, a sunny display position, arranged in the autumn and enjoyed in the spring. They look well in the front of the herbaceous border. They make a charming edging to the rose beds. Then move them to some quiet shady corner for their summer rest.

The old double primroses seem to be the most interesting of all the garden plants. So much beauty there is, so much variety, so many stories, legends, and myths. The dear old double white primrose (*Primula acaulis alba flora plena*) is mentioned in Gerard's Herbal (1957). The double lilac, with it's neat delightful flowers, is, one supposes, almost as old.

A collection may be started with the double white and double lilac. These are not difficult to obtain and often one can easily beg a plant of 'Bon Accord Gem'—a lovely rose-red double primrose and of 'Bon Accord Lavender'. These are the most hardy of the Bon Accord primroses raised by Messrs. Cocker of Aberdeen about 1900.

'Our Pat' is another variety well worth tracking down. It has a violet blue flower and pretty bronze leaves and came originally from the Daisy Hill Nursery at Newry. 'Marie Crousse' can still be found too, it hails from the famous Crousse Nursery at Nancy in France and it first appeared on the market about 1885 but its charming flower so much suggests a crinolined lady of a rather earlier date than one likes to think. It was about 1865 that its violet, silver edged petals first came to adorn the garden.

Primrose 'Tyrian Purple'

'Red Paddy' is a charming primrose—so neat and gay. It has bright red petals with a silver lacing, 'Arthur du Moulin', reminiscent of a bunch of double violets may easily be added to the collection. One should seek for 'Chevithorne Pink', it is easily obtained, and the lovely 'Tyrian Purple'.

And now the hunt is up. How many of the rarer double sulphur varieties can one discover? Will that tiresome (I do admit it *is* tiresome) double primrose 'Pompadour' live in your garden, or will it quickly die away? ('Pompadour', one gathers, was named for the colour, not for the lady—but the lady has somehow taken the primrose to herself and it is known as 'Madame de Pompadour'. The colour of the primrose is that very dark crimson known to the lovers of old china as 'Rose Pompadour'.)

Can you find 'Prince Silverwings', that delightful double polyanthus splashed with orange and mottled in mulberry and white? Can you seek out the splendid rarer varieties of the 'Bon Accords', the lovely 'Purple', the enchanting 'Blue', and my own favourite primrose 'Bon Accord Purity' with its frilled white petals and it's ice green heart?

One soon becomes very enthusiastic and collecting becomes an absorbing interest. There are the old single primroses too. Jack-in-the-green with its little early ruff of bright green leaves, and all the hose-in-hose varieties with their double row of petals.

Just pet them up a little and all will go well—do not leave them too long in the same place, and do not, oh do not, try to grow them on a dry and windswept rock garden.

Originally published in 1961. Volume 2, number 7

Western American Iris Species

by Le Roy Davidson

IT is an annual pleasure for a number of enthusiasts in the north western United States to make a journey out into the wilds of the Pacific Slope to study the wild irises growing there. Such a trek through the varied terrain, from the summits of the Cascades and Sierra Nevada westward to the Pacific shore, lends much knowledge as to why there are such great variations among these irises, and, through observing the soils, the conditions of moisture and temperature, and all the other things that we are told influence speciation, we come to better understand the plants themselves, as well as learn how to best succeed with them in our gardens.

This past season's trek was the most extensive and intensive organized so far, taking us, as it did, through no less than six California counties and three additional in Oregon, plus the distance back home, for some of us a distance extending nearly across the state of Oregon and half that of Washington. This is the strip of Pacific coast northward from San Francisco Bay to Coos Bay in Oregon, between the 38th and 44th degrees of parallel, an area cut into deep canyons by swift rivers, their steep slopes clothed with the coniferous forests consisting of pines and firs, redwood groves along the low fog-belt, and, in the southernmost areas, Monterey cypresses and blue gum eucalyptus forming groves from their ancestors, originally planted by man, while the major deciduous trees are various oaks of many species. There are in addition several of the evergreen oaks and a number of other broadleaf evergreen species, both among the trees and the lower shrubs. The temperatures in the area vary of course through the year, from a frost-free strip along the immediate shore to areas of heavy frost and deep snowfall in winters and daily temperatures from moderate along shorelands to over 100 deg. F. in the interior valleys during the dry summer period. It is an area of moderately heavy rainfall, but the precipitation comes mainly during the six cooler months, as rain in the coastal warmer belt, and, of course, much of it as snow at greater altitudes.

It is in this situation that the western American species of beardless (Apogon) irises classified as *Californicae* have spread to cover the sunny openings in the forests, to provide some of the most beautiful of the wild flowers of late April and May. The designated meeting place for the trek was Ukiah, Mendocino county, California, and on this morning we gathered early to go eastward into high Lake county, then south west through Sonoma county, to the shorelands in Marin county, northward along the Pacific coast of Sonoma and Mendocino counties, then inland and northward through Humboldt county where we reached the coast again at Eureka, again northward along the Humboldt and Del Norte county coasts, and, upon reaching Crescent City, inland to Josephine county, Oregon. The last day was spent exploring the coastward strip of Oregon, in Curry and Coos counties. In addition to many species of the Californicae Apogons, we encountered *Iris longipetala* of the Longipetalae Apogons, growing in quite a different kind of habitat; instead of the well-drained slopes, this species flourishes in the wet bottomlands of cattle pastures, particularly in Marin county, though further south it can be found on cooler slopes where it is able to succeed largely because of the summer fog-blanket of the San Francisco Bay area. This species does not spread far beyond the bounds of this cooler summer condition, from Monterey north along the peninsular San Mateo county, San Francisco and Marin counties, into southernmost Sonoma county, and somewhat to the counties immediately to the east. A handsome plant, though not of much variation in the wild, it will grow from two feet to a half-foot taller, bears up to four, frequently more, wide-spreading ivory or whitish classically-formed iris blossoms at the top of each stem, the flowers etched sharply in an intricate pattern of blue-violet lines converging toward the centre and marked with a brilliant golden blaze on the three lower segments (falls). Even in its native meadowlands it bakes quite dry in late summer, so much so that the foliage disappears, to begin growth anew with the first rains of autumn, and, in this habitat of little frost, it continues to grow during the wet winter months, to flower in April and May, the bold five-to-six inch blossoms quite lovely atop the masses of stiff, rich, deep bluish-green foliage fans. Transplanted northward it is subject to winter damage if there is enough warmth to encourage growth too early or during intermittent winter temperature periods of freezing.

The first of the Californicae iris species was the yellow form of *I. macrosiphon*, along the roadsides of northwestern Lake county, in a nearly treeless, summer-hot-and-arid area. The usual form of this species is blue or purple, but here the pale yellows were to be found exclusively. Later and higher we found the purples and blues, and, in a most exciting mergence-area, the resulting smoked, greyed and bronzed forms, resulting from the occurrence of both the blue-purple and yellow pigments in the same blossom. Later we were to explore a great slope south of Ukiah populated with only the blue form, many of them exceedingly near to the illusive true-blue so much sought in flowers. A very neat narrow-leaved plant, it could not be coarse or untidy in the most discriminating garden surroundings; the fans of evergreen leaves are powdered with a heavy glaucous bloom which can be wiped off like the bloom of a plum. The name '*macrosiphon*' means long-tube, alluding to the perianth tube, that part of the blossom connecting the petal parts with the ovary below; consequently the plant has a shorter stem, the blossom being elevated above the foliage by its tube.

In an area near the Petrified Forest of Sonoma county we next saw the delicate pale yellow *Iris fernaldii* with light green foliage fans tinged red at their base, and growing under the big deciduous oaks of the hot dry valley, but which allowed the iris sufficient light for their success in that they did not come into leaf until they were well on the way to flowering. The slender stem of this species is stiffly erect from the base whereas many of its kin are lax, a fault in the garden, and each bears two nicely formed flowers within the reddish-bronze spathe at the top. All about the rather restricted range of this species are to be found its many hybrids with *macrosiphon*, the vast majority of them not as attractive as either species, and they are a mottled effect of lavender and yellow.

Iris douglasiana is the tall, branched species of the headlands immediately fronting the ocean, where it enjoys the comparative all-season warmth and is rather limited to south of the 44th parallel because it is damaged by freezing northward of this, and in the garden as well. In its long north-to-south distribution it has the opportunity to intermix with a number of other species, which may contribute to its own variability; it is known in a very wide range of colours, the usual ones along the California coast being blue-purples from light to very dark some in near-black tones. In several notable areas is to be found a wide range of colours, embracing white, light to medium yellows, rosey tints and some quite blue, and not a few in attractive blended tints. The evergreen foliage of this very robust species is wide and relatively coarse, more so than most of its allies, and is not well suited to any but the larger garden, but valuable for its many-flowered stems, it being the only branching

Iris douglasiana

species of Californicae. It is to be suspected that many actual hybrid areas are to be found along the mergence-zones of this with other species, and we did find some that appeared to have been derived from it crossed with *Iris macrosiphon*, and among them some deep plum-coloured individuals on short, simple stems, and with short, deep green leaves. Ordinarily these hybrid areas hold much exciting anticipation because of the possibility of unusual individuals occurring therein; such was the case with the intra-species smoke-coloured macrosiphons, but not often are such combinations as unique nor as attractive. Nevertheless it is always interesting and educational to study such swarms, observing how the individuals differ, not only from both the parent-stocks, but also from one another, in those points botanists take as the separating criteria for identifying the species. We were later to find hybrids of several natures and were to select some few good ones for collecting. But quite within the limits of species ranges it is possible to find superior colonies and clones; such was the case in the next species encountered, away from the coast in an interior valley again.

Iris purdyi, locally called the redwood iris, because of its range being rather coincident with that of the Coast Redwood of Mendocino and Humboldt counties, is ordinarily thought to be a low growing and quite non-variable orchid pink or cream marked with rose-purple. The sunny opening between the groves of redwoods are numerously populated with these forms, but more open and higher areas have some variants, some of which at least might be resultant of ancient hybridization. One of the most spectacular finds on the trip was a wide-spreading colony of tall-growing plants, with tufts of wide foliage, and with large, wide-spreading, pale apricot-yellow flowers, lightly veined with violet or red-brown. The sheathing stem-leaves of this iris are short, stiff and bract-like, coloured a bright reddish tint. In flower form, this species is flattened in the manner of a both *Iris tenuissima* and *chrysophylla*, wherein the standards, rather than being erect in the conventional manner, flare outward in the manner of the falls, to form a perianth that is star-shaped, viewed from above. This giant form grew to 1½ ft (45cm) tall and with a blossom that spread over 6 in (15cm) across. We also saw much of the conventional orchid-pink form of this species on the northward segment of the trip in Mendocino and Humboldt counties, far smaller, very dainty, forming dense clumps rather than tufts. As a garden plant, *Iris purdyi* in its many forms is an excellent and floriferous one.

The next subject of exploration and study was to be found in northernmost California, in the Smith River Canyon of Del Norte county, *Iris thompsonii*, which is disputable as a 'good' species, much evidence having been presented to the effect that it actually is a vast hybrid swarm deriving from the purple form of *Iris innominata* and *Iris douglasiana* and our observations of wide variation in the foliage, particularly, but in general in all parts, would not stand up to close inspection of this entity as a good species. In general, it might be described as a refined *I. douglasiana,* yet many individuals might well be taken for taller, and slightly coarser, *I. innominata.* As one progresses inland along the highway, the population begins to vary as the Oregon source of the north fork of this river is reached, many individuals being pale cream. It is here that one of the rare tri–hybrid situations among these irises is to be found; *Iris bracteata* has crossed the mountaintops above here to make its Californian appearance, and these, its children, below, have the blood therefore of three species.

Although this had been a late spring, and we had accordingly delayed our trip, we were fortunate finding *Iris bracteata* in good flower across the Siskiyou mountain barrier in Josephine county, Oregon. Here in the gravelly plains of the Illinois river basin, an area bitterly cold in winter, as bitterly hot and dry in summer, this endemic species is highly successful, one of the prominent plants to appear with the drought resistant undershrubs such as *Arctostophyllos* under the yellow pines of the open forest, and the shining green tufts and clumps of yellowish green leaves are handsome indeed in this sere situation. This is the one species of this group of irises to be found only in yellow, and it is a lovely one, ordinarily veined on the falls with mahogany-red. The foliage is rather sparse as that of *I. purdyi*, its large forms, in tufts rather than in ordinary fans of many interfolded leaves, and each stem bears two large well-formed flowers, a very choice garden subject.

Curiously enough, the mountainsides, right down to the valley floor, to the north of here are covered with another species and yet there is little evidence of much extensive interbreeding. However the northernmost of the *bracteata* population is consistently smaller in stature and size of leaf and flower. The mountainside species surrounding is *Iris chrysophylla*, found exclusively in Oregon and a bit into California north of the Siskiyou mountains. It is one of the long-tube species and may have little or no true stem, the tube serving the function of elevating the star-shaped blossom out above the slender, yellowish foliage. Pallid yellow or nearly white, the flower is veined lightly or heavily with reddish or purple lines. In one area we found all the flowers much more brightly coloured, and atop a stem of quite some length this late in the season. Ordinarily

Iris innominata

this is among the first of these irises to flower, at which time the stems may be 1 in (2.5cm) or even less in length. Like most of these allied species, it can vary, even to being coloured orchid; an unusual feature is the erect, elongated and ornamentally 'feathered' trio of style-arms. This is a nice smaller species for the rock-garden and foreplanting to the shrubbery.

With this exploration completed, we returned to the coast and drove northward along a newly completed highway that was a joy to drive, but one that avoided all the better irises, and so we made some excursions inland into the reaches of *Iris innominata*. It is curious that this handsomest of iris species seldom grows within sight of the ocean, preferring the hot interior valleys of Curry county, Oregon. The southernmost forms in occurrence are purple in colour, and the northern ones yellow, or often in a mixed population. The most coveted colour forms are in the golden to orange colour range, and they are handsome, dainty things in the wild as well as in the garden, where they have in recent years become quite well-known, both in 'pure' form as well as in hybrids, particularly with *Iris douglasiana*; this hybrid combination is to be found in the wild, and in other places than in the hybrid *thompsonii* area; where the yellow form of *innominata* has been the parent, the progeny run strongly to yellow flowers of good size, form and substance. In fact, some of the finest things we have found on these trips have probably been this hybrid combination, and a total of ten flowers per stem has been counted on some of the best ones. In addition lilac and amber branched hybrids occur also. In areas where purple innominata has been the parent, the majority of the hybrid progeny resembles the Smith River *I. thompsonii*, and yellow is not represented, there having been no yellow in the parent stock.

Among the more interesting hybrids to be seen, are those atop Langlois Hill in northernmost Curry county, where an isolated remnant of a once larger *Iris tenax* population has interbred with the coastal *Iris douglasiana.* Here the greatest amount of variability in stature was displayed, from branched, tall plants of over 2 ft (60cm) down to 4 in (10cm) plants, leaves and foliage about equal, and with 2 in (5cm) flowers topping the grassy tufts. These miniature forms seemed all to have segregated in an eroded and weathered outcrop where they were tightly chinked in with club mosses and lichens, a situation I have not before nor since found any of these irises to choose.

Inland in the Wilammette Valley some attention has been given

Agapanthus 'Dorothy Palmer'

Anthemis tinctoria 'Wargrave Variety'

Paeonia mlokosewitschii

Lychnis chalcedonica

to a 'new' iris growing thereabouts, particularly toward the village of Noti, and for which we have tentatively applied the name '*notiensis*.' It has been described by a local biological authority as an ancient segregate from the hybrid combination of *Iris chrysophylla* with *Iris tenax*. It is in stature and season of blossom more like the former, though coloured as the latter, an orchid tint, and with erect standards and flower form also of the latter. This was nearly past flowering as we visited, and would have long since been gone in a normal season, for the surrounding areas had come into full flower in our absence, the surrounding species being the northernmost member of Californicae, the valley-bound *Iris tenax,* found only occasionally toward the seacoast. Among hybrids of this extraction have been found a number of most unusual and worthwhile individuals for garden use, and no two such populations appear to produce similar ones, though all seem to be attractive in themselves.

The low, broad valley of the Wilammette River was now beautifully carpeted with *Iris tenax*; in colour this is ordinarily an orchid-pink but here in the southernmost reaches of its range, it is very much deeper toned, and rich blue-purple and red-purple are the rule. This is a most handsome and graceful plant, a very hardy and tolerant garden addition, and the one member of Californicae to be deciduous. The slender stems bear one or two flowers, but an established plant is profuse with such stems. This species occurrs too as far north as the Nehalem River in southwestern Washington, in its orchid form, and in a small area in Washington County, Oregon, we have previously explored the area where its yellow-flowered form, once called *Iris gormanii* is found. Where this form has mixed with typical *Iris tenax* a profusion of beautiful pastel tints and blends, mostly adorned with a contrasting deeper pattern on the falls in addition to the traditional golden median blaze, and here we find in addition to white, cream and soft yellow, both plain and fancy, the deep raspberry and fuchsia shades and some that are as near to true pink as to be found in the Californicae Irises.

And so we return to carefully plant our collected prizes, and already with plans in our futures for another trip, one we hope that will include some of the other Californian species, those found on the slopes of the Sierras and in the mountains of northern California. It has been a strenuous but rewarding journey through the rainbow of Pacific Coast Irises.

Originally published in 1962. Volume 3, number 1

Cottage Garden Perennials

by Margery Fish

IT is very usual to hear the words 'Cottage Garden' used in connection with certain plants. These old favourites have definite qualifications for this description, they must be tough and easy to please, but not by any means without garden merit. A great many of the plants that have lived so long in our cottage gardens came originally from the big houses, thrown out when fashion decreed a change to elaborate bedding, or 'acquired' by gardeners in the form of cutting or seed. It is a very good thing they were, for many a good plant would be lost to cultivation had it not been for the care of the cottagers. Plants in a cottage garden were safe; they would never be disturbed, or neglected, and I am sure they were happy with their fellows crowding round them.

Nurserymen used to find the old cottage gardens a wonderful source of supply for lost treasures. Soon after we went to Somerset and I was busy buying plants from Scott's Nursery in Merriott, Mr Wallis the proprietor asked if I could help him. He had an enquiry for *Stachys byzantina* and thought perhaps I might be able to find him a plant in one of the cottage gardens in the village. I did, and from that scrap many thousands of plants have been produced.

On another day he offered me *Stokesia* as being an old-fashioned plant. I still have it, and appreciate its willingness to flower from July to October and its very good dark foliage in the winter. There are two improved forms being grown today, *Stokesia* 'Blue Moon' and *S.* 'Blue Star'.

This has happened in so many cases. The cottagers (and some of the rest of us) still grow *Campanula latiloba* in their gardens, but the better form which appears in nurseryman's lists is *C. latiloba* 'Highcliffe'.

Another campanula, *C. glomerata*, the clustered bell-flower of cottage gardens, is an excellent plant for dry shade and for any part of the garden where its running ways can be tolerated. There are several improved forms which are worthy of a place in the border, *C. glomerata* 'Joan Elliott' is early and fairly dwarf, while

Stokesia laevis

C. glomerata superba grows to 2½ ft (75cm). No cottage garden was complete without doronicum, leopard's bane, with its early golden daisies and good evergreen leaves. The improved forms being grown today are *Doronicum* 'Harpur Crewe' and the dwarf *D.* 'Miss Mason'.

Oxalis floribunda is one of the easiest plants to please. It will grow anywhere and all it asks for is the sun to shine. Its village name is shamrock and it is a useful plant for walls and odd corners.

Great strides have been made with erigerons in recent years but several of the cottage types are still seen sometimes, and they have a far longer season of blooming. *E. philadelphicus,* with its small hanging pink heads has an appealing beauty in a modest way, *E. speciosus* goes on flowering throughout the season, and *E. multiradiatus* does the same, with flowers of pink or mauve on long lank arms, which need firm staking to be attractive.

Veronica longifolia was one of the old well-loved plants, in varying shades of blue, because it is an inveterate seeder and the seedlings vary in colour. *Polemonium caeruleum*, our old friend Jacob's ladder, also seeds itself, and it has been greatly improved for modern gardens. *P. richardsonii* is the nearest to the old plant, but with bigger flowers, and a better habit of flowering.

How seldom now is seen the old goldenrod, *Solidago caesia*, with its whippy black stems and encrusted yellow flowers, and yet it is a good plant, with neat dark foliage and no bad encroaching ways. The helianthus we grow today have big flowers and a sturdy habit, a vast improvement on the old plant, *Helianthus rigidus*, which used to be called *Harpalium rigidus*.

Aster tradescantii has come back to popularity, for modern gardeners appreciate its graceful arching stems, with myriads of hovering white flowers late in the year. *Aster* 'Photograph' is still being grown, and more people are now growing *Aster lateriflorus horizontalis*, with its tiny crimson centred lilac flowers and dark foliage on horizontal stems. Neither *Aster* 'Empress' or *A. alpigenus* have a great deal of colour but they fitted into the colourful medley of a cottage garden.

When I was moving *Chrysanthemum uliginosum* recently I realized why it had survived so long, though it is seldom seen except in village gardens. Its strong fleshy roots defy extinction and are adequate anchors for the five foot stems furnished with green-eyed white daisies. Cottage chrysanthemums were real perennials, and remained in their appointed garden places year after year, flowering in October and November. Interest in them is gaining ground and we grow today 'Anastasia' in mauvish pink and her bronze counterpart, 'Dr. Tom Parr' in rose madder and 'Rob Roy' in glowing crimson. The tall double pink 'Emperor of China,' has good autumn leaves, and 'Innocence,' a delicate single pink, flowers generously. The tall cottage chrysanthemums can be stragglers unless they are staked early or grown to peer through shrubs or tall perennials.

The cottage variety of *Sedum spectabile* was robust but merely the pale sad pink which has been improved in *S.* 'Brilliant,' 'Carmen' and 'Meteor,' and the *Sedum telephium* they grew was tall and thin with small flowers, not to be compared with *S.* 'Autumn Joy' and 'Munstead Red.'

Omphalodes cappadocica and *O. verna* remain the same first-class shade plants and respond to an undisturbed life in the damp shade of a cottage garden. *Helleborus niger* used to be just a Christmas rose, with no fancy name to denote size, growth, time of flowering or pink shaded petals, but it was never disturbed and was as good as any we grow today. Solomon's seal, *Polygonatum* × *hybridum*, and lily-of-the-valley, crown imperials and *Dicentra spectabilis*, the graceful 'lyre' plant or bleeding heart, are all typical cottage plants.

Omphalodes cappadocica

There were phloxes, with small flowers and hard colours, which were seldom divided, and red penstemon and heucheras. Astrantias are simple, retiring plants, but quite indestructible. One of my greatest treasures is an extra large form of *Astrantia major,* with long petals heavily etched with green. A friend in whose family it had been for years, gave it to me, but I have heard recently that a form not unlike it has been seen in cottage gardens in parts of Gloucestershire.

Cottage pinks had a fragrance and stamina not always found in modern pinks, but the flowers were often blowsy and untidy. Poor 'Mrs Sinkins' has been largely superseded because of her regrettable habit of calyx splitting, and the old clove types, which had such a delicious perfume were not as shapely as modern pinks. There was a good scarlet, aptly called 'Rifleman', and two delicious pale pink varieties, 'Reine Hortense', in a delicate shade and 'Marie Antoinette' in a deeper colour. Laced pinks such as 'William Brownhill' and 'Little Old Lady' are still cultivated, and such old plants as 'Caesar's Mantle' and 'Sops-in-Wine' still exist.

Double primroses, auriculas and laced polyanthus are cottage plants, and so are double perennial wallflowers and double sweet rocket. Cottage gardens have given us many of our most cherished plants, and though the gardens may go we are lucky still to have the plants.

Originally published in 1962. Volume 3, number 1

Butter and Cream

by Alice M. Coates

NEXT to pink forms of yellow flowers, I have a partiality for cream-coloured flowers—using the terms in its widest sense, to cover the shades ranging from butter or lemon-yellow to sulphur, primrose and ivory. These fulfil the same function as do white flowers, of lightening and enlivening the border, but without any risk of being discordant or harsh. White flowers, lovely in themselves, require to be placed with some care; they are best by themselves, with grey or dark foliage or with certain blues. Painters know how sparingly pure white must be used, if it is not to distract the eye and jar the harmony of the whole; but cream-coloured flowers can safely be planted anywhere, and in any quantity. I am not one of those who believe that flower-colours never clash, but cream can pacify the warfare of orange and magenta, and look equally well with either. Even in spring, when white and gold is the proper wear, and the most blatant dandelion or doronicum does not look out of place, I prefer the paler daffodils, the ivory wallflowers. Later on, when the golds turn to brass, the superior value of silver-gilt is even more apparent.

On examination, the unexpected fact emerges that cream-coloured flowers are remarkably few. Take for example the innumerable families of yellow-rayed composites—only a handful of them have produced lemon or cream forms. The pale varieties of *Anthemis tinctoria* are among the best, and are excellent for cutting. The belauded yellow achilleas do not please me, but I like the silver-leaved *Achillea taygetea*, which opens lemon and fades to ivory. There is a good lavender-cotton, *Santolina neapolitana* 'Citrina', which even when kept hard pruned will cover itself in summer with tidy butter-balls; it makes a fine show at a distance, but close at hand the flowers have a slightly soiled appearance, suggestive of aged woollen underwear. Lemon forms occur among the newer solidagos, but lighter and more graceful in habit is the bigeneric hybrid, *Solidaster luteus* (*Solidago missouriensis* × *Aster ptarmacoides*), which can be relied upon to give a fine primrose-yellow display. But in the families of coreopsis, gaillardia, helenium, helianthus, heliopsis and rudbeckia I do not know of a single blonde; nor for that matter have I ever seen a cream-coloured dandelion, though I believe that many shades of this flower are cultivated in Japan.

Other families predominantly yellow have their rare but attractive cream representatives. Among the oenotheras there is a lovely pale variety of the biennial *O. odorata* that is well worth growing; the brassy hypericums are redeemed by the exquisite *H. olympicum citrinum*, and the lemon variety of *Alyssum saxatile* forms a much more pleasing contrast to its inevitable companions the purple and crimson aubretias, than the usual gold type. For a big mass of the desired colour, there is nothing to beat the tree-lupins, whose colours cover the whole range from milk through cream and butter to cheese; and the sulphur-coloured giant scabious, *Cephalaria gigantea*. But these are plants for the larger garden, where the silver-gilt *Cytisus praecox*, the paler forms of *Potentilla fruticosa* and the cream and apricot azaleas might also find a place. On a smaller scale, *Sisyrinchium striatum* can be relied upon for providing clumps of bloom over a long period, and there are rock-garden or front-of-the-border treasures such as *Anemone magellanica*. Cream and primrose forms are common among the narcissi, and fairly so among tulips, flag irises, gladioli and violas, but are rare among crocuses, and surprisingly infrequent among chrysanthemums, where they are particularly desirable, blending as they do as well with the pinks and purples as with the gold and bronze shades.

A few more names might be mentioned—the new kniphofia, 'Maid of Orleans'; and the stiff little bells of *Digitalis lutea*—but on the whole the list is a short one, and what is more, the items on it are not easily obtained. Few nurserymen stock the pale forms; they seem convinced that all the public wants is ever brighter and more brazen yellows. Attempts to raise the desired varieties from seed are often disappointing; the seed is seldom offered, and the seedlings too often fail to come true. I suspect that the cream and lemon varieties tend to be less robust than their darker cousins and are relatively short-lived, which would account for their rarity.

Originally published in 1962. Volume 2, number 1

Hardy Plants for Seaside Districts

by Christine Kelway

HAND in hand with increasing building development in coastal areas goes a growing interest in hardy plants suitable for seaside gardens, and since frost is not the bugbear within the sea's influence that it is inland, gardeners on the coast need not concern themselves as closely with the frost-hardiness of plants and would be able to include many a near-tender plant were it not for the damaging effect of sea-wind and salt-scorch. Where there is shelter from these there is little problem and there is practically no limit to what will grow successfully, but gales and salt are immensely destructive to unprotected plants.

Few plants really enjoy the buffeting of violent, salty wind straight off the sea, though fortunately for seaside gardeners there are some which endure this sort of torment better than others and even a few that appear to revel in such conditions.

For sandy, limy soils the huge dianthus family undoubtedly tops our list; border carnations and garden pinks of every description all relish the salty tang of sea breezes and their stiff grey foliage is unaffected by a drenching salt-bath. Thrifts or sea-pinks (*Armeria maritima*) are a common sight in summer when they have a long-flowering season on exposed headlands when their grassy tussocks are studded with pale pink flowers. These low-growing cushions make an ideal edging for a cottage path or for clothing a sea-facing wall and varieties in red, deep rose and white as well as the more common pink make a pretty patchwork quilt effect. For the front of the flower-border there are some with broader leaves and rounded heads on long stems.

In the same way that shrubs with grey or silver foliage are so successful by the sea because of the myriads of tiny hairs protecting their leaf surfaces, so we may confidently expect most perennial plants with similar leaves to do as well. Such beautiful foliage-plants as *Senecio cineraria* (*Cineraria maritima*), *Centaurea gymnocarpa* and *Senecio leucostachys* may be reduced by frost to horrid black messes inland, but stand a remarkable amount of exposure on the

Eryngium maritimum

coast and are hardy enough for warmer coastal areas. The sea holly, *Eryngium maritimum*, was once a familiar denizen on sandy dunes, and cultivated forms of it and the globe thistle (*Echinops*) are excellent seaside plants, but for very exposed situations I prefer such dwarf varieties as *Eryngium* 'Blue Dwarf' and *Echinops* 'Veitch's Blue', *Catananche caerulea* bears silvery scaly buds that open to exquisite mauve-blue flowers in June, and the dry papery flowers do well in trying conditions of drying winds. Among the achilleas, the grey-leaved *Achillea clypeolata* with flat yellow heads and the long-flowering *A.* 'Coronation Gold' are very good. Though *Anthemis cupaniana* may be too prolific a seeder for some tastes, it's ferny grey foliage and white daisy flowers are very decorative hanging down a wall in company with the trailing *Convolvulus sabatius* whose pale blue saucers fading to mauve with age continue on into autumn.

Kniphofias (red hot pokers) flourish even on the inhospitable north-east coast and though they benefit from moisture at the roots during the flowering season they resent a soil that gets waterlogged. There is now such a wide range both in height and colour that they may be had in flower from April to October. Spring planting is best and once planted they like to be left alone. Irises are very successful by the sea because of the rigidity of their stems and leaves and are worth the risk of a June gale destroying their all too short season of bloom. The dwarf *Iris pumila*, in purple, blue or gold, stands a better chance and is very welcome in April and May.

To achieve a striking, sub-tropical note the New Zealand flax, *Phormium tenax,* may be planted, but not too near the house, as it leaves makes a rattling sound that can be very disturbing in a gale. As well as those with sea-green or purple leaves there is a variegated form whose tall sword-like leaves are edged with yellow and the immense arching spikes of dull coppery-red flowers are borne in late summer. With similar foliage effect, yuccas make good accent plants either as a single incident on a lawn or at a corner or rising spear-like from dense ground-cover. One of the hardiest as well as one of the most beautiful is *Yucca filamentosa* which can be relied upon to throw up imposing spikes of creamy-white, bell-shaped flowers each summer. The yuccas are sun lovers and never flowered better than during the long hot summer of 1959. *Crambe cordifolia,* 5 ft (1.5m) tall, a showy relative of the wild seakale sometimes found on shingle beaches, has large panicles of white flowers and huge leathery leaves, so that rather after the manner of *Phormium tenax* it might be used to create a sub-tropical effect in a seaside garden. None of these plants requires staking; indeed this is almost an impossibility in a windy garden on the coast.

For low massed plantations there are few hardy perennials so indifferent to soil and so decorative and long-lasting in flower as *Sedum spectabile* with thick glaucous leaves and flat carmine flowers. It has at last received the Award of Merit which this useful late bloomer richly deserves. *Sedum spectabile* 'Brilliant' has flowers deeper and brighter in colour that contrast well with the type. The soft pinks and purples of perennial mesembryanthemums act as a foil to the exotic colouring of that old favourite, *Gazania splendens,* bright orange with a black centre and all the newer large-flowered hybrids in varied colours. Not hardy enough for colder inland gardens they make spreading mats of colour from May to September by the sea. Both 'mezzies' and gazanias like a light sandy soil and no spot is too hot for them.

Originally published in 1962. Volume 3, number 1

Agapanthus

by The Hon. Lewis Palmer

THE old-fashioned idea that agapanthus or African blue lily was not a hardy plant was largely the fault of the botanists of the last century, who included all the varieties of agapanthus that came from South Africa (and they are found wild nowhere else) under a single species *Agapanthus campanulatus*.

In fact it is now established that there are now some fourteen or fifteen different species of agapanthus that inhabit very different climatic regions in their native land, and the name *A. campanulatus* belongs to none of them!

Those that come from the coastal regions of the cape and Natal are usually not hardy and those were the first to be introduced into British gardens in the 17th and 18th centuries. But, those that naturally inhabit the dry cold high veldt and the mountains of the Drakensberg are generally perfectly hardy under English conditions.

Agapanthus have been cultivated for some two and a half centuries in African gardens and it is fairly safe to say that the vast majority of forms of garden origin are of hybrid blood. A great many of these hybrids have a greater or lesser dose of hardy blood which often give them the same hardiness as their hardy ancestors enjoyed. I have been breeding and selecting from these hardy strains for nearly twenty years and I have plants in my garden now that came through the winter of 1947/48 in the open. Last winter which was a very severe one for shrubs, killed 9 of my agapanthus in the open out of over 200 plants and some of those were recent acquisitions that had been planted out experimentally.

Hardy agapanthus are of all sorts, tall or short, deciduous or evergreen, early flowering (July) or late flowering (September) with open bells or hanging tubes dark blue, blue, pale blue or white. The leaves of deciduous varieties turn yellow and die down in the autumn, those of evergreen varieties stay green until frost comes to reduce them to a pulpy mush. One would imagine that the plants would be severely damaged by this but it is not the case. The

Agapanthus campanulatus

following spring the leaves come up again as strongly as ever and they flower just as well as the deciduous varieties.

All like a hot well drained position in full sun and are perfectly happy in a hungry sand or plain chalk. What they do not like is getting their roots wet in water or being dug round in the autumn since their long white fleshy roots extend for quite a distance all round the plant. I find they respond with increased vigour to an autumnal mulch of chopped bracken or of bonfire ash.

This year, like everything else, they are very late. Instead of beginning to flower in the middle of July, the first blossoms opened in the first week of August and now at the time of writing during the second week of August I can see from my window over a hundred flower heads making a haze of blue at the bottom and at the top of my rock garden.

Originally published in 1961. Volume 3, number 1

Iran and Turkey

by Paul Furse

IN 1962 my wife and I made a long journey in Iran and Turkey to collect plants and dried specimens for the Royal Horticultural Society and for Kew; a general account of the flora of this area has been published in the R.H.S. Journal, and articles on several groups of alpine and bulbous plants will appear in the specialist periodicals and Year Books. The following notes try to give an impression of some of the more handsome plants in the area which might be valuable in gardens; some of them are already in cultivation, and it was fascinating to see these growing under natural conditions.

Lack of water and intensive over-grazing are the two dominant factors affecting the vegetation of most of the area, and it is only on the slopes of the Pontus and Elburz ranges, above the Black and the Caspian Seas, that there is enough rain to support dense rain-forests; in the mountainous provinces of Armenia, Azerbaijan, Kurdistan, and the northern end of the Zagros range there is rain to produce rich vegetation and comparatively green pastures and even hay, and it is in these areas that most of the 'herbaceous' plants grow. The general altitude is between 4 and 6,000 feet, and the winters are cold and harsh, the summers dry and hot. Another favourable area is the extreme west of the country close to the Iraq border, where there is scrub oak; if it were not for the grazing a forest would grow up. The rest of the area is mostly very dry and not good country to find plants suitable for our gardens; indeed, we were told that Iran has the biggest area of the whole world which has no plants at all!

Campanulaceae

The campanulas were among the most showy families; white *C. alliariifolia* grows on all the rocky banks and cliffs above Trebizond, hanging out its long stalks of white flowers; the glades of the spruce forests above are often a solid mass of 6 ft (1.8m) dark mauve *C. lactiflora*, its glowing colour there being intensified by contrast with clumps of tall golden inulas and a shower of magenta sparks from the flowers of *Geranium psilostemon*.

Campanula rapunculoides grows in both the forests with

C. trachelium (or species very close to these), and a tall dark purple form of *C. glomerata* grew in the Elburz valleys and on the Armenian uplands. Another outstanding campanula was *C. stevenii* which is a large and graceful semi-erect harebell that swings its pale blue bells in the winds of the Azerbaijan and Elburz ranges; for contrast in these mountains there is *Michauxia laevigata* with almost unbranched stems up to 9 ft (2.7m) high, stiff and sticky, with white flowers opening irregularly over a long period.

Dipsaceae

Of the scabious families the most striking was the giant yellow *Cephalaria gigantea,* 6 ft (1.8m) high and in masses in the Armenian hay; in Iran there were shorter yellow species 18 or 6 in (45 or 15cm) tall and in thick mats (*Cephalaria pilosa* and *Pterocephalus canus*), both growing on stony slopes. There were attractive slender annual species too, such as *Scabiosa olivieri*, which makes bushy plants with thread-thin stalks, carrying pale blue or white flowers.

Boraginaceae

The borage family was always with us and often splendid, particularly blue acres of *Anchusa italica* and *strigosa* in Kurdistan in spring, on fallow ground; *A. officinalis* was a glorious sight in Armenia in August, masses of bushy plants smothered under deep and brilliant blue flowers. With the latter grew the very beautiful *Echium plantagineum,* its 18 in (45cm) clumps entirely covered in deep powder-blue flowers; in the Elburz there were two more lovely echiums, *E. italicum* which is a pale blue version of the British Viper's Bugloss, and *E. amoenum*, which sprawls and has very large crimson flowers.

Yellow arnebias and alkannas often covered large slopes, like deep yellow lithospermums, but we never found any species with the maroon spots of the Prophet Flower. Onosmas of course are a great feature throughout the Middle East, many of them tall enough to be valuable border plants if they proved hardy; they arc yellow and orange, salmon pink, pinky white, and even opalescent pale blue (*OO. dichroantha, pachypoda, rascheyanum,* etc). Brilliant blue *Moltkia coerulea* sometimes grew in masses on open grazing slopes, and we learned to recognise it as a signal telling us to hunt for irises and fritillaries which often grew in association with it.

Papaveraceae

The most surprising plants were the oriental poppies growing in drifts in the Elburz between 6000 and 9000 feet, sometimes mixed with yellow *Eremerus spectabilis* or *E. stenophylla*; the poppies were large-flowered, and always deep blood-crimson. On Kuh i Savalon, the greatest mountain in Azerbaijan, we found another large poppy, more slender and with pale vermilion flowers 4 in (10cm) across, like a crumpled meconopsis.

In Kurdistan and Armenia *Papaver armenaicum* and *P. triniifolium* were lovely, both with grey bristly leaves and thick stems, carrying a loose shower of rather small pale scarlet or pink flowers, and again very like a meconopsis.

The horned poppies were really fine, in all colours through crimson and scarlet, yellow and orange, and with a satiny texture to the petals; the loveliest was *Glaucinium grandiflorum*, and it is of interest that young plants grown from seed collected during 1960 suffered no damage during the winter of 1962–3 although growing fully exposed and under snow in our cold clay garden in east Kent.

Ranunculaceae

There were many beautiful species of the Ranunculaceae; the delphiniums included deep blue *D. tomentellum*, about 3 ft (90cm) tall with a loose spike of large flowers, and we collected another very striking species in Kurdistan, *D. macrostachyum*, which was about 4 ft (120cm) tall with a slender branched inflorescence of small bronze-black flowers in tight racemes. *D. saniculifolia* in the Elburz has slender spikes of purplish blue or blue-and-white flowers, and on high Armenian slopes at the end of the summer there was a species with foot-high stems and tight spikes of blue or sulphur or bicoloured flowers. Throughout the area we found many larkspurs ranging from tall deep purple *D. orientale* which covered whole hay slopes, down to single-flowered species making bushy little plants only a few inches high, such as *D. thirkeanum*.

Aquilegia olympica grows both above the Black Sea and the Caspian; in the Pontus it is low-growing with very large blue and white flowers, the form usually grown as *A. glandulosa* or *A. jucunda*, and it hangs its flowers above the young hay; in the Elburz valleys it grows beside streams and irrigation channels, even at 9000 feet, with 4 ft (120cm) stems carrying many smaller flowers of the same lovely colours.

We found only two monkshoods, both in the Pontus, one *A. orientale* made 4 ft (120cm) thickets in wet hayfields above tree level, with loose showers of mauvey-blue and white flowers, and the other was a yellow species in the forest glades which looked like *A. lycoctonum*. In similar wet and shady places in the Pontus and in the Elburz we found a lot of *Thalictrum minus*, tall, with small yellow tassels; and throughout the mountains of Iran we found several small alpine thalictrums with fine-cut grey leaves and stems less than 12 in (30cm) high, such as *T. isopyroides*.

Anemone narcissiflora

The only hellebore was *H. orientalis* in the Pontus, and always a strong white and green form, sometimes tinged with pink.

Anemone narcissiflora is one of the main constituents of the hay of the high yailas in Armenia and the Pontus, a strong-growing form 15 in (38cm) tall, its large clusters of brilliant white flowers untouched by pink. *A. coronaria* grows near the Iraq border, a slender graceful form with white or lilac-blue flowers, but we never saw pink or red forms. The very beautiful little *A. biflora* in pinks and reds, and the violet-black *Pulsatilla armena* are both small plants, suitable for the rock garden.

Ranunculus asiaticus we only found near the Persian Gulf, and it was almost always the strong-growing deep crimson form, very occasionally orange, never the slender graceful pink or white or yellow forms which grow in the Mediterranean area.

The large crimson-pink *Paeonia arientina* is common on sunny stony slopes in the Pontus, but we did not find the even more beautiful white peony (akin to *P. wittmanniana*) which grows in the Caspian forest.

Labiatae

The Labiatae were always with us, and often lovely; *Nepeta speciosa* made large violet-ultramarine splashes in Armenian hay, and *N. racemosa* and *N. fissa* were a feature in the Elburz on stony slopes. Throughout the Elburz and Kurdistan the same deep violet colour appeared with the loose and elegant *Teucrium orientale*, which makes clumps a yard across.

Salvias were almost innumerable, among the most striking being *S. virgata* with its spikes of deep violet flowers and its calices stained with chestnut; *S. pseudosylvestris* was of the same sort, but stronger and with very aromatic leaves. In Azerbaijan there was lovely small *S. suffruticosa* with large yellow flowers. Of them all we loved best *Salvia aristata*, with a loose much-branched and hairy infloresсense, carrying widely-spaced large flowers of an exquisite salmon-orange colour; we collected what seeds we could find of this, like blue apple-pips.

There were many *Phlomis* species, and we particularly liked *P. kurdica* with several slender 18 in (45cm) stems carrying loose whorls of old-gold flowers, and another much heavier species which made big clumps of robust 3 ft (90cm) stems, with crowded whorls of crushed-strawberry-and-cream flowers.

Another charming labiate was *Stachys lavandulifolia*, a spreading plant only a few inches high, entirely covered in a web of long silver hairs out of which come the large-lipped deep magenta flowers; a pearl-like white form was even more lovely. This plant is aromatic, and you can make a mint tea out of it, and locally it is called 'Persian Kittens'; altogether a delightful plant.

Scrophulariaceae

The Scrophulariaceae were most noticeable for the verbascums, particularly *V. olympicum* which was very common in the Elburz and Armenia, with masses of tall branched spikes of pale yellow flowers. Another beauty was *V. szovitsianum* in the corn of Azerbaijan, slender, two foot, with a graceful spike of large yellow flowers.

The best *Linaria* was *L. dalmatica* var. *grandiflora*, growing 30 in (76cm) tall with a curving spike of large yellow flowers; *L. fastigiata* is handsome in Kurdistan, but its untidy inflorescence spoils the effect of its toffee orange flowers.

Two foxgloves were lovely in Turkey; the tall orange-brown spikes of *D. ferruginea* in the Pontus forest glades, and woolly white *D. orientalis* on drier stony slopes; both of these are valuable self-seeding plants for untidy gardens.

Leguminosae

The Papillionaceae were numerous and often very beautiful, but probably not many would be useful outside the rock garden except for two or three large yellow astragalus species, about 18 in (45cm) high and as beautiful as lupins. A very large sulpher-coloured clover (*Trifolium trichocephalum*) in Armenia would be a good summer plant with its 12–18 in (30–45cm) stems, and in Iran *T. resupinatum* is grown for hay, and though its pink flowers are small and rather dingy, its scent is so fantastically sweet and strong that it would be valuable in the garden.

The well-known *Lathyrus rotundifolius* is common in the Elburz, and just as beautiful as it is in British gardens.

Carophyllaceae

There were many Carophyllaceae, including a lot of *Silene* species, both as alpine rock plants and as herbaccous campions up to 2 ft (60cm) tall and usually with whitish or pale yellow or green flowers, all of which would be handsome and unusual in a wild garden.

The majority of the *Dianthus* which we found were rather straggly and small-flowered, but they often made such large clumps with so very many flowers that they were spectacular; the only showy large-flowered species was 15 in (38cm) tall with several stems, each carrying large creamy flowers, deeply fringed, and laced with crimson.

The gypsophilas were not very remarkable, the usual clouds of white or pink flowers, such as *GG. bicolor, polychloda,* and *virgata.*

Geraniaceae

There were not many large geraniums suitable for gardens, and the brilliant well-known *G. psilostemon* was the outstanding species; *G. tuberosum* is very widespread, and though it varies a lot is always lovely with mauvey blue flowers which sometimes look purple and sometimes bright blue. *G. kotschyi* is another tuberous species with larger flowers, and there was *G. trilophium* in the valleys of the Elburz, making large clumps beside the streams with many 12 in (30cm) slender stems carrying large clear pink flowers.

Linaceae

Linums are beautiful throughout Turkey and Iran; in Armenia there is *L. anatolica* with strong leafy stems and clustered heads of white or pink or crimson flowers; in the Elburz there is *L. bungei* which is the most brilliant cobalt blue flax that I know, and in Kurdistan *L. austriacum* grew 2 ft (60cm) high with very slender stems crowned by two or three very large pale blue flowers. The beautiful glaucous and white *L. album* is very widespread in Iran, and so is *L. mucronatum* which makes a bushy plant with large yellow flowers, sometimes with a central crimson eye.

Compositae

Of very many Compositae the monumental thistles were outstanding, and the echinops as cornfield weeds; large golden inulas such as *I. helenium* grow in the damper places and in the forests, and in the Black Sea forest there was a splendid blue lactuca 6 ft (1.8cm) tall. Centaureas grew everywhere and the deep blue *C. depressa* made acres of flower-hay in Azerbaijan; another beauty was the pink and white *C. dealbata.*

Umbelliferae

Umbelliferae were one more omnipresent family, and many of the large plants such as *Heracleum persicum* and species of prangos and peucedanum would be fine in large wild gardens. The many eryngiums were attractive, varying from 1–6 ft (30–180cm) high; the most interesting was *E. wanturi* in Azerbaijan, which has the ensiform iris-like leaves which are characteristic of some of the South American species; it is interesting that the genus should produce this unusual leaf-form in two such widely distant places.

Cruciferae

The Cruciferae were always with us and among them were beautiful plants, particularly some of the smaller plants for rock gardens. The tall yellow isatis species are very lovely in the distance, and so are huge bushy white crambes which often grow mixed with scarlet poppies. *Hesperis persicus* is attractive with large long-petalled flowers in racemes, coloured green or yellow, olive or dusty purple; *Fibigia suffruticosa* had such beautiful red flowers that we always knew it as the 'Carmine Beauty'.

Malvaceae and Solanaceae

Hollyhocks grew beside the road all the way from Iran to Macedonia, either primrose-coloured, white or pink, always single and 3–4 ft (90–120cm) tall, growing on stony banks and slopes or in masses in the fallows. Another group of plants in these places was henbane, (*Hyoscyamus*), with primrose or purplish-pink flowers finely netted with dark purple veins.

Shrubby Plants

Small shrubby plants of great beauty included the prostrate trailing *Vinca libanotica* with starry blue flowers, and the Rose of Persia (*Hulthemia berberidifolia*) which makes small prickly bushes with glaucous leaves and yellow flowers blotched with crimson like a Cistus. Another treasure was *Plumbago europaea* in Azerbaijan and Armenia, its bushes 18 in (45cm) high and 3 ft (90cm) across, with masses of long-tubed purplish-blue flowers.

Woodlanders

An attractive woodlander was *Epimedium pinnatum* in both the Black Sea and Caspian forests, its yellow spikes coming out before there were leaves on the trees, just after the cyclamens and snowdrops. In drier scrub oakwoods in Kurdistan we found the beautiful pink *Acanthus discoridis*, which is only 6–10 in (15–20cm) high but has a very large showy flower. A second dwarf *Acanthus* grew on hot banks in Anatolia, but it was in seed and we do not yet know its colour.

Gentians

Only a few Gentians were suitable for places outside the rock garden. *G. asclepiadea* was as fine in the Pontus forests as it is in the Alps; above tree level in Turkey there was strong-growing *G. septemfida* which does so well in Britain, and pale yellow *G. gelida* which would probably do equally well in gardens as it looks strong enough to hold its own in a low border; it varies a lot, creamy yellow striped outside with pale green or purple, and usually with cluster heads, and it grows in quantity in the hay. In Armenia, too, there is *G. cruciata* as in the Alps.

Marsh and Water Plants

Marshy places in Kurdistan and elsewhere had lovely plants, including the slender ruby-purple *Gladiolus persicus*; *Scilla persica* was over 12 in (30cm) high with very many sky-blue flowers, and both marsh orchids and *O. laxiflora* were common and usually mixed with the tall yellow spikes of *Pedicularis comosa. Primula auriculata* was vigorous and its head of purple-pink flowers was often 12 in (30cm) high. Two swertias grew 18 in (45cm) tall, *S. aucheri* with spikes of dark indigo flowers and *S. haussknichtii* with greeny-white flowers: and there was sapphire-blue *Gentiana olivieri*.

In still lusher wetter places we found the yellow flag (*Iris pseudo-acorus*), *Sanguisorba officinalis*, purple lythrums and yellow lysimachia, flowering rush (*Butomus*), marsh mallows (*Althaea*) and sea lavenders (*Limonium*); a curiously British community.

Liliaceae

It would be impossible not to mention some of the tall liliaceae which are so suitable for growing among hardy plants in the garden, such as several eremurus about 3 ft (90cm) tall; yellow *EE. spectabilis*, *stenophylla* and *persicus*, and pink or white *E. olgae*. Another plant was *Ornithogalum leichtlinii* which grows among corn, 2 ft (60cm) tall with a big white spike, which would be splendid if it proved hardy.

Of the many alliums, some would be valuable; *A. noeanum* is only 12 in high (30cm) and has large heads of big pink flowers, *A. orientalis* is the same height but has tight balls of white flowers with very dark ovaries, *A. laceratum* is a tall purple ball-head; *A. ampeloprasum atroviolaceum* grows in cornfields, raising its tight violet-black balls 2 ft (60cm) slender stems so that they sway in the wind over the bronzing corn.

Finally, for more shady places there was tall *Veratrum viride* in the Pontus glades, and solomon's seals and *Paris incompleta* in deeper shade.

Originally published in 1963. Volume 3, number 2

Antique Plants

by Alice M. Coats

ANYONE attempting to construct an Elizabethan garden, using for the purpose only plants known to have been in cultivation before 1600, would be likely to receive some surprises, when he came to select the herbaceous plants eligible for inclusion. Some of the surprises would be unpleasant. Many apparently 'old-world' flowers are not truly antique, but only old-fashioned; the genuine period garden could include no perennial delphiniums or lupins, no bergamot, catmint or mignonette. The omissions would be particularly apparent in the autumn, for there were no chrysanthemums, dahlias, phloxes or Japanese anemones in the sixteenth century, and the only Michaelmas daisy was the Italian *Aster amellus*. Many heaths were known, but none were cultivated. The year's display finished with the late hollyhocks, snapdragons and carnations.

The easiest way of telling which flowers would *not* be available for such a garden, would be to look for their countries of origin. Our Elizabethan ancestors had nothing (with one possible exception) from the great floral regions of China and Japan; nothing from South Africa, western North America, Chile, or (again with one exception) Peru. They were limited to the flora of Europe and the Near East, plus a few Central American species from the West Indies, most of which had arrived by way of Spain. On the other hand, most of the garden-worthy European species had been introduced by 1600, including some which have been unfairly neglected but are now returning to fashion; and the early introductions from America included the sunflower, canna, yucca, 'French' and 'African' marigolds, and nasturtiums (*Tropaeolum minus*, not the more familiar *T. majus*)—not to mention the tomato, potato, tobacco, aloe and Marvel of Peru. Basil, balsam, cock's comb and globe amaranth, (all tender plants) had come by slow stages from India.

A list has been preserved which was made by John Gerard of plants growing in his own garden in 1599, two years after the publication of his famous *Herball*; it comprises over 900 species of plants, the majority of which would now be classified as being of botanical interest only. Nearly all the ornamental ones are still in cultivation, though usually in the form of 'improved' varieties. Even a selection from the list would be too long to print here; but it might be of interest to quote Parkinson's list of 'English' flowers in 1629. These, he explains, were plants that had been so long cultivated in English gardens that they had come to be regarded as our own, whereas most of the bulbous plants, of more recent introduction, were known as 'French flowers'—from whatever country they had come. The 'English flowers' were: various primroses and cowslips; single and double rose-campions; single and double Flower of Bristow or Nonesuch (*Lychnis chalcedonica*; the double form, a fine plant, is still available, though rare); double wild campions; wallflowers, stock gilloflowers (Stocks); Queen's gilloflowers or dame's violets (*Hesperis matronalis*); violets, columbines, larkspurs; double poppies, daisies and marigolds; French marigolds; gilloflowers, pinks, sweet Williams and sweet Johns; double and single paeonies (*P. officinalis*); hollyhocks, pansies and heartsease. Among our oldest flowers, though not on this list, are cornflowers, snapdragon, iris, lily of the valley and periwinkle. Our ancestors also cultivated a number of double or freak forms of native plants, such as galligaskins (a hose-in-hose cowslip), the

Cyclamen coum

hen-and-chicken or childing daisy, and the rose-plantain. We still have the double ladysmock, the double marsh-marigold, and the double buttercup (which Gerard found in a field 'next unto the Theater by London'—*i.e.*, Shakespeare's 'Globe' at Southwark), but I do not know whether the double ragged Robin or the double red campion, which Parkinson called 'Bachelor's Buttons', are still to be found.

These are the real antiques of the garden; but Gerard's list also included a number of species by no means common to-day, which would not readily be recognised as belonging to so remote a period. He grew, for example, *Onosma echioides, Cyclamen coum, Gentiana acaulis,* and sixteen iris species, including *sibirica, graminea, susianus* and (*Hermodactylis*) *tuberosus.* A wonderful Elizabethan 'mourning border' might be planted, using the last two species, the almost black *Geranium phaeum, Veratrum nigrum,* and the darkest forms of *Fritillaria meleagris* and *Lilium martagon.* The very dark annual scabious, *S. atropurpurea*, came shortly afterwards; if we extended our period to cover the plants grown by Parkinson thirty years later, this might be included, as well as other fine, non-mournful plants such as *Gentiana asclepiadea, Paeonia peregrina, Lobelia cardinalis* and *Nigella hispanica.*

My own choice from Gerard's garden would include *Dictamnus alba,* the white form (the pink is dingy); both Veratrums, *album* and *nigrum*; the shrubby *Phlomis fruticosa*; and possibly also *Lactuca perennis, Catananche caerulea*, and *Astrantia major.* But the most surprising of Gerard's plants is the exception already mentioned; he had a 'Blew Bell-flower of China', that has been tentatively identified as *Platycodon grandiflorum.* The identification is uncertain, because no picture or specimen remains to guide us; how he could have obtained such a plant must remain for ever a mystery.

Originally published in 1963. Volume 3, number 2

Plants for Shade

by Margery Fish

THERE are certain plants one thinks of immediately in connection with shady gardens, hostas, hellebores and bergenias among them, as well as lilies and campanulas, and many of the paeonies. There are many other plants that do well in the shade but whatever one introduces it is important to see that the soil is good and the plants do not dry out. It is so often forgotten that shade means trees, and trees mean poor, dry soil, which must be improved by the addition of humus and kept moist by watering and mulches.

Astrantias are receiving more attention these days and understandably as they are easy and rewarding plants and like to grow in shade. The one most often seen is *A. major,* with pale flowers touched with green and pink, on 2 ft (60cm) stems. It is not a showy plant but fits in anywhere and is sometimes called 'Hattie's Pincushion' or 'The Melancholy Gentleman'. Though not as bright as some of the others the plant has a long flowering period and seeds itself well. *A. carniolica* is so similar that some experts consider it synonymous with *A. major. Astrantia biebersteinii* has the same pale colouring with perhaps a little more pink in the flowers and leaves more like *A. maxima.* It used to be called *A. intermedia*, being intermediate between *A. major* and *A. maxima.* The latter which used to be called *A. helleborifolia*, is quite distinct with its three lobed leaves like those of a hellebore, its running white roots and flowers which are a definite pink inside and shaded green outside. It flowers in June and July then finishes for the season. *A. carniolica rubra* has the deepest coloured flowers of all, in dark crimson. It is not really as pretty a plant as the others but the colour break makes it quite popular. There are two others but they are not yet in general cultivation. One is a form of *A. major* with very large shaggy flowers, the long, shapely petals being tipped with green. *A. minor* grows to about 1 ft (30cm) and has smaller leaves and flowers which are not much more than little bunches of stamens.

Solomon's seal, polygonatum, has been grown in cottage gardens

Polygonatum × hybridum

for many years and is now enjoying a comeback because it is the type of plant suitable for informal gardening and like the astrantias looks after itself. *Polygonatum × hybridum* has several forms. The largest, *P. biflorum* grows to 4–5 ft (120–150cm), the normal variety grown is about 2½ ft (76cm) and the small one, *P. × h. falcatum*, about 12–18 in (30–45cm). The double flowers of *P. × hybridum* 'Flore Pleno' miss something of the grace of the single variety, but it is a rare and interesting plant. *P. verticillatum* is an uncommon British native which has leaves growing in whorls up the stems and small flowers also in whorls. There used to be a pink form, *P. roseum,* which had flowers of purplish-pink instead of white. The Solomon's seal with variegated leaves shows up well against a dark background but it is not as strong a plant as the other types. All the polygonatums look best above eye level so that one can see the green tipped white flowers hanging from the arching stems. The flowers are followed by black berries.

Smilacina racemosa is not unlike the polygonatums but it has its sprays of small feathery cream flowers at the top of the leafy stems.

Most of the geraniums flower as well in shade as in sun but some get rather big and leafy and are more suited to a woodland garden or for under-planting shrubs. The three double forms of *Geranium*

Tiarella wherryi

pratense with blue, purple or white flowers are worthy of any shady border. With me the purple and blue forms grow to 3 ft (90cm) or more but the white-flowered form is seldom more than 2 ft (60cm) *G. delavayi* has very good leaves and small, but interesting, reflexed flowers of dark crimson with prominent glistening red styles. The pale lilac flowers of *G. nodosum* hover above pale green leaves, which have a lacquered surface. It seeds itself mildly and mixes well with all other flowers. *G. atlanticum* has bulbous roots and is deciduous. It disappears completely in the summer and after autumn rain the well-cut leaves reappear, to be followed in spring by blue, red-veined flowers. Both *G. wallichianum* 'Buxton's Blue', with white-eyed blue flowers, and *G. grevillianum*, which has bright pink flowers, do well in shade and have beautiful leaves.

The leaves of the tiarellas are beautifully marked too and they all have feathery cream flowers which give them the name of foam flowers. *T. wherryi* is the most aristocratic with pointed leaves and neat habit but it seems to need a fairly damp position and does not increase quickly. Nor does *T. unifoliata,* which is rather woody and has large pointed leaves which colour well in autumn. *T. cordifolia* is the one most usually grown. It has running roots and rather flat leaves. There are two other species, *T. polyphylla,* with sprays of tiny pearl-like flowers and *T. trifoliata* which has small feathery flowers.

Some people advocate that *Liriope muscari* should grow in full sun but the best plants I have seen have been in shade and that is where I grow it. The encrusted spikes of blue or white flowers appear in autumn above the grassy leaves. *Reineckia carnea* also has grassy leaves and soft, pinky-mauve flowers which are sometimes hidden by the leaves.

One of the most exciting plants to grow in shade is *Arisaema candidissima*. It makes its appearance late but with great speed. About the end of June one looks for it. The ground is bare one day and the next a pointed spike is about 1 in (2.5cm)above the soil and the handsome white flower, marked with crimson and green, opens in a day or two, to be followed by very large leaves.

The toad lilies, *Tricyrtis*, have character too, with mottled flowers on 2 ft (60cm) stems. The flowers are curiously shaped and speckled with mauve or purple. *TT. maculata, stolonifera* and *hirta* have mauve flecked flowers and there is also a white form of *T. hirta.*

Speirantha gardenii caused great interest when it was shown at Chelsea a few years ago. It is somewhat reminiscent of lily-of-the-valley with leaves of the same type and spikes of small white flowers. *Rohdea japonica* is similar but has larger, more fleshy leaves and shorter flower spikes.

Some gardeners dispute the name of *Selinum carvifolia* and consider it should be *S. tenuifolium*, which is the plant the late E. A. Bowles grew. Both plants can be seen in the Oxford Botanic Garden and both have very fine, fernlike foliage. *Selinum carvifolia* is a rare British native sometimes found in Cambridgeshire fens and known as Cambridge parsley. Its red stems and large heads of lacy-white flowers make it a sensational plant for shade.

Originally published 1964. Volume 3, number 3

The Development of the Herbaceous Border

by Walter Gilmour

THE history of the herbaceous border is not a long one. Old gardening literature makes no specific mention of it, although a general reference to borders is not uncommon. It is entirely artificial in its concept, and a good herbaceous border is frequently the best loved and most beautiful of all garden features and this, in spite of the fact that it represents an instance in which man presumes to improve on nature.

The Persians, in ancient times, had a great love of flowers and this induced them to grow them in clumps, boldly displayed along their favourite walks. Most of the evidence of flower borders in the past comes from chronicles of mediaeval times and the physic gardens of the monastries.

Monastic gardens were essentially enclosures, and within the high walls all was quiet and restful. They were usually designed as a square plot with straight, narrow paths running through, a few trees and simple beds in which herbs and vegetables were tended with great care. A few flowers, especially roses, were grown for use in religious ceremonies, but most of the colour in the garden was to be found in the herbarium, where such things as violets, poppies and lilies were grown for their medicinal properties.

The next stage at which we find mention of herbaceous fashion is towards the end of the fourteenth and beginning of the fifteenth centuries, when noblemen and less important citizens owned residences round London and in other parts of the country.

Although fruit, vegetables and herbs were still given pride of place, men of this time were bringing back from other lands plants to add beauty to their gardens. In a way these men, unknown to themselves, were our first plant collectors.

Many collectors have passed, and been remembered, although many have, unfortunately, been forgotten. One of these was a young collector who brought together herbaceous material from all parts of Europe. This man was Patrick Murray, Baron of Levingstone.

It was during the middle of the seventeenth century that this young nobleman, in possession of an ample fortune, turned his attention to the study of natural history, and not content with farming at his own country-seat, he formed a botanical collection consisting of one thousand species of plants, a great collection in those infant days of science, and he traversed European countries with a view to increasing it. Having travelled over the whole of France, he was on his way to Italy, when smitten by a fever and died as a result. His death was deeply regretted by those friends who could estimate the worth of character displayed by a youth, who, in possession of an abundant fortune, could steadily devote himself to a praiseworthy pursuit.

Patrick Murray had been a friend and pupil of Sir Andrew Balfour, who, after his death, had his plants transported to Edinburgh where he added them to his own collection and laid the foundation of the first Botanic Garden in that city.

In 1827 Loudon listed border flowers under the titles 'perennials, bulbs, biennials and annuals—hardy and half-hardy'. Later on George Nicolson, then curator of the Royal Botanic Garden, Kew, advised 'the best results are obtained when a border is mainly made up of hardy herbaceous perennials'. This was only the start of this type of gardening and more ideas were on the way from William Robinson, a superb plantsman and writer of this time, also Gertrude Jekyll, who once said, 'I try for beauty and harmony everywhere, and especially for harmony of colour. A garden so treated gives a delightful feeling of repose and refreshment'.

Among the first to see the merits of carpeting borders effectively and who suggested the border in Robinson's *Hardy Flowers* was Frank Miles, an exceptionally fine flower gardener who improved and took great interest in his father's garden at Bingham. He wrote, 'We can never go back to the mixed border of our ancestors; we have been spoilt for such blank flowerless spaces as they had, by the gorgeousness of bedding out. But we have now a wealth of hardy plants especially bulbs, which they have never had, and this combination of bulbous plants and herbaceous plants will certainly lead to a preparation of the borders which have been hardly dreamt of by people who do not care what they spend on tropical flowers; for it seems to be forgotten that we have irises as big as plates and lilies as tall as a tree, all hardy and requiring little attention when once they have been properly planted'.

This country was quite content with its new term 'herbaceous border' though, unfortunately, the plants did not lend themselves to the beauty we have in our borders today. This may have been partly the reason for our American friends to change from their large collections of perennial plants to mass bedding plant schemes, however, the hybridizers changed the garden picture somewhat, and introduced many outstanding perennial personalities.

We hope these perennial personalities of the herbaceous border will give us joy for many years to come.

Originally published in 1965. Volume 3, number 4

Common Sense with Paeonies

by Donald Leatherdale

I USUALLY put off giving an answer when asked to name my favourite genus of plants, for as each season unfolds I realize increasingly that nearly all the plants in a garden are there for the main reason that each of them is a favourite at its appropriate time. At one time, it is obvious that so well-known a genus as the rose predominates; at another time, it may be a much less frequently seen plant that takes pride-of-place – such as *Kirengeshoma palmata*, blooming with serene beauty in half-hidden solitude. And so it would be that a visitor in May or June might be excused from imagining that paeonies were my sole passion in the garden.

As the years have passed, I have made more and more use of the genus *Paeonia* as I have come to understand both its potentialities and its limitations. Also with the passing of time, I have come to the reluctant conclusion that many writers on paeonies have over-simplified the care needed by these, the most magnificent of our hardy herbaceous plants, and it is difficult to see why they should have done so. They have tended to create the impression that paeonies are so long-lived and constitutionally robust that, once planted, the plants may be left to their own devices.

Paeonies most certainly are long-lived, yes, and robust. But let us not leave them at that. They make certain demands, and he who satisfies those demands will have the considerable satisfaction of knowing that in early summer his paeonies will be giving of their well-worthwhile best.

First of all, where shall they be planted? (I hope, by the way, that you are, to some extent, an experimental gardener—one who is prepared to try the unorthodox approach now and again.) Paeonies will tolerate a wide range of conditions, some of them flowering well in almost sunless situations and yet none of them being averse to full exposure to the sun. Generally, it may be said (as indeed of many types of plants) that paeonies in the shade will bloom for a longer period although less freely than those in a sunny site, but varieties vary considerably in this respect; in my experience, some of the singles fare better in moderate shade. All paeonies prefer a moisture-retentive soil, but that by no means rules them out on chalk or sand, for their needs are satisfied by the incorporation of manure, leaf-mould or possibly peat in the lower levels when planting. They are less happy in ground that becomes waterlogged in winter, but even here there may be suitable varieties, for I must admit that I have seen long-established clumps growing strongly in almost marsh-like conditions.

As paeonies are such long-lived herbaceous plants, their inclusion in a herbaceous border of the traditional type may well be an embarrassment, for when the time comes to give the border an overhaul it will usually be considered advisable to leave the paeonies as islands in the dug area. Please do not construe this as meaning that they must not be shifted; the oft-given advice that paeonies will not flower for several years after a move is no doubt prudent on the part of the nurseryman, but is misleading. Plants brought in from a distance usually do need a year or two in which to settle down, but blooming will not be retarded in the least when we move plants from place to place in the garden, provided that the majority of the roots are contained in a single, large lump of soil, for both shoots and roots are brittle. Last autumn I carried out an overdue digging of the single herbaceous border in our own garden and took advantage of the opportunity to move all the plants with the sole exception of dictamnus. Most of the other plants I dug up and laid in on a spare piece of land until I was ready to replant them in new positions, but the paeonies I left until last and then removed and replanted them in the same afternoon: all of them have bloomed well this year, including a plant of 'Sarah Bernhardt' that was exposed on the surface of the border for a fortnight with a sack wrapped around the lump of soil enclosing the roots.

But apart from this, I feel that the paeony is better suited to other parts of the garden than to the borders. The blooming of each variety does not last for long, and plants with as long a flowering period as possible are best chosen for such positions. This is not so important a consideration amongst shrubs, and paeonies provide one of the best types of plant for association with them. Their habit accords well with the spaces between shrubs at all stages in the growth of the latter, and paeonies in the darker colours give an illusory sense of depth to a shrub planting.

Autumn colour at a lower level amongst shrubs may be looked upon in the nature of an unexpected bonus. Too much emphasis has, to my mind, been placed on the foliage coloration of paeonies. Some of the species, such as *P. mlokosewitschii* and the even more difficult-to-obtain *P. tenuifolia*, have delightfully soft green leaves, but those with *officinalis* and *lactiflora* blood have a harder colour and a coarser appearance, and in autumn the chances are that the leaves will change to an untidy wither of brown. In some seasons and in some locations they will take on subtle, pleasing shades of the painter's earthen colours—ochre, umber, sienna, and even a dull purple—but we all know how capricious autumn tints can be. If autumn colour you must have, then perhaps such varieties as 'Mistral', 'Kelway's Supreme' or 'Festiva Maxima' are more dependable in this respect than many other cultivars.

If the space is available, paeonies probably look their finest in beds to themselves—or nearly so. We have a long, narrow bed on the northern side of a privet hedge, the roots of which are kept under control by an annual trimming with a spade. They bloom particularly well in the partial shade thus provided, and are preceded by narcissus and followed by such robust lilies as *Lilium henryi, pardalinum, regale* and *auratum*. This border is pleasing in early spring, when the narcissus contrast with the ruby-shaded emergent leaves of the paeonies, again in June, when the paeonies are at their finest, and in summer, when the lilies spread sideways over the greenery to give the appearance of a bed devoted entirely to them.

The planting of paeonies entails deep preparatory digging, the provision of rough drainage if the soil is inclined to be stodgy, and the inclusion of a liberal amount of dung, compost or leaf-mould. The plants may be moved at any time while they are dormant, but there is little doubt that plants moved as soon as their foliage has died down will be having the very best done for them. Plant with the eyes no deeper than a couple of inches–less is preferable on heavy soils. The planting distance for the general run of varieties would be 2½ ft (76cm), although 4 ft (120cm) apart would not be too much for robust ones: treated well, a paeony can become a large plant in surprisingly few years. I usually complete the planting operation with a scattering of bone-meal, but I must admit that I am addicted to its use in general and I have not compared growth both with and without it.

Most plants will require staking before the flower buds have developed far, and I beg of you to disregard any advice to the contrary. Paeonies do not belong to that fashionable no-staking-

Paeonia emodi

required group of plants. For some years I thought that they did, but so frequently were superb blooms suddenly weighted with rain and bowed ignominiously into the mud that I came to realise that some form of support was essential. I use three or four canes ringed with a single strand of fillis, with crossing strands to quarter some of the larger clumps, but any unobtrusive support would be suitable. One would be justified in giving many of the larger-flowered double varieties a cane to each bloom. The only exceptions to staking that I make are for some of the early-flowering species, and for such later varieties as are purposely allowed to bow down to achieve a desired result in association with architectural features.

Plants derived from the Chinese paeony (*P. lactiflora*), as well as *P. emodi* and *P. veitchii*, produce more than one bloom on a stem. This is a desirable attribute in the garden, where I have not found disbudding to be worthwhile, but some rubbing out of the side buds would doubtless be necessary if show blooms were required.

We used to be advised to retain the shrivelled foliage during the winter to protect the plants, but it has been found in more recent years that the remains of the leaves harbour a fungus, *Botrytis paeoniae*, which is unfortunately becoming more prevalent as a disease. In any case, all except a few species are fully hardy; and even with the others it is more a case of protecting them from the sun after spring frosts, as with tree paeonies, rather than from winter cold.

The manurial requirements of paeonies are simple but essential—few plants respond more bountifully to good treatment in this respect. Annual mulching in the autumn with dung or compost will keep the soil sufficiently retentive of moisture, but an application of bone-meal or superphosphate at 1 oz to the square yard should not be omitted in alternate springs.

The selection of suitable varieties is a very personal matter. A wide range is stocked by many nurserymen, but their catalogue descriptions often fall short of describing the varieties adequately. To my way of thinking, the best way of choosing varieties is to see plants in bloom in public and private gardens; then, having made a list of those that particularly appeal, search through the catalogues and order them accordingly. You will have to hunt for them by name (and learn a few synonyms in the process, no doubt), for classification is a somewhat haphazard business. The Japanese paeony of one supplier is the Chinese paeony of another, and whilst one will list all single varieties in a comprehensive category another will differentiate (perhaps somewhat arbitrarily) between 'Imperial' paeonies and others.

Many of the varieties are too much alike, although it is true that two cultivars of similar substance and colour may well differ in other characters, such as their time of blooming and their degree of perfume. The great majority of varieties have been derived from the June-flowering *P. lactiflora* (syn. *albiflora*) so do not forget that most of the other species bloom earlier and thus extend the season. The species have a delicacy that precedes or complements the full-petalled form of the more commonly-known varieties, and the diligent searcher will find that they have a greater range of colour and habit. Some hybrids and varieties of striking appearance are slowly becoming available, and if their cost precludes their immediate purchase they are well worth saving for.

The selection of varieties for your garden should therefore not be undertaken in too much of a hurry. Develop a critical approach to them and select those that survive your own criteria: you will probably find that the paeonies you want are not necessarily those most lauded in the horticultural press.

Originally published in 1965. Volume 3, number 4

A Brief Survey of the Genus Trillium

by Kenneth A. Beckett

FEW genera have a more appropriate name, for trillium is derived from *trilix*, meaning triple, and as anyone who has even cursorily examined a trillium will know, the trimery of its parts is the most outstanding feature.

The wood lilies, as species of trillium are popularly known, are primarily North American in origin, with some species in east Asia extending from the Himalayas to Japan and Kamchatka. Approximately 40 species names are recognised by some authorities, but it is doubtful if as many as half of these merit separate specific rank. Probably little more than a dozen are in cultivation in Great Britain. (If there are keen trillium enthusiasts with more, I should like to hear from them.)

Practically all are natives of woodland or other moist shady habitats. In cultivation similar situations should be found. Ideally, light woodland with a moist, but not waterlogged, soil, rich in humus should be chosen. A north facing border, preferably sheltered from the north-east, or the north side of a shrub or shrub border is equally good. On the other hand, a number of species will flourish in the open border provided that there is shelter from wind and the soil is always adequately moist.

Propagation is usually by division of the rootstock, which in mature specimens is a cluster of rhizomes. In some species the rhizomes are fleshy and tuber-like, in others they are more slender, with an accompanying growth of fibrous roots. It is stated that division should be done during the dormant season, late summer to autumn being ideal. From personal experience I have found that they also move very satisfactorily just as they finish flowering; rather like snowdrops. The operation must of course be done with care, and the divisions must not be allowed to dry out under any circumstances. Seed may be sown and if one is patient it is the best way to increase one's stock numerically. However, even when the seeds are sown as soon as ripe, germination usually takes 18 months and the subsequent seedlings take up to five and more years before they flower.

Unlike many of the genera of *Liliaceae*, for example, *Lilium*, *Tulipa*, *Scilla* and *Convallaria*, which have petaloid sepals, those of trillium are clearly differentiated and are generally green and smaller than the petals. Indeed, so distinct and clearly definable is the genus trillium, in this and other characteristics, that some authorities place it in a family of its own—*Trilliacea*—along with its only other near ally, *Paris*. *Trillium* may be roughly divided into two main groups; one where the flower sits stemless at the junction of the three leaves—as typified by *T. sessile*, and the other where the flower is borne on a peduncle from the same junction, as in *T. grandiflorum*. It will be easier, however, for the purposes of this survey to discuss the names in the literature alphabetically.

T. album Small, comes from North Carolina, Georgia and Tennessee. It is little more than a white-flowered form of *erectum* and need not concern us further.

T. × *amabile* Miyabe and Tatew., is an alleged hybrid between the Japanese *smallii* and *kamtschaticum*, with larger flowers than either and well developed, ovate orbicular, purple petals. It is known only from the island of Hokkaido.

T. catesbaei Elliott is similar to *cernuum* in appearance, but the petals are undulate, arching and much longer than the sepals. Dr Rendle considers this plant to be a distinct form of *stylosum*, which in turn is only a variant of *cernuum*. It is now rare in the wild and may even be extinct.

T. cernuum Linn, has the delightful vernacular name of 'bashful Benjamin'. It has a wide distribution in the USA and Canada, being found in the woods of Newfoundland west to Manitoba and south to Minnesota and North Carolina. This is a species with a more or less fibrous root system surrounding the ascending rhizomes. The leaves, which can range up to 6 in (15cm) long, are rhombic-ovate, tapered to a point and narrowed to a short petiole. They are set on a stem approximately 5–8 in (13–20cm) tall. The flower is white or pink and borne at the end of a short peduncle so strongly nutant as to all but hide it beneath the foliage—hence the common name. The pink form is designated *T. c. tangerae*. A broadly ovate, dark-red berry follows the sweetly-scented flower. It is easily grown in a peaty soil.

T. chloropetalum Howell, is, in the strictest sense, the large western form of *sessile* with greenish-yellow petals. It was at one time considered to be a form of *giganteum*, which in turn is only the large western form of *sessile* with the usual maroon-purple flowers. When it was realised that the western form varied in the colour of its flowers and that therefore only one name was needed to represent it, *chloropetalum*, being the oldest was given priority over *giganteum*. It is a variable plant, but easily distinguished from *sessile* by its more robust habit, attaining a foot or more at flowering time, and brownish-purple mottled, broadly ovate leaves, approximately 6 in (15cm) long. The flowers can be as much as twice the size of *sessile,* ranging to 3 in (7.5cm) long and varying in colour from maroon through red, pink to greenish-white and yellow. It occurs in the wild from Washington State down into California. Cultivation is easy and it will flourish in the open border.

T. crassifolium Piper, is no more than a dwarf form of *ovatum* with curiously thickened leaves.

T. declinatum Gleason, is a white-flowered species which would seem to have close affinities with *grandiflorum.* It is not in cultivation in this country as far as can be ascertained. C. H. Grey maintains that this native of Ohio, south Michigan and Missouri will thrive in full sun in a moist position.

T. decumbens Harbison, was found in 1901 in the Sand Mountains of north-east Alabama. From Grey's description it appears to be an aberrant form of *sessile.* The stems are almost prostrate and densely pubescent; flowers brownish-purple. Not in cultivation.

T. discolor Wray, is undoubtedly a form of *sessile* and has, in fact, been known as *sessile* var. *wrayi.* However, it is convenient to discuss this somewhat puzzling entity under the above heading. Grey's description suggests that it is a distinct form of sessile with more handsomely marked foliage and sulphur-yellow flowers. *The R.H.S. Dictionary* states that the flowers are 'dark purple varying to green'; Farrer comments 'greenish'. Who is right, I wonder? A plant of this name was shown by the firm of Veitch in 1890 and received an Award of Merit. Certainly the yellow-flowered plant of Grey would seem to be worth obtaining.

T. erectum Linn. (syn. *rhomboideum* and *acuminatum*) has some quaint vernacular names: stinking Benjamin, birthroot and squawroot being a few of them. It is not uncommon in the eastern United States and Canada, extending as far south as Pennsylvania to Tennessee. From a stoutish rhizome a number of sturdy stems arise, topped by prominently nerved, broadly rhombic-ovate, acuminate leaves. The peduncle is usually straight, up to 4 in (10cm) long, but often less and topped by a 1 in (2.5cm) long flower that may be crimson or dark purple. *T. e. cahnae* has purple and white flowers, *viridiflorum* greenish, *luteum,* clear yellow and *albiflorum,* white. Generally speaking the scent is rather unpleasant, but in *blandum,* with fuller, creamy-white flowers, it is described as 'not ill-scented'. As with some other species polymery occurs and a form designated *polymerum* has its parts in multiples of four or more.

T. flexipes Raf. would appear to be close to *cernuum*, and is distinguished by its courser growth, sessile leaves and much larger white flowers. *T. f. walpolei* is similar, but with maroon or purple flowers. Almost certainly it is not in cultivation.

T. govanianum Royle, is interesting from a taxonomic point of view, in that it may well represent a link between *Trillium* and *Paris*. Although the leaves and perianth parts are in the usual multiples of three and not the four and more of *Paris*, there is still a strong resemblance in the erect flowers with long, narrow, purple petals and comparatively long spreading stigmas. It is a small species, rarely exceeding 4–6 in (10–15cm) high in its native Himalayas. The slender, rigid stems and 3 in (7.5cm)-long, ovate, shortly petiolate leaves are a bright green and distinctive. This little species is more quaint than showy and of no great garden worth, and is probably not in cultivation.

T. grandiflorum Salisb. is the plant most people visualise when the names trillium, wood lily or wake robin are mentioned. It is an extraordinarily variable species in its native North America. Indeed, in the past many of its forms were given separate specific rank. In cultivation in this country it is usually represented by a vigorous form with broadly ovate, lustrous-green leaves with strongly impressed veins, and glistening white flowers. The latter may be as much as 3 in (7.5cm) long, with wavy-margined, obovate petals and set upon sturdy peduncles somewhat inclined at the top. This robust species is a good garden plant and will tolerate drier conditions than some of the others. It is the only species grown at all widely in this country.

The following names represent forms of mutants of *T. grandiflorum*, or entities closely allied: *T. g. chandleri*, is a mutant without leaves, their place being taken by enlarged sepals; *gleasoni*, is a large-growing form, with broadly rhombic-ovate, sessile leaves borne on stems that may reach 2 ft (60cm) in height; *elongatum* has lance-elliptic leaves and very narrow petals; *lirioides*, has ovate leaves on definite petioles; *T. g. parvum*, as its name suggests, is smaller in all its parts, and has flowers that soon turn pink, fading purplish-pink. Along with *chandleri*, the remainder are teratological forms: *polymerum*, has its parts in multiples of four, five or more and *dimerum*, in twos. A number of double-flowered forms are known, and at least one or two are in cultivation. One such form gained an Award of Merit at the R.H.S. Chelsea Flower Show this year (1966), when shown by Major and Mrs Knox-Findlay, Keillour Castle, Perthshire. *T. g. petalosum* covers the extreme double form in which ovary and stamens are petaloid.

T. hugeri Small, (syn. *cuneatum* Raf.), is of the *sessile* group, from North Carolina south to Florida. It would seem to be a distinct form of *T. sessile* with scarcely mottled leaves and shorter petals. According to Grey, the flowers have a musk scent.

T. kamtschaticum Pall., is also *pallasii* Hulten (and *obovatum sensu auct.* Japon., *non* Pursh). This species comes from Kamchatka and north Korea, where it occurs in birch woods. It grows to 20 in high with 4–5 in (10–13cm) long, rounded, acuminate leaves. As the synonymy suggests, this species can be thought of as a western extension of *T. ovatum* across to north-east Asia. It would appear not to have been in cultivation in Great Britain.

T. ludovicianum Harbison, is also of the *sessile* group and should be thought of as a form of that species.

T. luteum (Muhl.) Harbison, again is of the *sessile* group, but very distinct. The sessile, strongly purple-mottled leaves are ovate and borne on stout glabrous stems. The flower is large for the group, with petals 2½ in (6cm) long. In the best forms the lemon-scented flowers are buttercup yellow, but more greenish-yellow forms are not uncommon. This desirable plant is not difficult to grow and should still be in cultivation in Great Britain. Although distinct in appearance it is obviously so close to *sessile* as to be considered merely a variety of it. In the wild it is only found in the Cherokee Indian Reserve of North Carolina.

T. morii Hayata, was collected in the island of Formosa in 1910 and differs from *kamtschaticum* in minor characteristics only.

T. nivale Riddell, is a charming little species from Ohio to Wisconsin and may be thought of as a tiny *grandiflorum*. Overall size rarely exceeds 6 in (15cm) high and the petioled, ovate-obtuse leaves range from ¾–2in (2–5cm) long. Thc short peduncle is topped by a 1 in (2.5cm)-long blossom of white, with oblong petals striped pink at the base. It is almost certainly in cultivation in this country.

T. ovatum Pursh., is also *obovatum* of Hooker—but not of Pursh., which is synonymous with *erectum*. It represents *grandiflorum* on the western side of the USA and is obviously closely akin. The main distinguishing characters are narrow leaves and petals and the rapidity with which the petals turn pink after anthesis. *T. o. stenosepalum* is a minor variant, with a more slender habit and purplish stems. *T. scouleri.* Rydberg and *venosum* Gates are probably synonymous with it.

T. petiolatum Pursh., is another sessile-flowered wood lily, but amazingly distinct by reason of its cordate, long-petioled leaves. It has been found in Idaho, east Oregon and Washington States.

T. pusillum Michaux, includes *ozarkanum* of Palmer and Steyermark. It is a slender species, with narrowly oblong, sessile leaves, on stems that may be as little as 4 or as much as 12 in (10–30cm) high. The lanceolate petals are usually less than 1 in (2.5cm) long, white, soon turning pink and aging purple. Like *catesbaei*, this species has affinities with *cernuum*.

T. rectistamineum (Gates) St John, appears to be an ally of *sessile* from Georgia and Florida. Mottled, deltoid leaves and erect purple flowers with reflexed sepals are its main characteristics. Not in cultivation.

T. recurvatum Beck., from Grey's description sounds very much like *petiolatum,* but with ovate-acute, long-petioled leaves—often mottled grey or whitish—and flowers with incurved, concave, maroon petals. A native of moist woods in Ohio, Mississippi and Arkansas.

T. rivale S. Watson, is a real little rock garden gem among the trilliums, occurring in the wild on stream banks in the mountains of Oregon. The ovate acute, subcordate, petioled leaves often almost hug the ground, but may be on stems 6 in (15cm) or more high in shady places. They rarely exceed 2 in (5cm) long and subtend the relatively long peduncle with its inclined tip and terminal white flower. Individual petals are triangular-ovate-cordate, glistening white, often splashed and spotted pale purple; (rose-carmine according to Grey). This species is akin to *nivale* of south-east USA and resembles it in many respects. It should be in cultivation in Great Britain and presents no cultivational difficulties.

T. rugelii Rendle, comes from the mountains of North Carolina and Georgia, and would seem to be of the *grandiflorum* group. It is of similar size, with broadly rhombic, strongly three-nerved leaves. The flowers are small for the size of the plant, somewhat nodding, the petals and sepals of equal length. Not in cultivation.

T. sessile Linn., has been frequently mentioned in this survey as the type for a number of allied or otherwise similar entities. It is a sturdy species, with dark green, thickish stems and sessile, ovate, or nearly orbicular, dark green leaves frequently mottled pale green or whitish. The sweetly-scented, erect stemless flowers sit tight in the centre of each leaf whorl. They may be maroon purple or greenish-yellow. The petals stand erect like rabbits' ears at anthesis, gently splaying out soon after. They vary from narrowly oblong to oblanceolate, acute or sub-obtuse, up to 1½ in (4cm) long. The sepals are a little shorter and spreading. In its native eastern USA it is sometimes known as toadshade. *T. sessile viridiflorum* Beyer, is the name given to distinguish the yellowish flowered forms.

T. simile Gleason, may be dismissed as akin to *rugelii*, but with petals a little longer than the sepals.

T. smallii Maxim, is a Japanese species from moist woods and wet meadows. It is a pity the earlier synonym of *apetalon* Makino could not be retained for it adequately described the most distinctive characteristic of this species, namely its lack of petals. The stems may reach 8–9 in (20–23cm) but are usually less, with sessile, broadly rhombic-ovate prominently nerved leaves. The purple-brown flower sits on an arching peduncle which may be nutant at anthesis. It consists of three, thick-textured, ovate oblong sepals, each about ¾ in (2cm) long. Occasionally, petals are present, but if so they are very small. Although it has no great garden value it may well be in cultivation. It certainly is in Great Britain, because I brought back a couple of plants from Japan this spring.

T. stamineum Harbison, is another of the *sessile* tribe, with mottled leaves and foetid-smelling, dark purple flowers.

T. stylosum Nuttall, (syn. *T. nervosum* Elliott,) comes from Carolina and Tennessee, south to Georgia and Alabama. It is doubtless a pink-flowered form of *cernuum,* with possibly narrower, more ovate leaves. It may be synonymous with *T. c. tangerae.*

T. tschonoskii Maxim., is a white-flowered species from Japan and Korea, where it is found in shady places in the mountains. It ranges in height from 6–18 in (15–45cm), with rhombic, orbicular leaves, prominently five-nerved. The nodding flower is set upon a slender peduncle. Both sepals and petals are approximately 1 in (2.5cm) long, the petals sometimes a little longer and more broadly ovate. Possibly in cultivation. *T. t. violaceum* has pale rose-purple petals.

T. underwoodii Small, is a good form of our old friend *sessile*, with musk-scented, purple flowers up to 3½ in (9cm) long. The typical foliage is mottled in various shades of green. A native of Florida, Alabama and North Carolina.

T. undulatum Willd., is the painted-lady or painted wood lily, of woodland throughout the north-east quarter of USA. It will tolerate drier conditions than most trillium species—I have found it in quite dryish conifer woods in Main—though it grows more vigorously with adequate moisture. It is a slender, elegant plant, with distinctly petioled, broadly lanceolate leaves that taper to a fine point and are often wavy-margined. A short peduncle carries the 1½ in-wide blossom, each white, wavy-marginal petal prettily marked with a basal horse-shoe of carmine-purple rays. This is followed by a conspicuous ovoid red berry. There are a number of forms, mainly of aberrant mutant types *T. u. polymerum* has its parts in multiples of fours to eights, (there is a dimerous form recorded); *cleavelandicum* has the sepals enlarged to almost leaf size and the leaves in whorls of three to six; *striatum* bears white-striped sepals.

T. viride Beck (syn. *viridescens* Nutt.) is similar to *sessile viridiflorum*, with narrower green petals often exceeding 3 in (7.5cm) long. The leaves too are narrower, tapering to a fine point.

Originally published in 1966. Volume 3, number 5

A Reassessment of the Willow-Herbs

by A. P. Hamilton and V. Thakur

THE family *Onagraceae* contains many genera that have provided great beauty for our gardens. *Fuchsia, Oenothera, Godetia* and *Clarkia* are probably the best known. One genus, however, has provided almost nothing but trouble. This is, of course, *Epilobium,* the willow-herbs.

Epilobium is a fairly large genus containing about 160 species that are native of the temperate and arctic-alpine regions of both hemispheres. It exhibits a wide morphological range and many species are of considerable beauty. However, attempts to turn the willow-herbs into respectable garden plants have always failed. In the case of one species in particular, *E. nerterioides* A. Cunn., the attempts were disastrous. Because of its minute size (about 3 in (7.5cm) tall when flowering) and its dainty white flowers that contrast against the reddish-bronze foliage and stems, this little New Zealander has value in the rock-garden. It also has a very effective reproductive capacity! First recorded in the wild in 1904 by the Firth of Forth it now occurs in at least 300 localities throughout the British Isles, ranging from the Orkneys to Land's End and from Co. Kerry to Essex. A similar story of rapid spread can be told about the rosebay willow-herb or fireweed, *E. angustifolium* L., which conquered much new territory with the aid of the railways.

It is perhaps superfluous to say that the seeds of *Epilobium* are wind-dispersed. Probably every gardener, at one time or another, has had the problem of trying to cope with weeding out the willow-herbs before their long capsules dehisce, releasing clouds of fluffy seeds to the four winds. A very effective means of dispersal it is too, for not only does it ensure that the seeds blow to every part of the garden where they readily germinate, but they will also happily grow on walls and in gutters where they can rain seeds onto the luckless gardener below!

But there is another side to the coin. Many *Epilobium* species are of undoubted beauty and have found a welcome place in gardens—for a while. Of our eleven native species, two have horticultural potential and have been grown in the herbaceous border. One of these has the delightful name of the great hairy willow-herb, *E. hirsutum* L. Another name for it is codlins-and-cream, because the fragrance of the flowers is said to smell like stewed codlin apples, and the name apple pie can be found for it in some parts of the country. The 'cream' presumably refers to the colour of the stigma. *E. hirsutum* grows by streamsides and in damp meadows and is common throughout most of the country except Scotland and the north-east. This species, with its long stems reaching 5–6 ft (1.5–1.9m) high and bearing purplish-rose flowers, is certainly suitable for damp spots in the wild garden.

E. angustifolium is obviously the other candidate for horticulture and it has deliberately been introduced into gardens many times especially around the turn of the century when a white form was also grown.

In the 1930s renewed interest in the rosebay willow-herb arose and once more attempts to turn a beautiful wild flower into a garden plant were made. In 1934 and 1939 the R.H.S. gave Awards of Merit to two cultivars of this species. However, while their beauty was not questioned, their habits were, and these plants have been discontinued in commerce for some time now.

Of the 150 or so other species that are found outside the British Isles several have been grown by rock-gardeners. For instance, *E. fleischeri* Hochst., from the European Alps, *E. glabellum* Forst., from New Zealand and *E. obcordatum* A. Gray, from the mountains of Oregon and California.

Can anything be done to reduce or eliminate the phenomenal ability of *Epilobium* to colonize disturbed and bare ground? It now appears that it can—by hybridization. The willow-herbs hybridize freely, but generally only with those species in their own division of the genus. These hybrids are currently popular for research, primarily because they exhibit the curious phenomenon of cytoplasmic inheritance. During recent work on these hybrids at the University of Durham, one of us (V.T.) crossed *E. hirsutum* as the maternal parent with a dwarf yellow-flowered species from North America, *E. luteum* Pursh., that occurs over a wide area from Alaska to the Cascade Mountains in Oregon. This cross had been made many years earlier by Dr P. Michaelis of the Max Planck Institute and the results were published in 1933. However, no notice appears to have been taken of the horticultural possibilities of the F_1 hybrids and also the back-crosses that were made.

The first generation hybrids can be separated into two types. First, there are the extreme dwarfs that grow only to 1–2 in (2.5–5cm) high and are barely viable. The second group are those that normally grow 8–9 in (20–23cm) tall. It is this latter group that has provided some extremely decorative plants. These taller hybrids are virtually identical in appearance and are characterized by possessing vegetative characters generally like *E. hirsutum* except for the greatly diminished height. The flowers, on the other hand are morphologically closer to *E. luteum*, but in their colouring they have developed a shade that is unique. It is a dark purple that the R.H.S. Colour Chart describes as doge purple (732)—i.e. the colour of *Primula* 'Wanda', which is made even more striking by a long, pure white cruciform stigma that protrudes well out of the flower even up to two days before the flower completely opens. The flowers are larger than *E. hirsutum* and are borne in pairs; the first partner opening about a day ahead of the second. Like most of the willow-herbs these F_1s show closing movements of the flower in the evening. A noticeable improvement is in their perfume which is stronger and sweeter than in *E. hirsutum*. These plants seem to have all the advantages of both parental species and some of their own. However, the most useful character is their high infertility. Indeed, if self-pollinated their seed production is virtually nil; they are virtually self-sterile. The capsules simply turn a golden colour and drop off. This, of course, eliminates the main reason for the unpopularity of willow-herbs as garden plants.

It was felt that further crosses should be made with these two species, this time with the aim of producing worthwhile garden plants only. Back-crosses have been made, but those produced from *E. luteum* have all been unsatisfactory. The usual results are that the buds drop off and the plant never flowers. Some seedlings in this cross do flower, if it can be called flowering, and produce everything except petals! This behaviour Michaelis attributes to an unsatisfactory reaction between the different cell components contributed by the parents. For a detailed account of this phenomenon readers will find E. Caspari's paper helpful. Ironically, these apetalous plants are the most strongly-scented so far produced!

When the *E. hirsutum* × *E. luteum* hybrids were back-crossed with *E. hirsutum* a good range of segregates resulted covering various shades of pink and purple, and differing degrees of floral production and size of flower. Perhaps it should be stated at this juncture that all the crosses mentioned in this article are arranged in the order of the maternal parent first. One of the seedlings from the back-cross with *E. hirsutum* is quite exceptional. Essentially it is similar to the best of the F_1 hybrids but the colour is definitely more intense and the bud colouring is well within the range of colour described by most gardeners as 'black'. The white throat, that in the F_1 is hardly noticeable, has increased to such an extent that it almost is the most striking feature. However, the character that puts this plant in a class of its own is the size of the flowers which average 1¼ in (3cm) in diameter. This is partly accounted for by the flowers being flat rather than the open bell-shape of the F_1 plants. Another pleasant feature is the light covering of white 'fur', a perfect foil to the dark purple flowers. Altogether there is a formidable set of desirable characteristics in one plant.

Looking through the seedling boxes this season two other crosses seem to offer possibilities for the rock-garden. One is derived from *E. lanceolatum* Sebastiani and Mauri, pollinated by *E. luteum.* Their seedlings carry attractive white hanging bell-shaped flowers and look more like *Linnaea borealis* L. than an *Epilobium*. They are very dwarf and reach to only 4 in (10cm). The other cross, *E. hirsutum* × *E. parviflorum* Schreber., is very decorative if one looks down on it, for it holds all its flowers up to the sky. The flowers are a clear pink and rather over ¼ in (0.6cm) in diameter. Perhaps their best feature is that their leaves are so covered in down that they appear grey-green and this acts as a perfect background to the bright pink flowers. The 6 in (15cm) plants that are completely regular in their appearance have obvious possibilities for the creation of uniform carpets of colour in the rock-garden.

A very considerable number of new crosses has been made during the 1966 season and if the new seedlings are as interesting as those so far raised there will be few dull moments next flowering season.

A few notes can be added here on the cultivation of these hybrids. We find they give their best performance in poor soil as they will produce excessive leaf in good garden conditions. In the alpine house best results are obtained when the plant is pot-bound. The ideal situation is certainly the rock-garden and the rockier the better. In the case of the very dwarf ones good places are the edge of paths and crazy-paving where they can run wild. The larger hybrids obviously have 'filler' potential in the margins of borders that are disturbed infrequently, but more especially in shrubberies where shearing at appropriate moments will not only ensure an increase in floral production but also a dense canopy of shoots that will help to suppress weeds. One of their most attractive features is that, as they gradually exhaust the soil, so the ratio of flower production to leaves improves; a feature also shown by many *Tropaeolum* hybrids, the garden nasturtiums. Surely, these *Epilobium* hybrids are the ideal lazy-gardener's plant.

The new willow-herbs, like their parents, begin flowering in the second half of June, reach their peak in July and finish in August. They are readily propagated by stolons.

Since we published our first note on these plants Mrs Sanecki has drawn our attention to some similar work that was done by H. C. Pugsley on the section *Chamaenerion* Tausch., the rosebay willow-herbs. Two species were used by Puglsey in his crosses (*E. angustifolium* and *E. latifolium* L.) and his interesting results were subsequently published in the *Bulletin* of the Hardy Plant Society.

From his article it is clear that we were not the first to think of making willow-herbs acceptable garden plants by sterilizing them. However, while both Pugsley and ourselves had the same aim we have used different methods. Pugsley hoped that by crossing *E. latifolium* whose chromosome number is listed as 2n = 72 with *E. angustifolium,* 2n = 36, the resulting triploids with number 2n = 54 would be sterile because of the chromosomal imbalance at pollen and ovule formation. However, the plant of *E. latifolium* that was counted came from Iceland and appears to have been atypical as the chromosome numbers of all the other European *Epilobium* species that have been counted are all 2n = 36. The *E. latifolium* used by Pugsley came from the Rocky Mountains from seed collected by Will Ingwersen. When the F_1 hybrids were counted they were found to be the usual 2n = 36. This suggests that the *E. latifolium* parent was also 2n = 36. A further point is that, in contrast to our plants, the rosebay seedlings were fertile. This result of Pugsley's work is interesting since it suggests that species in the section *Chamaenerion* do not show the sterility mechanism that we have encountered in our species that come from the section *Epilobium* (= Sect. *Lysimachion* Tausch.). It was, of course, this mechanism that we used for sterilizing our plants; a mechanism that is not based on imbalance of chromosome numbers but rather on some subtle physiology. We feel that our method has some advantage over Pugsley's approach because it does not close the door to further hybridisation at the F_1 stage, as triploidy normally does. The presence of some residual fertility enables one to continue breeding for many generations. At the present state of knowledge it seems perfectly possible to keep adding to the hybrids *ad infinitum*. The range of variation that this should produce ought to provide plants for every taste.

Many thousands of willow-herbs have been raised at Durham since 1963 and it is clear that most of the hybrids of *Epilobium* species are highly infertile. We would suggest that if readers are tempted to hybridize the willow-herbs for themselves, they should note carefully just how sterile their seedlings are. Michaelis has found that some strains have quite a high degree of fertility. Fortunately we have not encountered these in the plants mentioned, but it cannot be emphasized too strongly that if very fertile seedlings are produced it would be best to destroy them before they spread like wildfire. Pugsley's results could be explained by assuming he used fertile strains but more work is needed on the rosebays before firm statements can be made. A series of crosses has been carried out on them at Durham this season. It can be added here that all crosses between section *Chamaenerion* and the other willow-herbs have failed; a result which supports the existing taxonomic division of the genus.

This preliminary analysis that we make of the Durham work on *Epilobium* hybrids does suggest that willow-herbs, in general, can be tamed and made to produce worthwhile garden plants.

References

Caspari, E., (1948) *Cytoplasmic Inheritance* Adv. Genetics. 2. 1–66.

Pugsley, H. C., (1959) *Extracts from the proceeds of the Scientific Committee* Journal R.H.S. Vol. LXXXIV. Part 2. 52.

Pugsley, H. C., (1960) *Interesting Hybrid Willow-Herbs.* Bulletin Hardy Plant Society Vol. 2. No. 5. 102–104.

Thakur, V., (1965) *Biosystematics of Some Species of Epilobium* University of Durham. Ph.D. thesis.

Hamilton, A. P. and Thakur, V., (1966) *New Epilobium Hybrids as Garden Plants.* Journal R.H.S. Vol. XCI Part 7. 304–306.

Harvey, M. J., (1966) *An Experiment with Epilobium angustifolium* Proc. Botanical Society of the British Isles. No. 6. Part 3. 229–231.

Mosquin, Theodore (1966) *A New Taxonomy for Epilobium angustifolium L. (Onagraceae)* Brittonia Vol. 18. No. 2. 167.

Originally published in 1966. Volume 3, number 5

Spotlighting Salvias

by Cornish Torbock

THERE are so many salvias which can be grown in this country that I am surprised I have never come across a book on them and thought that perhaps some observations on my first fifty might be of interest. I am treating them entirely from a gardener's point of view—I am no botanist—and my experience of growing them is in a really cold and rather wet climate in Westmorland.

First of all there is the common sage, *Salvia officinalis*, which is not to be despised, and would be much more grown in the flower garden if we had not all been so familiar with it in the kitchen garden since childhood. The purple and pink variegated form is charming but needs replacing by cuttings, as it appears less hardy when old and woody. On the other hand, the white flowered *S. canescens* lives to a ripe old age and I have two plants which must be 30 years old. I find the grey foliage admirable for picking in March to go with primulas from the greenhouse.

Salvia superba, which we used to call *S. virgata nemorosa*, is, in my opinion, one of the six best herbaceous plants. It never needs replanting or tying up and remains in flower for a long time. The dwarf form *lubeca* which I was given from Holland has never done so well with me, but I have great hopes of the new early variety 'May Night' which I bought at Chelsea last year.

Salvia pratensis makes a wonderful display in the Swiss meadows and I have often thought of trying to establish it in the grass here. I believe it is indigenous, but not in the north. It seeds all over the path but can be razed flat after flowering and survives all the traffic after that. *S. s.* var. *baumgartenii* is a particularly fine deep violet form and the pink *rosea* is pretty too, but I pull up the odd white seedlings that do not appeal to me. *S. hians* from Kashmir is a useful deep blue dwarf with a surprisingly large flower and I once saw at Lochinch a brighter blue of a similar type *S. evansianum* but have never grown it. Another good dwarf is *S. jurisicii* with lavender flowers and a cut leaf which did particularly well at St Pauls', Waldenbury. It has a white form too. I used to grow *S. nutans* which is a brighter blue than most about 3 ft (90cm) high, but I have not been able to find the true plant since the war. Nothing I have been sent nods any longer, so how can it be nutans?

Salvia przewalskii is prettier than its name and the flowers are somewhere between mauve and heliotrope, and rather more bell-shaped than most salvias, but as it is a late starter, I seldom get it tied up as well as I should. I have seen a rosy form of this 3½ ft (100cm) salvia at the Edinburgh Botanic Gardens. *S. castanea* is unique in colour, maroon with a black blotch. *S. forkskahlei*, which is very near what we used to call *S. gardneriana*, is almost as speckled as a schizanthus and grows about 2½ ft (76cm) with me.

The pale blue *azurea* and *uliginosa* are too late to come into flower with me and reluctantly I sent them to warmer homes in the south.

All the foregoing are in shades of blue and mauve, as a general rule. The yellows I class as really wild garden plants. *S. glutinosa* a rather straw yellow in late July and *S. bulleyana* is a better yellow with a chocolate lip. The whites are usually grown for their wonderful grey velvet foliage and as such need keeping dry in winter. This is why *SS. aethiopis, argentea* and *rhodopaea* (which I saw once at Edinburgh but did not think was sufficiently distinct from *argentea*) and the *globosa* once seen at Ingwersen's, are not regular members of my establishment. With these exceptions, *all* the foregoing are perfectly hardy; that is to say they have survived 40°F. from which I feel few readers have experienced!

My next section are the so-called perennials which in our conditions are much better treated as biennials, as they are so easily raised from seed, and as perennials cannot be relied upon here to come up again every year. I have never known the difference between *S. sclarea* and *turkestanica.* All I know is that there are good coloured forms, and a few poor coloured forms. I can usually pick up enough self-sown seedlings for a nursery row for next year. They are worth looking at from June till the frost.

Salvia haematodes is a charming, easily raised plant with its lavender sprays about 3½ ft (100cm) high in July, but needs careful placing, as if you have a large patch there is a blank with practically no foliage when you cut it down. *S. dichroa* 4 ft (120cm) with a pronounced white lip is good, but has never survived flowering with me.

What we used to call *S. verbascifolia*, but what Edinburgh told me is really *brachyphylla,* is very exciting and the lavender flowers look as if they had a velvet bumble bee on them. When you get them nearly 6 ft (1.8m) high in June they really look remarkable.

An equally remarkable plant is the annual *S. carduacea* with grey velvet leaves like a miniature onopordon and flowers about 9 in (23cm) high, mauve with a white lip. I grew it up to the war but have not found seed anywhere since. The annual clary is a good standby in borders particularly pink-tipped clary, which has now got 'with it' to such an extent that it is designated 'Pink Sundae'. As *S. horminum* was introduced in 1596, so I think it can survive on its merits without being given fancy names.

Almost the only hardy salvias which I do not think worth growing are the native *S. verbenaca* which does neither salvia nor verbena any credit and *S. taraxacifolia* from Morocco which is an indeterminate pink.

I seem to have left out *SS. hierosolymitana, lyrata* and *verticillata.* I know I have seen them, but they have not left any impression on me!

The next sections of salvias I could not honestly call hardy—but they have all been grown outside at various times and those with a more fortunate climate than Westmorland may like some account of them.

S. ambigens and *S. caerulea* appear to be the same plant, which has good, rich, deep-blue flowers and grows outside at Forde Abbey. A smaller and brighter blue *S. chamaedryoides* about 2 ft (60cm) high used to be grown by Professor Lyttel near Southampton. *S. patens* and its Cambridge blue form are well-known as bedders—I cannot really say whether from seed or stored tubers do you get the best result. It seems an easy and useful plant either way. *S. coccinea* about 2½ ft (76cm) is equally easy from seed, cutting, or boxed for the winter in a cold frame and has a long flowering season *S. farinacea* is used rather more abroad than in this country but its slender, blue spikes are very attractive. *S. leucantha* has woolly leaves and heliotrope flowers and makes a pretty, low hedge in South Africa but is seldom met outside a greenhouse here.

The next section are the sub-shrubby ones. *S. candelabrum*, flowers purple with a white throat, is more commonly met with than the similar *S. interrupta* which has longer leaves. *S. ringens* is a dwarfer plant about 18 in (4.5cm) and its var. *romanica* which I saw once at Kew has flowers like a pale blue candelabrum.

One of the best new plants I saw last year was *S. recognita* at Bressingham which looked like a pale pink candelabrum. Mr

Bloom also had quite a new colour to me in salvias; *S. buchananii* which I should call puce. I have never seen any salvia approaching that colour before. I suppose some people would call *S. involucrata* magenta, but rosy crimson sounds nicer. The var. *bethellii* is the one usually seen, which has a fat globular bud on the end of the spike which never seems to unfold; nor do I really want it to, as that gives the plant so much character.

Some nurserymen in the past seem to have been confused between *SS. grahammii, greggii* and *neurepia* but the first is deep crimson and smells of black currants and the second is carmine and has a shiny leaf and the third is somewhat between the two but perhaps a carmine flowering *grahamii* is the simplest description.

Salvia fulgens has bright scarlet tubes of hairy velvet and *gesnerifolia* is supposed to have more abundant and showy flowers, but I have never grown the latter to prove it. The only other scarlet I know of a similar height is the pineapple-scented *S. rutilans* which I have never seen outside a greenhouse.

Two dwarf scarlet shrubs are *S. blepharophylla* which is worth trying on a sunny, sheltered rockery and has dark stems and *S. roemeriana* which I saw in the Botanic Garden at Munich, but it may have been put out for the summer. I forgot to ask that excellent gardener, Dr Schacht. I see that Robinson says it should be wintered under glass. It struck me as being cherry coloured rather than scarlet. *S. cacaliifolia* I remember once seeing at Parcevall, but Sir William Milner was such an incurable optimist that he would plant any tender thing outside. I never saw it on subsequent visits and do not remember meeting it anywhere else.

S. splendens is such a harsh colour that I can find no place for it in this garden. I tried a so-called purple only to find it was a muddy chocolate and a salmon pink got by mistake was equally unfortunate.

This does not pretend to be a scientific or even an exhaustive account of the salvias—but it may remind other enthusiasts of plants they have seen or grown in the past and encourage others to attempt to cultivate more of a race which provides so many winners and such a small proportion of losers.

Originally published in 1967. Volume 3, number 6

The Genus Potentilla

by Will Ingwersen

THE name potentilla derives from *potens*, powerful, from the supposed medical properties of some members of this large and very garden-worthy family of plants. It is yet another group in the vast and valuable natural order of *Rosaceae*, and among its 350 or more known species plus many cultivars and hybrids, are to be found shrubs, rock garden plants and hardy herbaceous perennials. In nature potentillas are widely distributed throughout the northern hemisphere.

Within the confines of a short article it is impossible to deal in an exhaustive manner with such a large and important family. I can do no more than describe a selection of the most usually encountered kinds. In the *Bulletin* of the Hardy Plant Society it might be thought more proper to confine myself to those which are strictly herbaceous perennials, but nowadays it is common practise to associate shrubs with border flowers, and to use rock garden plants as ground-cover and for edgings. I shall, therefore, be in no way arbitrary in my selection.

A rather neglected but useful species is *P. alba*, native of central and southern Europe. It is a vigorous, spreading plant and is extremely valuable as a ground-cover for sun or shade. The prostrate, rather woody stems are adorned with dark green leaves divided into five leaflets and the 1 in (2.5cm)-wide white flowers are carried freely from spring until late summer in loose terminal clusters. In gardens it is frequently confused with *P. ternata*, which is similar, but can be detected by its three, instead of five leaflets, and by its rather smaller flowers.

Another white-flowered species, *P. alchemilloides*, which comes from the Pyrenees and Italy, has leaves with five to seven leaflets, smooth and green above, but silvery beneath. It is a sun-lover, and a good plant if given rather spartan treatment. In rich soil it tends to develop foliage at the expense of blossom.

The typical *P. argentea* is not a plant with any great garden value, but in its cultivar 'Calabrica' it has considerable merits. The spreading, prostrate stems are decorated with small leaves cleft into many leaflets which are intensely silver. It makes a handsome grey carpeter and it carries, from May to July, quite pleasant, if not very large yellow flowers. It should be given gritty soil in the fullest possible sunlight.

P. argyrophylla is a robust herbaceous perennial and has been concerned, together with *P. atrosanguinea* and *P. nepalensis*, in the parentage of a race of invaluable hybrids of which, alas, too few are now available. Forty or fifty years ago a score of named cultivars could have been found offered for sale in the catalogues of herbaceous plants. Today, it is remarkable to discover a quarter of that number. It is not that they have been superseded by better plants; for some reason or other they went out of popularity and some of them have been lost altogether. This is one of the many reasons why I am so anxious that, somewhere or other, there should be a 'plant museum' of living examples of the good old plants which are in danger of extinction.

Among the names of these fine, colourful, free and long-flowering hybrids are 'Gibson's Scarlet', 'Vesuvius', 'Van Dyck', 'Chameleon', 'Heroine', 'William Rollison', 'Archimedes', and many more. If you come across any of them, obtain and treasure them. 'Gibson's Scarlet' and 'William Rollison' are still fairly widely cultivated. They all grow to a height of about 18–24 in (45–60cm) with handsome foliage and large flowers which may be, according to variety, single of semi-double, and red, crimson, terra-cotta, orange, yellow, vermilion, or a combination of intense tints.

P. aurea is a low-growing, June to August flowering plant from the European Alps with bright yellow flowers and there is a form with double flowers too. Not unlike it is *P. crantzii*, sometimes grown as *P. alpestris*, which is looser in habit and a little more erect. This plant has a very wide natural distribution, being found in North America, in Asia and in Europe.

If it were more generous in the production of its large, rounded pure white flowers, *P. clusiana* from the Eastern Alps would be a really good plant. As it is it deserves space for the sake of its tufts of cleft, shining silver leaves. It is particularly handsome when grown in spaces between rather dark stones.

Still to be found in some catalogues as *P. flagelliformis*, or *P. fragiformis*, but more correctly, *P. megalantha*, is a very valuable and handsome, easily-grown plant from Japan. The leaves are large, palmate and softly hairy and form dense tufts up to 9 in

(23cm) high. The large, nicely rounded clear yellow flowers are carried in abundance during the summer months. It is not too large for a rock garden and not too small for the front of a flower border, or for use as an edging to border or path. Even when not in flower its ever-green foliage is distinctly handsome.

A plant which will grow in almost any soil, is long-lived and blossoms from spring until autumn is assured of a welcome in any garden and no potentilla better qualifies for praise on these points than *P.× tonguei*. It is a hybrid of rather obscure parentage, but is most probably the result of a marriage between *P. aurea* and *P. nepalensis*. The sprawling, leafy stems require a fair amount of space. A mature plant can easily spread over an area of 2 sq ft (0.2 sqm) and should be kept at a distance from small rarities, which it might smother.

Given gritty, open soil, either alkaline or acid, and full sun, it will flower from May until October, producing a seemingly endless succession of round, flat flowers, about 1 in (2.5cm) in diameter. The colour is not easy to describe and is really a suffusion of rich apricot, orange and terra-cotta with markings of crimson on the petals. If there were such a thing as a list of 100 indispensable plants I would certainly include *P. × tonguei*.

A fine border plant is *P. nepalensis* 'Miss Willmott', a selection from the type, which originated many years ago in the once-famous garden at Warley, in Essex. The branching, 18 in (45cm) stems carry a long succession of rose-pink flowers and it has a worthy companion in *P.n* 'Roxana' which is similar in all ways but has orange-red blossoms. When checking on its present availability I found it listed in several catalogues, and at the same time noted a few good hybrids in the *argyrophylla-nepalensis* clan which I ought to mention as they are to be had. 'Arc en Ciel' is good in blended shades of red and orange. 'Etna' has crimson flowers and 'Glory of Nancy' sets off its semi-double orange-crimson flowers against grey foliage. 'Jupiter' is also semi-double and a fine deep, rich crimson.

An unusual species from New Mexico and California, *P. thurberi*, although not very frequently available, is worth seeking. In general appearance it resembles *P. nepalensis* but the flowers are an unusual shade of deep brown red-purple. They are not very large, but plentiful, and appear during July and August as a rule, on stems of approximately 18 in (45cm). Another very useful border potentilla is *P. recta* 'Warrenii', an 18 in (45cm) plant with sheets of soft yellow flowers from mid to late summer. The type is a native of

S. Europe, Algeria and Siberia and the cultivar is usually, but incorrectly, catalogued as 'Warrensii'.

No list of potentillas could be considered adequate if it did not contain at least a brief mention of the absolutely invaluable forms, clones and hybrids of *P. fruticosa*. Their name is legion and there has been a useful trial of them at Wisley recently which has served to sort out at least some of the confusion surrounding their nomenclature. Some muddle is inevitable in a plant which seeds and hybridises freely and produces a multitude of worth-while seedlings, many of which are named and launched into commerce without careful reference to existing cultivars.

There are no more useful dwarf shrubs for any soil, sun or shade, than the various forms of *P. fruticosa*. On their own, or in association with other plants, especially in the heather garden, they provide a summer-long succession of flowers. Where all are good it is inviduous to single out particular forms, but among the best are 'Elizabeth' (once *P.f.* 'Arbuscula') *vilmoriniana, mandschurica*, 'Sunset', *farreri*, 'Kathleen Dykes' and *purdomii*.

Originally published in 1968. Volume 3, number 7

Polemonium

by Kenneth A. Beckett

UNDER such quaint local vernacular names as 'Jacob's ladder', 'Jacob's walking stick', 'blue jacket', 'charity', 'poverty' and 'ladder to heaven', the common *Polemonium caeruleum* has been cultivated in our gardens for centuries. The reference to 'ladder' is not hard to appreciate, for each leaf with its many pairs of narrow leaflets does resemble a primitive ladder of sorts. Why 'Jacob's' is more obscure, but at least one authority puts forward the hypothesis that Jacob slept with a stone for a pillow and the native habitat of the plant is often in stony places (scree and rock ledges; but also in grassy areas). This, combined with Jacob's vision of a ladder descending from heaven, would appear to be the somewhat obscure origin of the most frequently used common name which now covers many of the American and Asian species as well.

At the most recent count, there are reckoned to be 50 species in the genus *Polemonium*. Most of these are native to North America, but others occur in Mexico, Chile and Europe eastwards to Japan. It is doubtful if all the 50 names represent clearly distinct species and certainly no more than about a dozen are in cultivation at the present time.

The genus falls roughly into two groups from a cultivation point of view, those small plants from high altitudes like *PP. viscosum* and *eximium*, which are not too easy to grow, and the tall species exemplified by the familiar *PP. caeruleum* and *foliosissimum*. The latter group are mostly easily pleased in any good garden soil, alkaline or acid, sun or partial shade. Generally speaking the dwarf mountain species can be cultivated quite satisfactorily providing one prepares a well-drained sunny nook on a rock garden. They can also be grown in pots or pans in the alpine house or frame.

All the species in cultivation are perennials, though some are short-lived. All are characterised by having shortly creeping rhizomes which may be tufted or spreading. In the latter case they are often somewhat woody. All have pinnate leaves, but in some cases the leaflets are lobed and arranged in whorls around the mid-rib in a most distinctive fashion, *P. eximium* being a good example.

Most of the species here described have been in cultivation in Great Britain at one time or another, but to the best of my knowledge the following are not now grown by anyone, though they may lurk in a botanic garden: *PP. mexicanum, micranthum, grandiflorum* and *glabrum*.

It seems likely that the 'true' Jacob's ladder, *P. caeruleum*, is no longer the commonest representative of the genus in our gardens, forms of the very variable, but usually superior, *P. foliosissimum* having taken its place. If one takes the modern view that the former *PP. vanbruntiae* and *occidentale* are only subjects of *P. caeruleum*, then this plant has the widest distribution in the wild, being found in Asia, North America and Europe, as far north as the Arctic Circle.

It has long been known as a native in England, being first recorded in 1666 in Christopher Merrett's *Pinax*. John Ray, one of the true fathers of British botany and an excellent all-round naturalist, found the plant five years later at Malham Cove in the West Riding of Yorkshire where it may still be found to this day. *P. caeruleum* has a very limited distribution—mainly on limestone rocks—from Staffordshire and Derbyshire north to the Cheviots. It does, however, appear in many other parts as a garden escape.

There is no doubting its value as a fine plant for the herbeaceous border, the tough stems seldom requiring staking. The tufts of pinnate foliage create a ferny effect which forms an excellent foil for the erect leafy stems topped by loose spike-like inflorescences composed of small corymbose axillary clusters of blue flowers. These have a short corolla tube and five rounded lobes or 'petals', which partly overlap and create a somewhat bell-like appearance. The stamens are a little shorter than the corolla lobes and the style barely as long or slightly longer. There is a lovely pure white form *P.c.* 'Album' which has the same overall appearance as the type and the same long flowering period.

Polemonium caeruleum subsp. *vanbruntiae* is the form from eastern North America and is mainly distinguished by the stamens and style being longer and exserted in a prominent fashion. *P.c. villosum* is like the type species in its short stamens and style, but it is more glandular, the calyx lobes are ciliate and the inflorescence looser and distinctly branched. The stem leaves, too, are somewhat reduced. It comes from the Bering Sea area growing both in Siberia and Alaska.

Polemonium foliosissimum

P.c. ssp. *occidentale* is the western North American form, occurring in Yukon southwards down the Rocky Mountains into California and Nevada; also in the Cascade Mountains. It has a narrow inflorescence and a slightly exserted style.

As might be expected there are numerous forms of *P. caeruleum* throughout its European and Siberian range, mainly differing in flower size and shade of blue and other relatively small botanical features. Most probably the plant sometimes listed in catalogues as *P. cashmirianum* belongs here. This is an attractive form with larger pale blue flowers that expand widely and often touch each other in a head-like inflorescence.

The best forms of *P. foliosissimum* are more robust and richly coloured than *P. caeruleum* and better as border plants, though I find that they are less wind and rain resistant than that species. In its western USA homeland it is a very variable plant, so much so in fact that forms have, in the past, been given specific rank. Such names as 'robustum', 'filicinum', 'grande' and 'albiflorum' (white flowered) are still sometimes used. There is further confusion in cultivation, because it seems quite likely that it has hybridised with *caeruleum*.

It is usually represented in gardens by a robust leafy plant with branched stems plentifully set with rich blue-purple flowers. Such a plant received an Award of merit from the R.H.S. when shown by Alan Bloom in 1964. In my experience this form comes fairly true from seeds, and I raised one almost the same from botanic garden seeds under the name of 'filicinum'. The most distinctive morphological characteristic of *P. foliosissimum* is the way the terminal leaflets, of the stem leaves in particular, fuse together at their bases and form a deltoid wing on either side of the main midrib.

P. reptans is not infrequent in cultivation and is a most useful plant for the front of the border or on a large rock garden. Fairly common in the wild in moist spots in its native north-eastern USA this species forms bushy mounds of slender, branched, stems rarely more than 1 ft (30cm) tall. The flowers are rather small and usually of a pale mauve or lilac-blue shade, though some forms are of a clearer blue. Once again, the foliage is distinctive, the leaflets, particularly of the basal leaves, being broadly ovate and strongly nerved. On moist soils this species soon forms wide tufts, but hardly merits the name of *reptans* in the accepted sense of 'far creeping by stolons', though some forms are reported as stoloniferous.

As previously stated, *P. micranthum* is probably not in cultivation, and if it is, few, if anyone, outside of a botanic garden would want to cultivate it. Setting aside the fact that it is one of the few annual species, sparsely branched and with tiny white or pale blue flowers hidden by the calyx, it is not lacking in interest. Most interesting of all is its distribution in the wild, being found in desert regions in western North America and in similar situations in Chile and Argentina. In the north it flowers from April to May, and in the south from August to January.

P. mexicanum has affinities with both *foliosissimum* and *micranthum*, oddly enough, and is not worthy of cultivation even if it were available. It is an annual or short-lived perennial with a branched inflorescence of tiny flowers.

Originally published in 1969. Volume 4, number 1

Perennials with Appeal to Flower Arrangers

by Madge S. Green

MOST gardeners like to bring a few cut flowers indoors from time to time so that they can admire them close at hand in a flower decoration. But people who rate flower arranging high among their hobbies have discovered that it may not only be the flower produced by a plant which is decorative and worthy of a place in arrangement. Many bracts, leaves, seedheads, even stems, of hardy herbaceous perennials can be equally decorative, and perhaps twice as eye-catching as the flower when thoughtfully displayed in an arrangement designed to bring out some special character of the plant's beauty.

'Flower' arranging today embraces all forms of natural plant material and certainly encourages us to keep our eyes open and to really look at plants and the way they grow. There are very few hardy herbaceous perennials which do not provide something lovely at some stage for cutting and bearing indoors with pleasure. There can be very few keen arrangers who do not place hardy perennials top of the list of desirable garden plants.

Hosta species of every kind are much grown and loved for their foliage, especially in spring and early summer when the colours are young and bright. The lavender or white flowers occurring in summer and autumn are invaluable, as are the intriguing green seed capsules of late summer or autumn. I have even seen the winter-bleached white seeding stems effectively used in late winter and early spring in the advanced 'free-style' designs now becoming popular.

Hosta fortunei 'Albopicta' has foliage which is specially attractive, not only for cutting, but as a spring garden plant. The new leaves are bright butter-yellowed, edged with soft green. As summer advances the colour darkens to an overall green. *H. sieboldii* (*albomarginata*) forms clumps of green leaves, each one banded with white and these are pleasing in all-green and white

Hosta fortunei 'Albopicta'

designs. The handsomer blue-grey leaves of *H. sieboldiana* are large and important enough to grace a town-hall-sized pedestal arrangement, and indeed they often do!

Hosta foliage, especially the early leaf growth, must be stood in ½ in (1.25cm) or so of very hot water. When this has cooled off they should be placed for an hour or two in deeper cooler water. After this the leaves will be crisp and fully charged with water and may be expected to last for some weeks before their colour fades and they must be thrown away. They are best arranged in deep water or on pinholders in shallow dish or bowl containers where there is a wide expanse of water.

During early autumn hosta leaves preserve for winter decoration if they are left in an arrangement until they have turned themselves into gently twisted soft-brown shapes. These arrange well with gold, bronze or apricot chrysanthemums, or may be sprayed dull gold or shimmering silver at Christmas time.

Most arrangers have perennial poppies in the garden somewhere. In my not specially sheltered Surrey garden I am able to cut their pretty leaves right through the cold days of winter to add to seasonable flower arrangements. The flowers of such handsome plants as *Papaver orientale* 'Watermelon', 'Perry's White' (excellent for church wedding decorations), 'Stormtorch' and 'Indian Chief' (mahogany red) give first-class flowers for dramatic effect, used either in mass arrangements or more sparingly in simple one, two, or three-flower designs. These flowers, too, should be given a hot water drink before arranging. The flowers last longest if picked when just breaking bud or still at the stage where their new opened petals are looking slightly crumpled. When the petals have dropped, the dusky-eyed flower centres are still attractive and can be added to another flower decoration.

Poppy seedheads, hung up to dry out for a week or so, are invaluable later on in the year when eking out winter or late autumn flowers. By picking them at different stages one may preserve them in a variety or soft colours from blue-green to faded brown. If oriental poppies are left unstaked in the garden they will produce seedheads on stems with lazy curves that most arrangers find so attractive.

Have you ever noticed how blue-tits sometimes get busy on poppy seedheads, pecking out the seeds and leaving behind appealing little poppy skeletons, like tiny cages on stalks? These paint and glitter charmingly for Christmas decorations, and every year in early autumn I make some 'cages' for myself by leaving a bunch of poppy heads soaking for a week or so upside down in water in the garden. When the flesh of the seedheads is really soft it is fairly easy to scrape it and the seeds away, leaving behind the small, cage-like shapes.

All species of *Rodgersia* are worth growing but *R. aesculifolia*, with its pinkish-mahogany leaves in springtime and plumes of creamy flowers, is a delight. *R. pinnata* 'Superba' provides large bronze-green leaves and the prettiest rose-pink flowers. The nicely tinted young leaves of all species are often to be seen included in arrangements in the floral art tent at Chelsea. If steeped in hot water then packed carefully so that the large, rather soft ears do not tear, they travel and last well.

Phytolacca, more commonly known as Virginian poke weed, gives useful late-summer spikes of blackberry-like berries. These start pale green, slowly turning to purple-pink then purple-black. A fine plant in the garden, it makes a striking cut fruiting head, with the berries neatly carried close together on a good length of stem. *P. americana* is the one usually recommended to flower arrangers, but I have found *P. clavigera* an altogether more pleasing plant, both in the garden and when cut. All these plants are poisonous and should therefore not be planted or arranged where young children play.

Originally published in 1969. Volume 4, number 1

Plants That Dry Well

by R. B. Pole

ALTHOUGH I am a member of a flower club I confess that I am not a flower arranger, but, being a nursery gardener, I grow flowers for others. Also, as chairman of The Hardy Plant Society, I grow them in order to have plenty of material for publicity stands at shows in various parts of the country.

Specialist societies are allotted space in the Royal Horticultural Society's Halls at the first and the last shows of the year; this limits the exhibits to dried material. In consequence, I have experimented for some years with drying many flowers, foliage and grasses.

A total of sixty hardy herbaceous subjects were shown on our stand in November, 1968. Thanks to the skilful arrangement of these by our (and your) treasurer, Mr E. M. Upward, the stand was admired by many visitors, including artists, gardeners and flower arrangers, and there were numerous enquiries about how they had been harvested and dried. Many N.A.F.A.S. members, florists, and others, are expert at this, using borax, glycerine and other methods and so it was with some diffidence that I agreed to the suggestion that I should reveal my methods.

Briefly, I cut everything I think might dry and tie into bunches with a 'Twistem' wire, which also holds a loop of string, this is then hung on a coat hanger. In my tiny cottage the only place they are not in the way is my bedroom, fortunately it has a picture rail so they hang festooned around the walls. Occasionally I tighten the wires as the stems shrink and then, when dry, they are stored in large flower boxes ready to be taken to the shows.

A few words about some of the less usual material, the stage at which it seems best to cut it, and in one case the peculiar behaviour while drying, may be of interest.

Agapanthus seed-heads, cut when green, dry to a golden brown looking as though they have been lightly sprayed with gold.

Alchemilla mollis is cut when green and before it is fully open.

Anaphalis, both the tall *yedoensis* and the shorter *triplinervis* dry successfully.

Alchemilla mollis foliage

Antholyza (now *Curtonus*) *paniculata*, both the seed-heads and the foliage are cut when green and also after they have turned yellow.

Artemisia lactiflora, cut in full bloom, dries to a sandy colour; it is also good when it has turned brown.

Aster ericoides 'Golden Spray' is cut in flower.

Astrantia, flowers of both *carniolica* and *maxima* (*helleborifolia*) will dry.

Cedronella foeniculum is cut in full flower.

Centaurea, the seed-heads of *glastifolia* and of *macrocephala* dry well.

Chelone obliqua seed-heads are harvested and the flowers of its white form, *alba*, which dry to a pale fawn colour, are attractive.

Cimicifuga, quite a find as I have two varieties (but some doubt as to which), one has white flowers growing to a fine point and dries white, the other, with broad cream racemes, dries cream. They both produce seed-heads which are attractive at the green stage and the brown.

Dictamnus albus (*fraxinella*) seed-heads were the most spectacular subjects on one of the stands. Only one visitor knew what they were. Cut as an experiment, when the little star-shaped seed-pods were a rather dull brown, they were stood in a dry jar as the stems were already quite stiff. After a few days little black seeds were being shot all over the room as the pods opened showing a cream lining. Next followed loud cracks as the cream cushions, on which the seeds had lain, dried and shot out leaving stars facing in all directions, brown outside and cream inside. So beautiful are these that I have vowed to cut all I have this year.

Eupatorium purpureum is useful if cut before it is fully open. There were many enquiries as to its name.

Morina longifolia is another attractive, though savagely prickly, seed-head which dries well both at the green and the brown stage.

Phlomis russeliana seed-heads also dry well when both green and brown.

Many of the polygonums dry well and keep their colour, *P. affine* 'Donald Lowndes' being particularly good.

The brown centres of rudbeckias are good and salvias are useful in mixed arrangements.

Scabiosa ochroleuca seed-heads are useful when several are bunched together.

Sedums I find are temperamental. Some years *S. spectabile* 'Meteor' keeps its brilliant colour but another year it fades to a pinkish-grey. 'Autumn Joy' is always good, giving large almost black heads.

Thalictrum aquilegifolium has green seeds which stand well if cut as soon as they are formed. If left until later they shatter.

Of foliage, we have staged pressed yellow bracken, bergenia, epimedium, autumn coloured peony and hosta, the latter being cut green and kept in water in a shed until they turned yellow, after which they were pressed under the carpet. Attractive coloured leaves of *Astrantia carniolica, Alchemilla mollis* and *geum* are sometimes to be found in late autumn and all press well.

These are some of the successful experiments with hardy herbaceous plants. There are others to be tried in future years.

Originally published in 1970. Volume 4, number 2

Helleborus niger Hybrids

by Eric Smith

HELLEBORUS × *nigricors* (*H. niger* × *argutifolius*) is occasionally mentioned in books on gardening, but only a small number of plants appear to be in existence. Rather varying opinions seem to have been expressed on its horticultural merits, but though I have not seen the plant myself, I have been shown a fine, large flower from one of these plants.

As I wished to grow this hybrid myself, I decided to attempt a deliberate cross. My first two efforts were unsuccessful, although on both occasions seed appeared to have been set. However, the first time the flower stem rotted, and the following year the seed capsule suddenly disappeared—probably eaten by a rabbit! Such accidents are certainly disappointing, but are more than compensated for by the excitement of eventually seeing the first flowering of one's hybrids.

It was a case of third time lucky, however, though the cross was not what I had intended. Having a *H. niger* ready for pollination, I then found that no pollen was available on *H. argutifolius*; so instead, I used that of *H.* × *sternii* (*argutifolius* × *lividus*). From the one capsule I obtained at least 60 seeds, and almost all of them must have germinated. The majority of the seedlings were almost indistinguishable from *H. niger*, but 14, though rather variable, were much more like the pollen parent (*H.* × *sternii*).

The seeds were sown fresh, and it was interesting to note that the *H.* × *sternii* type seedlings came up in October at the same time as the ordinary *H.* × *sternii*, but those like *H. niger* did not appear until mid-January, which is about normal for *H. niger*. As soon as they were large enough to handle, the seedlings were potted and all flowered the following year (1970). When in bloom, the plants were about 1 ft (30cm) high, but, of course, may become somewhat taller as they grow older.

The largest flowers were about 3 in (7.5cm) in diameter and could be divided about equally into two groups—one being more or less of a *H. argutifolius* type, and the other bearing more of a resemblance to *H. lividus* in both shape and colour, the pinkish-purple flushing being quite distinct.

There was also just one seedling which was similar to *N. niger* but flushed with pink and green, and becoming very pink as it aged. In all cases, the stems were nearly horizontal at first, but gradually straightened up as growth advanced.

A good number of flowers were produced, particularly when it is considered that the plants were then only about 18 months from germination. The *H. argutifolius* type was probably the most spectacular, as so many of the flowers were open at the same time.

As was rather to be expected from a hybrid of this type, all the plants proved to be sterile, though the ovaries did develop to a considerable extent.

Last spring I repeated the cross on a larger scale, so, if all goes well, I should have more plants for evaluation in 1972. A genuine *H. × nigricors* cross also produced a small number of seeds so it will be possible, I hope, to compare the two hybrids in due course.

Originally published in 1970. Volume 4, number 2

Six years later Eric Smith wrote:

Now that I have retired from the retail nursery business, I hope to have much more time for the hybridization and selection of those plants which for a number of years have been my main interest, in particular *Hosta* and *Helleborus*.

It is now six years since I wrote a note for the H.P.S. *Bulletin* on my *Helleborus × nigristern* (*niger × (× sternii)*) in which I concluded by saying that I had a few seeds from crossing *H. niger* with *H. argutifolius* (*H. × nigricors*) but unfortunately, did not get any germination (probably due to neglect on my part). I intended to try this cross again, but in the meantime had crossed *H. niger* with *H. lividus* (*H. × nigriliv*), and the resulting seedlings are the main reason for this note.

Helleborus lividus is a particularly elegant and attractive plant, but, unfortunately, I have not found it satisfactory for outdoor cultivation, and however beautiful a plant may be, it does not seem worthwhile if it barely survives the winter. It is for this reason that I decided to make this cross. Of course, it may thrive in some gardens, and I should be very pleased to hear from anyone who has achieved success. In my experience, it is best grown in an alpine house.

The *H.* × *nigriliv* seedlings were surprisingly similar in appearance, in fact at a casual glance one might have thought that they were all one clone. In contrast, the *H.* × *nigristern* had shown considerable variation, though this was not unexpected as *H.* × *sternii* is, of course, itself a hybrid (*argutifolius* × *lividus*). The general growth and leaf shape of the *H.* × *nigriliv* seedlings was clearly influenced by the seed parent (*H. niger*) but with the bluish green, silver veined leaves characteristic of *H.* × *lividus*. The flower stems, usually up to about a foot in height, carry about three or four *niger*-like blooms but with the pinkish/buff reverse as in *lividus*. With aging the whole flower becomes pinkish.

I flowered the plants for the first time 1974 and the buds even began to open before Christmas, and this year the same thing has occurred on the one plant which I have here (near Castle Cary, Som.). However, this may be due to the mild winters which we have experienced recently. It will be interesting to see how they behave when we get a cold winter, not only with regard to the time of flowering, but also as to hardiness. I hope that they will prove as hardy as *H. niger*. It does appear that as with the 'Christmas Rose', the flowers of all the *H. niger* hybrids last longer when cut than those of the *H. orientalis* group. However, they also have the disadvantage of being completely sterile, so to produce a number of plants it is necessary to repeat the cross. Propagation of all these hybrids is possible by division when they are about three/four years old, but they take time to establish, and, as with most Hellebores, they do not seem to have the vigour of seedlings.

As all the *H. niger* hybrids have several flowers to a stem (particularly those where the influence of *H. argutifolius* is dominant) they make an additional attraction in the winter garden. No doubt, this would be even greater if *H. niger* could be crossed with members of the *H. orientalis* group for this should increase the colour range. Unfortunately, this does not seem possible, for it appears that *H. niger* can be crossed only with Hellebores of the *caulescens* group (*argutifolius, lividus,* × *sternii* and, possibly *foetidus*). However, I have not heard of a *H. niger/foetidus* hybrid, and my own attempt at this cross was a complete failure.

Originally published in 1976. Volume 5, number 2

Perennials for Shade

by Kenneth A. Beckett

MANY gardens, especially those in our towns and big cities are either shaded for much of the day or have areas which may not receive direct sunlight from one year's end to the next. Apart from these special conditions, gardens almost everywhere have shaded spots, perhaps beneath trees or on the north sides of houses, walls and high hedges. Although there are numerous plants suitable for growing in shade, many gardeners think of a shaded site as a problem area and seldom take full advantage of it. Before listing and describing suitable plants, however, it might be of interest and value to consider the characteristics of various kinds of shade and how they affect what sorts of plants can be grown.

Broadly speaking, there are two kinds of shade, that of trees and of solid objects such as walls and buildings. Sometimes the two are combined in various ways. Tree shade can be subdivided into that cast by deciduous and evergreen sorts and it will largely depend upon the actual species as to what can be grown beneath them. Most small-leaved trees such as birch and open-branched trees such as our native oaks, cast dappled shade, whereas sycamore and other large-leaved species and such trees as native beech with a close-set horizontal branch system cast a dense shade. One could make similar comparisons among broad-leaved and evergreen conifers.

There are comparatively few higher plants from temperate regions that tolerate dense shade the whole year round, and even in deciduous woods the bulk of the smaller herbaceous plants grow and flower during the early part of the year before the trees are in full leaf. Plants that continue to grow after the tree canopy is complete usually have large or thin textured leaves to take full advantage of every dapple of sunlight or the continuously diffuse light. In very dense woods, such as young plantations of conifers, which exclude all direct light, there are usually few if any herbaceous flowering plants; mosses and perhaps a few ferns are all that survive.

Shade cast by buildings and hedges is usually less of a problem if there are no trees to complicate the picture. Even when there are other buildings or walls nearby there is open sky above which allows both direct and reflected sunlight or radiation to penetrate much more effectively than when screened by dense trees. On the other hand, the dappled shade of well-spaced open-branched trees is much to be preferred to the area in a city surrounded by high buildings and which never sees a direct ray of sunshine the whole year round.

Whatever the source of shade, however, it is important to choose plants which either grow in shaded sites in the wild or are known to tolerate it and still thrive and flower at least moderately well. Fortunately the choice is a wide one, provided the site is not also very dry or can be artificially watered to maintain adequately moist conditions. This moisture factor cannot be over-stressed, especially if one is gardening beneath large trees having dense shallow root systems which quickly rob the soil of any moisture that falls. The narrow border at the foot of a high wall may also need special watering and of course a hedge such as privet can, on a lesser scale, be as troublesome as a large tree.

Although adequate moisture is an absolute essential, one must not overlook soil fertility if vigorous healthy growth is to be expected. Ideally, plenty of compost, leaf-soil or peat should be worked into the soil before planting and a mulch applied of the same material each year if possible. Plants grown in woodland or even under a solitary tree will receive a natural mulch, particularly if the trees are deciduous, but make sure that the plants are not completely buried under fallen leaves for long periods. To prevent a natural mulch from blowing away, place pieces of chicken wire on the surface until the leaves begin to rot.

Although shade is not essential to their well-being, most hellebores are natural shade dwellers and always look at home beneath trees or between larger shrubs. The common Christmas rose, *Helleborus niger*, is well worth growing, especially in one of its selected forms, such as 'Potters Wheel', with large bowl-shaped flowers that sometimes open just in time for Christmas. Not every one's choice is *H. viridis* with vivid yellow-green flowers that seldom fail to open in early January. Although a native of many European countries and sometimes locally common, it is also a rare British native with the apt name of 'bear's foot', descriptive of the large fingered leaves.

There is much confusion over the correct names for many of the taller hellebores, collectively called 'lenten roses' by some people. In cultivation they generally seem to be forms and hybrids of *H. orientalis*, the best kinds having fancy names such as 'Georgina Nightingale', with shell-pink blossoms; 'Nancy Smith', with rich velvety-purple flowers; and 'Snow White', pure white. All flower over a long period, generally from February to April. Rather

Helleborus orientalis

similar is the plant listed in catalogues as *H. atrorubens*. It often begins to flower a little earlier and in some seasons bears its red-purple, green-tinted flowers before Christmas.

Quite distinct from the foregoing are the sub-shrubby hellebores with persistent stems and evergreen leaves. Best known is *H. argutifolius*, the Corsican hellebore, with bright yellow-green flowers, but this is not a true shade plant and prefers a moderately sunny site. Ideal for shade is our native *H. foetidus*, a plant with several vernacular names including 'stinking hellebore', 'setterswort' and 'bear's-foot', sharing the latter name with *H. viridis*. The dark green palmate leaves are divided into nine slender-pointed narrow lobes and are an excellent foil for the rounded cluster of nodding, purple-edged, yellow-green cup-shaped flowers, which begin to open during February or March. Contrary to its vernacular and Latin specific epithets, the plant does not 'stink', though a rather pungent odour is given off when buried or roughly handled. Although not showy, *H. foetidus* is very shade tolerant and will grow beneath evergreen trees.

With equally dark green, but spoon-shaped, leaves and also growing quite well in heavy shade is *Euphorbia robbiae*. An extensive coloniser and an excellent ground-cover plant, 'Robb's spurge' sends up erect stems topped by neat rosettes of foliage. In deep shade the stems may reach 15–18 in (38–45cm) tall, but are usually much less. The flowering stems overtop the leaves by 9–12 in (23–30cm) and the greenish-yellow bracts contrast well with the dark foliage, lasting for several months. Our native wood spurge, *E. amygdaloides* is also well worth growing. For those who like variegated plants, *E. a.* 'Variegata' is even more garden-worthy, having the leaves marked with creamy-white and pink. Probably the most showy of all the hardy herbaceous spurges is *E. polychroma* (also known as *epithymoides*), with densely-borne, flower-like heads of bright sulphur-yellow bracts in spring. It needs more sun than the others mentioned, but does well in partial shade.

The lungworts (*Pulmonaria* species) are all useful plants for dappled shade. Also known as 'Jerusalem sage' and 'spotted dog', the common lungwort is not to be despised. Its pink and blue-purple tubular flowers often open in February and are particularly welcome at such a time. Later, the silver-spotted leaves expand rapidly and although rather course, help to brighten up a shady spot. Superior in this respect is *P. saccharata* 'Argentea' in which the silver spots unite to create a completely silver patinous surface to each leaf. There is also a bright rose-pink selection called 'Pink Dawn'. Dazzlingly blue is *P. angustifolia*, a green-leaved species with very freely borne flowers from March to May.

Belonging to the same family as the lungworts (Boraginaceae), *Mertensia virginica* is a much more elegant plant with nodding

Euphorbia robbiae

sprays of sky-blue flowers that mature from pink buds. The leaves are smooth and grey-green. This distinctive woodland plant from moist rich woodland in eastern USA has such charming vernacular names as 'Roanoke bells', 'Virginian cowslip' and in USA, simply as 'bluebells'. It received the coveted First Class Certificate award from the Royal Horticultural Society in 1962. As its habitat preferences suggest, this mertensia must have a moist, but not waterlogged, soil with plenty of humus to do really well.

It is always difficult to appreciate that the dissected, spiraea-like foliage and small clusters of fluffy, creamy-white flowers of *Actaea spicata* fit it for inclusion in the buttercup family (Ranunculaceae). *Actaea* is found in woods and in mountain gullies around the Northern Hemisphere. Several species are described with only slight differences of leaf and flower. Nowadays botanists consider them all to be variants of *A. spicata*. Although elegant of foliage, they are mainly grown for their colourful berries which mature in late summer and persist into winter if the birds do not find them. The two best sorts for the garden are *AA. rubra* and *pachypoda* (*alba*), red and white fruited respectively.

Also mainly grown for its fruits is the uncommon 'umbrella-leaf' *Diphylleia cymosa*, another native of moist mountain woods in eastern USA. Sometimes reaching 2 ft (60cm) in height the erect stems of this plant bear two leaves only. Each leaf is rounded in outline with pointed toothed lobes and having the stalk attachment near the middle (peltate), thus the allusion to 'umbrella'. Small spikes of white flowers give way to ovoid blue berries about ½ in (1.25cm) long.

Prussian-blue berries are produced by *Clintonia borealis*, also a woodland plant from North America. In growth, this member of the lily family rather resembles lily-of-the-valley, but sends up slender stems topped by small greenish-yellow nodding flowers rather like miniature lilies. Later, the striking blue berries develop, carried on now erect pedicels. The vernacular name of 'bluebead-lily' is most apt.

Columbines of all kinds are suitable for a shady site. The species tend to be seen less often, being replaced by coloured forms of *Aquilegia vulgaris*, quaintly known as 'grannies bonnets', or Long-spur Hybrids. For an informal site beneath trees, however, the true species take some beating. Highly attractive is *A. canadensis*, which, in its best forms has elegantly poised moderately long-spurred blossoms of contrasting red and yellow. Somewhat similar is *A. formosa*, but with slightly larger, shorter spurred flowers. Both these species are about 1½–2 ft (45–60cm) tall, sometimes less, whereas *A. longissima* is usually at least 2½, often 3 ft (76–90cm) or

Anemone nemorosa

more. This latter species has great charm with flights of yellow flowers each with long slender spurs that may be as much as 4 in (10cm) long. A native of mountain woods in the southern USA and Mexico, it is the main parent of the long-spur hybrids.

Making suitable companions for the columbines, the so-called Japanese anemones are ideal for dappled shade. The original Japanese anemone is *Anemone hupehensis japonica*, but this is less commonly seen nowadays, being replaced by hybrids with *A. vitifolia* and called *A.* × *hybrida* (formerly *A.* × *elegans*). Among some fine-named selections is the lovely pure white 'Honorine Jobert', so common in cottage gardens and often just referred to as *the* 'Japanese anemone'. Also white, but with semi-double blooms is 'Louise Uhink'; equally semi-double but in deep pink is 'Margarita'; and 'September Charm' is a single pale pink flushed lilac on the reverse.

Another superb woodland anemone is our own native windflower, *A. nemorosa*. It has given rise to several slightly larger flowered and coloured forms, noteworthy being *A.n.* 'Robinsoniana', with lavender-blue blossoms and 'Allenii' having the petals rosy-lilac outside and soft blue within. White and double-flowered is *A. n.* 'Alba Plena', whilst 'Rosea' is similar to the true wild 'wind flower' but with a deeper flush of pink.

All the species of *Bergenia* are suitable, though *B. ciliata* with distinctive hairy leaves is a bit too tender for reliable outside planting in much of Britain, mainly because the flower buds get frosted and the plants weakened if too many leaves are killed during winter. Much more reliable are such species as *BB. cordifolia, purpurascens* and *crassifolia*. The latter is the common sort in cottage and older gardens with clear pink flowers that usually open around Christmas time. Its large, oval, lustrous green leaves are a perfect ground cover, as indeed are those of most of the other species, except perhaps *B. stracheyi*, the smallest species with rather erect leaves.

Most colourful are the later-flowering *BB. delavayi* and *beesiana*, now combined under one species name as *B. purpurascens*. They are characterised by tall, robust flowering stems topped by a panicle of pendulous rich rose-purple, bell-like blossoms. There are also many fine hybrids, notable being 'Ballawley Hybrid', a cross between the former *BB. delavayi* and *beesiana* and also known as 'Delbees'. Having rich crimson-purple flowers and copper-tinted leaves is 'Evening Glow' ('Abendglut'), whilst 'Silver Light' ('Silberlicht') has white flowers delicately suffused with pink. Named 'Margery Fish', after the late lamented plantswoman of Lambrook Manor, is a choice cultivar with distinctively rounded leaves and pale pink flowers centered with conspicuous green stamens.

Several very garden-worthy species of *Campanula* are either natives of light woodland or tolerate and flower well in shaded sites. For informal areas our native 'nettle-leaved bellflower' or 'bats in the belfry', *C. trachelium* is well worth growing, but is too invasive for choicier spots. It has sharply angled, erect, almost woody stems bearing somewhat nettle-like leaves and terminal racemes of blue-purple bells, each up to 2 in (5cm) long. More slender of growth and bearing elegantly flared bells of a similar or paler shade of purple is another wilding, *C. rapunculoides* (not a true native, but well naturalised here and there). However, this 'creeping campanula' is so invasive it must be confined to the wildest areas of the garden. Most desirable of the native bellflowers is *C. latifolia*, a stout tufted erect perennial often reaching 4 ft (120cm) or more in height. The leaves are pale to mid-green and lanceolate in outline with irregular teeth. Blue-purple bells up to 2½ in (6cm) long are borne in long racemes during July–August. There is a rich violet-purple form known as 'Brantwood' and 'Alba' is pure white.

The 'peach-leaved bellflower', *C. persicifolia*, in all its forms is highly desirable for dappled or partial shade. Its narrowly lanceolate leaves (not really very much like those of a peach tree) and wide, nodding bells of blue are well-known in gardens. Double and cup-and-saucer forms are known and the colour varies through various shades of blue and purple to white. Recommended cultivars include 'Beechwood', pale soft blue; 'Snowfire', pure white; 'Telham Beauty', large bells of pale china-blue, and 'Blue Spire', having large bells of clear purple-blue.

Quite distinct among border campanulas is *C. lactiflora*, with large terminal panicles of shallow, wide-open bells facing outwards and upwards. The colour of the wild species is a pale milky-blue, but a number of different shades including white and pink are available from nurserymen. Of course, 'Prichard's Variety' is the richest in colour being a lovely shade of violet-blue; it received the Royal Horticultural Society's Award of Merit in 1964. A delightful shade of soft lilac-pink, *C. l.* 'Loddon Anna' is particularly desirable, whilst 'Alba' is a somewhat more compact form with white blossoms.

No woodland spot or shaded site should be without its clump of Solomon's seal. Usually referred to as *Polygonatum multiflorum*, this, the commonest member of its genus in gardens is now known to be a hybrid with *P. odoratum* and should be called *P.* × *hybridum*. It is a sturdy plant with erect unbranched stems that arch gracefully over at the summit. From the leaf axils of the arched portion numerous narrow bells of white and green dangle during May and June. Quite distinct and seldom seen in gardens is *P. verticillatum*, a native of mountain woods in parts of Europe and Asia and also a very rare British native. More erect than the other species mentioned, it has slender stems set with whorls of pointed, narrowly-lanceolate leaves and rather small, greenish-white bells. The fruits which follow are red, whereas those of *P.* × *hybridum* and its parents are blue-black.

One hesitates to mention really reliable species of *Lilium*, though many are true woodland dwellers. Two of the most persistent perennials are *LL. martagon* and *pyrenaicum*, both with so-called Turk's-cap flowers, their petals rolling back on themselves in fully expanded blooms. *Lilium martagon* can reach 4 ft (1.2m) in height when happily situated with racemes of pendant flowers which range in colour from white ('Album') to glossy claret-purple ('Cattaniae'). *Lilium pyrenaicum* is invariably sulphur-yellow, usually with dark-purple spots. It has a very heavy fragrance, which, if sniffed close to is rather unpleasant; well diluted with air, however, it is remarkably sweet. Another reliable lily is the western North American *L. pardalinum*, also with Turk's-cap blooms. It also can attain 4 ft (1.2m) or more and produces long-pediceled blossoms of bright orange-red, spotted with purple towards the lower half.

Many more lilies are worth giving a try, provided one has naturally acid soil conditions and plenty of humus. Most majestic of all is *Cardiocrinum giganteum* (formerly *Lilium giganteum*) which may reach 10 ft (3m) and is rarely less than 7 ft (2m). Unlike true lilies it has broad, heart-shaped basal leaves and is monocarpic (dying after flowering) though small offset bulbs remain. One disadvantage is that these small bulbs may take from 3 to 6 years to reach flowering size. Nevertheless, the wait is always worth while when the great stems soar upwards, topped by magnificent racemes of slender trumpets each about 6 in (15cm) long. The flowers are white, marked with maroon within.

A surprisingly large number of members of the lily family (*Liliaceae*) seem to require a shaded site. Common lily-of-the-valley hardly needs a mention, but its variegated leaved form, *Convallaria majalis* 'Variegata' might well be grown more often because its creamy-white-striped leaves add interest and colour after the flowers have faded. There is also a soft-pink-belled form which is really more interesting than showy.

Carrying brighter pink nodding bells is *Streptopus roseus*, a North American plant somewhat like a branched Solomon's seal, whilst its near ally and compatriot *Uvularia grandiflora* is a real 'must'. This latter plant sends up slender branched stems and pale green ovate leaves with great rapidity in spring and almost immediately bears flared yellow bells with elegantly twisted petals. Much dwarfer and far less showy, though built on similar lines, is *Disporum smithii* (often wrongly referred to as *Prosartes oreganum* or *P. menziesii*). The flowers are tubular and of a greenish-yellow shade that is not displeasing. Later, semi-translucent orange berries develop and, in some gardens, the foliage takes on yellow or orange hues as it dies down in autumn.

Rarely cultivated, though commercially available from at least one nursery-man in England, is 'fairy wand', *Chamaelirium luteum*. It is a slender plant up to 2 ft (60cm) in height, with a wand-like spike of fluffy white flowers that nods over at the tip. The name is an unfortunate one; *Chamaelirium* means 'dwarf lily', but the plant is neither dwarf or lily-like; and *luteum* means 'yellow', but the flowers are white!

'Lily-grass' or 'lily-turf' are names of American origin coined to cover the various species of *Liriope* and *Ophiopogon*, practically all species of which are very shade tolerant. Only one species is really showy, however, and has the stature to be included among hardy perennials of concern to our Society. This is *Lirope platyphylla*, the correct name for what is still generally known as *L. muscari*. Mainly of dense tufted growth, this plant has evergreen, narrowly strap-shaped leaves and erect wiry stems that bear narrow, spike-like panicles of purple buds that give it a superifical resemblance to a grape hyacinth (muscari). Not only will it thrive in quite deep shade,

Cardiocrinum giganteum

but it begins to flower in late summer and continues into late autumn. It received an Award of Merit in 1930 and Award of Garden Merit in 1963. The form in cultivation often has the tip of the flower spike forked or slightly fasciated and this very distinctive characteristic is also a feature of the cultivar known in USA as 'Majestic'. Almost certainly they are one and the same clone. Well over a dozen cultivars are known in America including a good white ('Monroe White') and it is hoped that some enterprising nurseryman over here will import them. All make good pot plants for a cool room. One other form sometimes encountered in gardens over here is *L. p.* 'Variegata', with yellow striped leaves, particularly desirable for brightening up a gloomy spot.

Now on a rising crest of popularity, *Hosta* is probably one of the best-known members of the *Liliaceae* at the present time. At least a dozen species are readily available, plus several hybrids and forms, often with variegated foliage. Although essentially foliage plants many have a very pleasing floral display, producing spikes of trumpet-shaped flowers in shades of purple or white above the leaves. Finest of the large-leaved sorts must be *H. sieboldiana* with large blue or grey-green foliage, though the flowers are often somewhat hidden. Only a little smaller is *H. fortunei*, usually represented in cultivation by its variegated forms, the most colourful of which is *H. f.* 'Albopicta', with bright, pale yellow leaves edged with green during the spring; later, as the leaves expand they become suffused with green. Having distinctive wavy-margined leaves with a twisted, pointed tip, *H. crispula* is much lower-growing and more suited to a confined space or the smaller garden. Each leaf is dark green with an irregular white margin. Pure green and smaller still is *H. lancifolia*, a very useful species that flowers freely during August and September.

Several bulbous genera are also very much at home beneath trees, notably our native bluebell and the so-called 'Spanish bluebell'; *Hyacinthoides non-scripta* and *H. hispanica* respectively. Such flowering onions as *Allium triquetrum* and *A. unifolium* are suitable and *Camassia leichtlinii* is particularly garden-worthy.

No shady spot should be without its clump of wood lily, a vernacular name often used to cover most species of *Trillium*, but specifically applied to *T. grandiflorum*. This white-flowered species is not only the showiest, but the best 'doer', from a gardener's point of view. Also known as 'wake robin', particularly in its North American homeland, it produces sturdy stems topped by three lustrous green ovate leaves, from the middle of which arises a solitary three-petalled blossom which may be as much as 3 in (7.5cm) long but is usually a little smaller. Many forms are known both in the wild and in cultivation, though few are commercially available. A double-flowered mutant is sometimes seen, also ones with rose-flushed blooms (most forms tend to flush pink as they age, but there are forms that start off pink).

Phlomis russeliana (samia) is good for drying

Introductions by Miss Pole, *Kniphofia* 'Lye End' (above) and *Achillea* 'Coronation Gold' (below)

'Birthroot' is one of a number of vernacular names for *T. erectum*, though even this name is seldom used in Britain. It is a less spectacular plant with 1 in (2.5cm) wide maroon flowers that nod when young. Slightly smaller is *T. undulatum*, charmingly known as the 'painted wood-lily'. The young leaves of this species are flushed with copper and have undulant margins, and each blossom is white with a basal horseshoe pattern of carmine rays on the petals.

The most distinctive characteristic of *T. sessile* is that the flowers sit stalkless amid the three leaves. It has long, narrow erect petals like rabbits' ears which only begin to open outwards as they age. Robust in habit, it is probably as easy to grow as *T. grandiflorum* but less obviously attractive to most people. The usual form in cultivation has deep red-purple petals, but yellowish flowered kinds are known. However, any yellow flowered trillium of this sort grown in Britain is almost invariably *T. chloropetalum* an even more robust plant from the western side of USA (*T. sessile* is native to eastern USA). Both these species usually have attractively mottled leaves; *T. chloropetalum* with purple and *sessile* with paler green or silvery-white.

All the species of *Dicentra* currently cultivated in Britain at the present time have decorative fern-like foliage and delightful sprays of unique heart-shaped flowers. Most spectacular is undoubtedly the well-known 'bleeding heart', *D. spectabilis*. Regrettably, this native of Manchuria, China, Korea and Japan, has a rather brief life above ground. In spring robust succulent reddish shoots erupt from the ground with great speed and soon mature elegant leafage and arching stem tips from beneath which depend rose-red 'hearts' with white points. Usually by the end of July all is over and by August not a trace of the plant is to be seen. The plant should in fact be carefully marked to prevent damage by hoe and fork during its dormant season.

Dwarfer and even more fern-like are *D. formosa* and *D. eximea*, the former from western and the latter from eastern USA. Both are tufted plants having unbranched flowering stems that overtop the mound of leaves and arch over gracefully, dripping with narrowly heart-shaped flowers; rose-red in *D. eximea* and pink in *D. formosa*. Both have a flowering season from about April–May to June–July, sometimes later. The cultivar *D. formosa* 'Bountiful' will often still be sending up flowering spikes in autumn.

Foxgloves look right in shade, although they grow perfectly well in full sun also. Our native *Digitalis purpurea* is quite the most decorative and has a number of garden forms, by some persons considered to be superior. More robust in habit and with flowers all around the stem is 'Excelsior', in various shades of pink, purple and cream. In similar shades, but more akin to the wild foxglove are 'Gloxinioides' with larger flowers and 'Shirley', the most graceful of all. Several species *Digitalis* are ideal for dappled light areas, noteworthy being *D. grandiflora* (*ambigua*) with smooth, dark green leaves and creamy-yellow flowers and *D. orientalis*, bearing cerise-purple-veined, biscuit-yellow blossoms, each with a curious tongue-like outgrowth of the lower lip.

Somewhat invasive and really ideal for the wilder type of garden is the silver variegated form of our native 'yellow archangel', *Lamiastrum galeobdolon*, sometimes known as *Lamium galeobdolon* and *Galeobdolon luteum*, depending on which botanist you follow. It is a perfect ground-cover plant if regularly sheared over after its 12–18 in (30–45cm) tall stems of strangely attractive hooded yellow flowers have finished.

Common honesty, *Lunaria annua*, is almost too well-known to mention, but its variegated form *L. a.* 'Variegata' is all-too-seldom seen. This bright mutant cultivar has the leaves splashed pale creamy-white and brightens up the shady spot it occupies.

Meconopsis are obvious candidates for light shade beneath trees or for a north border. Finest of the true blue poppies is *M. grandis*, much more of a perennial than the better-known *M. betonicifolia* and with slightly larger flowers. Producing panicles of yellow flowers, *M. dhwojii* is well worth growing for its foliage alone. This species from Nepal has delicately cut pale green foliage covered with purple-based, yellow, bristly hairs. Much taller (up to 5 ft (1.5m) or more) and also a native of Nepal is *M. napaulensis*, with large terminal panicles of poppy-flowers that can be in shades or red, pink, purple, blue or white. Small and delicate by comparison and a true perennial is *M. quintuplinervia*, with obovate or lanceolate basal bristly-hairy leaves from amid which arise slender wiry stems carrying a nodding terminal flower of lavender-purple.

Primula is another must for shade, providing it is not too dense. For the deeper shade of deciduous trees, forms of *Primula vulgaris*, our common primrose are ideal, providing the soil does not get too dry in late spring. Of similar habit but rather more choice is *P. gracilipes*, one of the easiest of the Petiolarid primulas, most of which only do really well 'north of the border'. This species has neat, sharply-toothed leaves and large primrose blossoms of rosy-purple which are usually borne in some abundance. Of the same group and also doing quite well in a cool spot in the southern half of Great Britain is *P. whitei*, with bright lilac-blue, chrome-yellow-eyed flowers.

Some of the Candelabra primulas are good, especially *PP. japonica, pulverulenta* and the lovely bright yellow *helodoxa*. The 'redhot poker primula', *P. vialii* with its unique tight spikes of pale purple and scarlet flowers, and *P. nutans* with heads of large lavender bells, are two really unique species.

Really at home under woodland conditions are some of the Cortusoides primulas, finest of all being the Japanese *P. sieboldii*. Having boldly-toothed, hairy, pale green leaves which shoot up quickly in spring, this variable species has umbels of rose-purple primrose blossoms in May. It is a favourite of the Japanese people, who have selected many different forms varying in colour and shade and floral formation, some being fringed or toothed. At least a dozen or so of these selected forms are commercially available in this country.

Boldly handsome in foliage and with frothy spiraea-like flowers, all the *Rodgersia* species in cultivation are worth growing. They combine well with hostas and thrive in dappled shade. Most species have compound leaves rather like those of a large horse-chestnut, but one species, *R. tabularis*, has circular leaves with the stalk in the middle and looking like flat, green parasols.

Having similar leaf form, though on a smaller scale, *Podophyllum emodi* is equally appealing. Actually, the leaves are quite deeply lobed and borne in pairs at the summits of tough erect stems. Between the pair of leaves nods the fleeting, solitary white flower to be followed by an ellipsoid 'berry' which may be 2 in (5cm) long when fully grown and turns bright red. The form known as *P. e. chinensis* has slightly smaller pinkish flowers and handsomely mottled foliage. Similar, but with pale green leaves and larger bowl-shaped white flowers is the North American 'May apple' or 'mandrake', *P. peltatum*, with equally showy red fruits which are edible.

One gentian is very much a woodland dweller. This is *Gentiana asclepiadea*, the willow gentian from mountain woods throughout much of Europe. Of tufted habit, the slender wiry stems arch gracefully outwards bearing typical gentian blossoms of purple-blue in the upper leaf axils. There is a white-flowered form which comes true from seeds.

Also a native of mountain woods, but this time in Japan, is that unique member of the saxifrage family, *Kirengeshoma palmata*. So distinct a plant is it, that it has been given a family of its own (the *Kirengeshomaceae*) though not generally accepted among taxonomic botanists. Oddly enough, at least one reliable authority now classifies it under *Hydrangeaceae*, another split off from the *Saxifragaceae*. *Kirengeshoma* is a robust, tufted species, with almost woody-based stems set with opposite pairs of sharply-toothed and lobed palmate leaves. Plants in rich, moist soil may reach 5 ft (1.5m) tall and bear large terminal panciles of tubular, somewhat lily-like, fleshy-petalled canary-yellow flowers during late summer and autumn.

Originally published in 1971. Volume 4, number 3

A Chain of Daisies

by Trevor Bath

I USED to despise daisies. It is so easy to become snobbish about flowers, and I decided that daises of all kinds were 'common'.

It was a photograph that changed my outlook. In the garden of my home in Dorset there was an enormous clump of *Chrysanthemum maximum* which my mother, who took great pride in them, called 'Marguerites'. They are also known as 'Shasta daisies'.

When we moved out of that house, after more than 40 years, I took a photograph of them as a memento. Looking at it afterwards, I was increasingly impressed by the classic simplicity of the flowers, and their cheerful effect, offset by the dark green stalks and foliage.

Having moved into my present house in Surrey, with the intention of creating a cottage-type garden, I found that among the few existing plants were single and double forms of *Chrysanthemum maximum*, though they were neglected, and surrounded with ground elder. I divided and replanted them, and soon they had made flourishing colonies.

I have been given a fimbriated form of the single daisy, which may or may not be 'Phyllis Smith'. It took me a little time to become reconciled to this one, owing to the rather untidy appearance of the characteristic petals (florets)—they look as if they have been washed but not ironed! However, like the other forms, they seem to thrive in most situations, creating a bold effect *en masse*, and are excellent for cutting. They also glimmer magically at dusk, for those who are addicted to surveying their gardens by summer twilight. Indeed, at least one article has been written which recommends them for growing in commuters' gardens for this very reason.

Doronicums were the next breakthrough in the daisy chain. I like them because they make such a happy contrast to the bulbs, polyanthus and other spring flowers. They have the advantage of novelty, as they appear long before the summer borders are filled with family likenesses.

I acquired seed of *Erigeron mucronatus* from the Royal

Horticultural Society's distribution scheme after reading about it in a book by Margery Fish. Now it is taking over in certain parts of the garden, but as it is mainly colonising dry walls and cracks in paving, this is not too serious. It seems to do best in these rather austere conditions and is seldom without a flower, in shades of pink ageing to white.

A similar flower, but in a pink which remains constant, belongs to *E. philadelphicus* with upright stems about 1–1½ ft (30–45cm) tall, and hanging buds which turn upwards as they open. It is an old-fashioned plant not seen very often, though I noticed it had seeded itself about at Bodnant. I have been given one of the large-flowered erigerons—name uncertain, but it may be 'Gaiety'. The purple florets make a gem-like combination with the bright gold centre. It soon makes a good-sized clump and is easy to divide. I love the colour of *E.* 'Darkest of All' but I am quite unable to grow it. After the statutory three failures I have now given up.

In the marvellous garden at Tintinhull, I was very taken by a white daisy with silvery-grey leaves, used to great effect in the White Garden section. This turned out to be *Anthemis cupaniana* which looks as if it should be tender but proves to be as tough as nails. I now have it in several dry and hungry spots, but it romps away and quickly spreads a mat of ferny leaves. It is also good beside steps. There is a stunning mass display of flowers in May–June, then odd flowers for the rest of the season. Cuttings root easily.

The old-fashioned pompon forms of *Bellis perennis* with small heads of tightly quilled florets in red or pink shades, seems less commonly grown now, judging by the surprise with which spring visitors to my garden greet it as an old friend. In fact, mine are a modern cultivar and came from a packet of Sutton's 'Double Carpet Mixed'. I long to try the 'hen and chickens' sort which was such a favourite of Margery Fish, but alas, it seems to have vanished from her nursery catalogue.

Another daisy successfully raised from seed, this time from Dobie's, is the compact form of *Chrysanthemum maximum* called 'Little Silver Princess'. Its taller progenitors tend to flop about unless staked in good time, as many of the places where I have them are less open than the ideal sites, so that they get drawn up. But 'Little Silver Princess', compact and not exceeding 1½ ft (45cm), is excellent alongside paths and at the front of the border. The single daisy flowers are lavishly produced and long-lasting. Like all the

Chrysanthemum uliginosum

others so far mentioned, it increases easily and soon makes robust plants from divisions.

One more survivor from long ago—*Chrysanthemum uliginosum*, which originates from Hungary. This has white flowers of great distinction and comes late in the season to accompany the Michaelmas daisies (too vast a tribe to even touch on here). The rather leggy, branching stems are woody enough not to require staking. It increases by underground rhizomes and also seeds itself about gently.

And so, from lumping together all these, and many more, under the single derogatory term of 'daisies', I have begun to appreciate their many excellent qualities—their long displays of flowers which seem largely unaffected by weather, pests or diseases, and their ease of cultivation and propagation—which qualify them for that old-world term of gardening approval, 'obliging plants'.

What next? A parcel of plants I recently received from a nursery included, as a substitute, a plant labelled *Erigeron compositus**, which I have never heard of, and have so far been unable to trace. I am looking forward with great anticipation to see what this 'unknown quantity' will produce. It is another link in a chain of which I can see no end.

**Erigeron compositus* has a wide altitudinal range in the mountains of Western North America, extending north to Alaska and Greenland. It is a tufted or cushion-forming plant with deeply dissected leaves. The flowering stems seldom exceed 6 in (15cm) and are usually less. Each stem carries a solitary daisy with numerous narrow ray florets, though in the wild there is a form (*discoideus*) which lacks these. The plant in cultivation has soft lavender flowers, but it can vary from white through shades of lilac to purple. It blooms in spring.—*Editor*.

Originally published in 1972. Volume 2, number 2

Fair Weather Flowers

by Joyce Forty

AFTER the prolonged periods of drought during the past two summers, it is interesting to take a look at the plants which have best survived the ordeal.

My garden is on poor, hungry Surrey sand and in spite of frequent soaking with the hose (Water Board permitting), the soil soon becomes a veritable dust bath for the sparrows during rainless spells. Every autumn, most of my plants are given a general mulch of garden compost and peat, with a little bone meal for good measure. This is done in the autumn for the simple reason that I know there will never be time in the spring, when a quick scattering of general fertilizer is about as much as I can manage.

Top marks in dry conditions must of course go to the Sedums, in particular *Sedum* 'Autumn Joy' which provides almost year-round interest. The large flat flower heads, beloved by bees and butterflies alike and held erect on 2 ft (60cm) stems, gradually change colour from pale green to bronzy-red, then to deep bronze through the winter. When the old stems are finally cut down in early spring, the new shoots are already making attractive clumps of delicate green foliage. I find it best to divide the plants every other year as the stems on large clumps tend to splay out leaving a bare mid-rib. I have even moved this *Sedum* in full flower on a hot summer's day to fill a gap elsewhere; replanted at once and given a good drink, it did not bat an eyelid (or perhaps I should say petal?) 'Autumn Joy' goes with most other plants, but particularly with those having purple leaves, silver foliage plants and Ceratostigmas.

Sedum 'Ruby Glow' has 9 in (23cm) lax stems and the dark ruby heads do not hold their attraction as long as 'Autumn Joy'. However, the fleshy, glaucous foliage is always pleasing and blends well with Stokesias and purple sage. A valuable addition to the foliage garden is *Sedum maximum* 'Atropurpureum', if a good mahogany-leaved form can be obtained. It does not seem to increase with the same vigour as the two previously mentioned cultivars, but is an excellent foil for silver, glaucous and gold plants making a pleasing group with *Helictotrichon sempervirens*, *Artemisia* 'Lambrook Silver' and a pale pink phlox.

Sedum maximum 'Atropurpureum'

Some years ago I was given a variegated *Sedum* which I imagine to be *Sedum telephium* 'Variegatum', it has pale yellow, green-edged leaves which are touched with pink, but has increased very little. Shoots occasionally revert to plain green and have to be cut out. The flowers are of no value but flower arrangers are apt to deprive the plants of all its foliage—if permitted!

Until recently, I grew only one *Anthemis, A. tinctoria* 'Wargrave Variety', which smothers itself for weeks on end with pale yellow daisies on 3 ft (90cm) stems. It is advisable to tie the clumps up loosely as they can be flattened by a summer gale. After flowering, towards the end of August, the stems should be cut right to the ground to allow in air and light, to produce new shoots before the onset of winter, otherwise they may not survive. Cuttings taken from basal shoots in spring are easily rooted.

Last year I was given *Anthemis cupaniana*, a low-growing species which has rapidly spread into silvery mats of finely-dissected foliage covered with a succession of glistening white daisies. Growing in an exceptionally dry spot it did on one occasion show signs of distress, but soon revived after watering. Achilleas on the other hand show no discomfort. My two favourites, *A.* 'Moonshine' and *A. taygetea* certainly give a long run for their money. If the first crop of flowering stems is cut right down when fading, a second batch soon appears. I like to grow these pale yellow Achilleas with white-flowered plants such as *Chrysanthemum parthenium* 'White-Bonnets' and *Viola cornuta* 'Grovemont Blue'. The sheeps-bit scabious, *Jasione* is not often seen, yet the 1 ft (30cm) high, *J. perennis* blooms non-stop from June to September with azure blue, scabious-like flowers. It is easy to grow in sun and well-drained soil, but as it resents disturbance, seed is the easiest method of propagation.

Similar to the *Jasione* is the plant now known by the rather ugly name *Knautia macedonica* (formerly *Scabiosa rumelica*). The much-branched flower stalks produce endless quantities of small ruby flowers over a very long period, but the plants tend to get untidy and floppy as the season progresses. A few discreetly placed twigs will usually keep it in order. In early summer, *Allium azureum* grows beside it, then a pale mauve *Erigeron* takes over, and by the time *Anaphalis triplinervis* is in flower on the other side, the *Knautia* is still in bloom.

The flaxes are another family of sun lovers for well-drained soils. *Linum narbonense* makes neat, bushy plants 2 ft (60cm) high, with airy stems and greyish green, narrow leaves. The cup-shaped flowers are china blue, and although they are individually short-

Linum narbonense

lived, there are always more to take over. It has the advantage of being practically evergreen though I cut mine back—somewhat timidly—in early spring. Last summer I saw a very peaceful grouping in a Gloucestershire cottage garden with *Linum narbonense, Alchemilla mollis, Hosta sieboldiana* and a few pink astrantias and dianthus growing round a rectangular pond (if that is possible!).

A marvellous little plant for the front of the border or the edge of the path is another non-stop performer, *Diascia cordata* from South Africa. Given the addition of a little peat and leaf mould when planting, it soon spreads into wide mats of pale green foliage from which arise masses of 6 in (15cm) spikes of salmon pink flowers. Reputedly rather tender it has survived the past two mild winters, but there is a hardier form, 'Ruby Field' which I have just received. The *Diascia* combines with *Ajuga* 'Delightful' a bugle which lives up to its name, rapidly covering the ground with foliage shading from pale pink to deep purple and occasionally splashed with cream.

Being particularly addicted to white flowers, I am full of admiration for *Epilobium glabellum*, a New Zealand willow herb, forming prostrate mats of bronze green leaves. The creamy white, funnel-shaped flowers are about 1 in (2.5cm) across and are freely borne over a long period. It does well in full sun and half shade, but so far has not blessed me with any offspring.

Euphorbia is a large genus of which many grow very well in dry conditions, I think *E. sikkimensis* must prefer moist soil as it shows no signs of increasing, but *E. robbiae* does so only too well and is busily filling an arid corner in deep shade, under an ash tree and also in dust-like conditions round a very large conifer in full sun. Mrs Robb's spurge grows about 18 in (45cm) high and the rather sombre dark green leathery leaves contrast well with its yellow green bracts which remain presentable for many months. An aristocratic relation from S.W. Asia, *E. niciciana* is much better behaved and needs to be grown in full sun. The narrow, glaucous foliage remains tidy all the year. In early summer the flower stems are covered with greeny-gold bracts which glisten in the sun after a shower of rain as if covered with myriads of tiny diamonds. Growing about 1½ ft (45cm) it is easily increased by cuttings, and also, I believe, by seed. I grow it under *Berberis thunbergii* 'Atropurpurea' with *Spartium junceum* behind. It also compliments *Campanula portenschlagiana*. Of the taller *E. griffithii* 'Fireglow', I have mixed feelings. It took several years to establish, but now threatens to take over a whole bed, even popping up into the lawn in places. The roots are tough and woody and not easily eradicated, but when the gorgeous flame-coloured bracts appear in late spring, all is forgiven. When the nearby *Rhododendron* 'Goldsworth Yellow' deigns to bloom, it makes a lovely combination, but this rhododendron seems to blossom only in alternate years. It is now, however, in danger of being smothered by the *Euphorbia* whose stems eventually reach 4 ft (1.2m) in shade.

Alstroemeria 'Ligtu Hybrids' increase rapidly in this sandy soil seeding themselves in all kinds of unlikely places. The exotic Brazilian *A. pulchellum*, the parrot lily, is more refined. Doubtfully hardy, it has remained with me for three years on the south wall of the house, with the aid of some peat heaped round the base for protection in winter. The green and red flowers are unusual and last for a very long time. In fact there are still a few now at the end of November despite several severe frosts. I am agreeably surprised that the dwarf wand flower, *Dierama pendulum* has done so well, though admittedly the corms were planted in a polythene-lined pocket with plenty of peat and compost. From clumps of Iris-like foliage, 1 ft (30cm) stems appear in June, gracefully arched and covered with pendent pink flowers. They look enchanting, dancing in the wind beside the pond.

The last performer is a star turn, *Chrysanthemum* 'Mei-Kyo' introduced from Japan by Will Ingerwersen. It does not start flowering until the middle of October, but from then until the end of November it is a mass of silvery pink, inch-wide pompons. It is perfectly hardy and increases well, the clumps dividing with the greatest of ease, though it is perhaps safest to do this in the spring. I am not a chrysanthemum fan, but this one has great charm and the late splash of colour is most welcome. In front of mine *Senecio* 'White Diamond' enhances the pink flowers, and another autumn bloomer, *Serratula shawii*, with darkish mauve mini cornflowers and finely-cut bronze green leaves, make a colourful corner.

These and many others, such as oenotheras, hardy geraniums, campanulas, dianthus and eryngiums to name but a few, have proved their worth.

If next summer should turn out to be cool and wet, these stars may not perform so well, there is always the consolation that others such as pholoxes, aconitums, astilbes and kirengeshoma will fill the bill, but that will be another story.

Originally published in 1973. Volume 4, number 5

Tiarella cordifolia

by Keith Bower

TIARELLA *cordifolia* was introduced into this country in 1731. To have survived in cultivation for more than two centuries must surely be proof that its modest charms have appealed to generations of gardeners during that time, and still continues to do so. The vast woodland areas of eastern North America are the home of this little member of the saxifrage family. Partial shade and leaf mould, therefore, are the ideal requirements for success in this country. However, *T. cordifolia* is very amenable and will grow almost anywhere providing the site does not dry out excessively.

A thriving plant will produce large mats of vigorous rhizomes and runners clad with small, hairy, maple-shaped leaves that turn bronze in autumn and persist all winter. During late April and May numerous 6–10 in (15–25cm) long flowering stems arise with the young leaves. Each stem terminates in a raceme of tiny ¼ in (0.6cm) wide flowers of white or palest pink. The myriads of tiny flowers on a large plant give a graceful, feathery, almost foamy effect which is most appealing. This observation was obviously the origin of its most widely-used common name in this country of foamflower.

At least three forms occurring in the wild have been described. Two of these, *T. c. parviflora* with very small flowers and *T. c. tridentata* with three-toothed petals are distinctive. My own plant is of the latter form. It would be interesting to hear from fellow members whether they have the type or one of the forms to ascertain which is the commonest in cultivation.

Originally published in 1973. Volume 5, number 5

Jeffersonia diphylla

by Kenneth A. Beckett

IN its native eastern North America, *Jeffersonia diphylla* has the apt and descriptive name of twinleaf. No other name could more adequately describe the quaint leaves of this little woodland plant, for each individual leaf is composed of two identical elephant's-ear-shaped leaflets. A characteristic duly noted, and made full use of in both its common and Latin epithets.

More robust than its aristocratic and lovelier cousin, *J. dubia*, it is, nevertheless a charming species and well suited for a choice position either in light woodland or on sheltered northern slope. Acid leafy soil and adequate moisture are essential if it is to do really well, however.

Quite early in the year, a drift of fragile-seeming pinkish bronze foliage emerges through the soil, and grows rapidly if the weather remains mild. At this stage, the growth is rather reminiscent of that of an epimedium. Flowering takes place when the foliage is about half grown, usually in April when approximately 6–8 in (15–20cm) high. By this time the foliage is much greener though still suffused with the bronzy pink tint that pleasingly foils the white flowers. These latter are eight-petalled, about 1 in (2.5cm) across and held just above the leaves. In shape and appearance they resemble the bloodroot (*Sanguinaria canadensis*), but lack the glistening purity of that species. Unfortunately, each bloom is of rather ephemeral nature, lasting rarely more than a couple of days. However, a well established clump will provide a succession of flowers for about ten days or so.

Flowering over, the foliage expands rapidly indeed, and the last few blossoms are often swamped by the rapidly growing leaves. In summer maturity, the clump may reach the height of 18 in (45cm). All hint of the pinkish shade is gone and the foliage now assumes a pleasing light green hue.

Quaint and decorative capsules succeed the flowers which when dry and open resemble gaping gargoyles in the Gothic style.

Jeffersonia diphylla is native to the States of New York, west

Jeffersonia diphylla

through South Ontario to Wisconsin and northeastern Indiana south to Alabama. It was introduced to England as long ago as 1792, but as far as I can ascertain it is now rare in cultivation over here.

Seed is a ready means of increase, but must be sown as soon as ripe if a good germination is to be expected. Even then one has to wait four or five years for flowering size plants. Sowing *in situ* would seem to be the ideal method, as root disturbance is not appreciated.

Originally published in 1974. Volume 4, number 6

Euphorbia robbiae does well in quite deep shade

The double primrose *Primula* 'Marie Crousse' is an old favourite

Dactylorhiza fuchsii forms large clumps and self-sows itself around

Another Look at Kniphofias

by Beth Chatto

I WISH you could see my pokers, or I should say kniphofas! On this mild mid-October morning they look like a sun burst, massed slender spikes of cool wax-like texture. In spite of the Big Drought these plants have maintained a successive show of colour since August. Now, with the welcome rain of the last month the display is quite spectacular.

My interest in kniphofias was decidedly cool until about fifteen years ago. Large clumps of straggling ragged leaves whipping their unfortunate neighbours, topped with a few intermittent spikes of a crude red and yellow, did not draw me very much. Then I bought a few plants of *K.* 'Maid of Orleans', impressed by the fine form as well as the delicate ivory colour. To this I added a few of the smaller kniphofias, all of them hybrids, I am sure, of the *K. galpinii* type. But although I liked the luminous orange colour the stems of my particular plants were very feeble and what is more seemed to be the favourite delicacy of slugs, so the flowers were always rather tumbled.

One autumn, instead of throwing away the few seed heads that had been produced I decided to sow them in a row across the vegetable garden. Next spring they germinated readily, and the following year a few of them flowered. I spaced them out to grow on again, and the third year I had flowers on most of them. I kept only the ones that appealed to me, that is, had narrow heads of closely set flowers. The large ones with short stubby heads I threw out.

A visit, again in autumn, to my old friend Sir Cedric Morris's garden (always a joy and inspiration) found me rummaging in my pockets for a handkerchief to tie up a handful of seeds collected from *his* kniphofias. Over several years I sowed seed and saved only those plants I thought were the best.

My first real excitement was the appearance of a green poker which I have called *Kniphofia* 'Green Jade'. This makes a medium sized plant, the flower spikes standing about 4 ft (120cm). It is the most delicate shade of green throughout, the colour bleaching slightly as it matures so that the tubes show pencilled green veins. It does not flower so generously as some of my other pokers, but it is a unique colour, and looks particularly good placed against a blue conifer. I originally planted it against *Chamaecyparis* 'Triomphe de Boskoop', where its pallor was shown up to perfection.

Since then another seedling has occurred of similar habit, but with large, fuller heads of greenish tubes which become very faintly flushed with orange, the effect still being green. 'Chartreuse' seemed a good name for this handsome plant.

Then, among the growing number of hot colours, a very dainty little creature appeared whose flowers opened green and faded through cream to ivory white. In colour it reminded me of *K.* 'Maid of Orleans', except that there is no hint of orange, but it is so much smaller, standing in full flower no more than 2 ft (60cm). The long slim line of this poker with its green and ivory tubes set closely along sometimes more than half the length of the stem make it a lovely plant to pick, while its small neat habit makes it perfect for the edge of the border. At the Great Autumn Show, Sept. '75, *Kniphofia* 'Little Maid' was awarded a Certificate of Preliminary Commendation as 'a flowering plant suitable for the Herbaceous Border and Cutting'.

Among my other smaller pokers, up to 4 ft (120cm), are several in warm shades of yellow, orange, coral and red. These are all one-toned, although some, like *Kniphofia* 'Burnt Orange' start with such deep toned buds they are almost brown. All of them have very narrow slender spikes, with the flower tubes set a long way down the stem. The stems themselves while slender are sturdy enough to stand up well without support. Flower arrangers love them, and my nursery rows are a great boon to local harvest festivals (which saves a lot of dead-heading!)

Coming along are several blocks of plants in tones of cream and coral pink. One we already list as *K.* 'Strawberries and Cream', a small summer flowering plant with another flush in autumn. A slightly larger, and we think better form, has not yet been named, being insufficient yet to list.

My interest in kniphofias now wide awake I bought some of the named larger hybrids as I fortunately have room for some of the big ones. *Kniphofia* 'Yellow Hammer' is a very handsome plant opening its acid yellow flowers beneath a crown of bitter green buds, very fetching. Another plant I call 'Prince Igor' was given me many years ago and has large short heads of brilliant orange scarlet standing on thick rigid stalks up to 8 ft (2.4m) tall! It is spectacular against the glaucous blue foliage of *Eucalyptus gunnii*. It is a superb plant for large openings in large shrubberies, or beside a large pond,

Kniphofia 'Little Maid'

provided it is planted well up in soil that does not become waterlogged.

Two more that I grow predominantly as foliage plants are *K. caulescens*, and *K. northiae* (after that amazing Victorian lady painter Miss Marian North). *K. caulescens* forms increasing clumps of inch wide leaves of a soft grey-green colour tightly banded at their bases to form a small trunk which, if you pull the old leaves away is revealed delicately pin-striped in purple and fawn. The flower head is somewhat stubby, but one morning this late September I was caught by its glistening beauty as the pale golden stamens emerging beneath the softly orange tubes sparkled in autumn sunlight.

Kniphofia northiae is reputed to be tender, but I have had it for the last 10 years growing in gravel on the south facing wall of my greenhouse. It is probably the most spectacular foliage plant we can grow in the Dry Garden. It makes a mound of enormous rosettes of leaves 6 in (15cm) across at their base curving 6 ft (180cm) away to end in a dry curling wisp. This 'untidy' dead end is not approved of by gardeners whose aim is perfection in all things, but to my mind it is part of the character of the plant. I can imagine a great group looking superb against the tall mellow wall of a stately Georgian house with those swirling bright green leaves overlaid with a waxen grape-like bloom making a pattern across the paved walk or terrace. Of course, it needs to be tidied up occasionally—we trim ours every spring. The few flower spikes are dull, and could be dispensed with, except that we are glad of the seed.

Finally, we have a few plants of *K. snowdenii*, very elegant with its slender stems of widely spaced curving tubes in shades of coral and red. These have not yet been tested by a genuine East Anglian winter.

On the Nursery the kniphofias are grown in a poor gravelly soil which we try to improve by rotavating in masses of old cow manure. They are split every May, and so far flourish well with this treatment.

Elsewhere in the garden they stand untouched for many years, in similar stony soil. Plenty of humus is dug into the soil before planting, and they are covered with a good mulching of anything available, usually rotted straw around the large growing kinds, or crushed bark on the fronts of the borders. This is for weed control as much as for moisture conservation.

Originally published in 1976. Volume 5, number 2

Plants Introduced by Miss R. B. Pole

by Michael Upward

THE curious fact about the plants introduced to horticulture by the late Miss R. B. Pole, is that none of them were raised through any deliberate or scientific hybridising.

Achilleas seeded about the nursery with profligate abandon and it was her very keen eye, so tragically affected in later life, that enabled her to select variations from the norm. Of course, it was *Achillea* 'Coronation Gold' that gave Miss Pole her deepest pride. It is a plant that fits modestly into today's gardens, where *A.* 'Gold Plate' might be too large. It has deservedly been given the Award of Garden Merit by the Royal Horticultural Society.

There were more selections of *Achillea* seedlings: 'Lye End Lemon', which has a self-explanatory colour; with heads perhaps not so tight as 'Coronation Gold'; 'Lye End Ivory', which is a variable creamy colour; 'Lye End Pink', which really is not yet stable enough in its colour consistency; and 'Canary', which is a lighter and brighter yellow. It may well be that further seedlings will materialise, as we are continuing to watch the seedlings as they flower.

Others of Miss Pole's perennial introductions include *Kniphofia* 'Lye End', at present on trial at Wisley Garden; it has peach and cream flowers, borne on sturdy stems and gives good value with two periods of flowering.

One of her favourite genera was *Aster*, probably because *A. amellus* and its cultivars were a challenge to grow; however, it was in the *novae-angliae* group that Miss Pole found two seedling variations: 'Lye End Beauty' and 'Lye End Companion'. The latter is a deeper pink that 'Harrington's Pink', but of the same habit and height, whilst 'Lye End Beauty' is an interesting plum colour.

The only plant of Miss Pole's to have received an Award of Merit from the RHS is *Salvia* 'Lye End'. It is a pity that such an attractive plant should have a rather dubious parentage. However, Graham Thomas, in his latest book *Perennial Garden Plants*, puts the record straight by stating it is a form of *S.* × *sylvestris*, which is the name

Achillea 'Coronation Gold'

given to hybrids between *S. nemorosa* and *S. pratensis*. Its lavender blue flower spikes last well and even the purplish-brown calyces are attractive when flowering is over.

Michael Upward adds the following note. It is fair to say that since the above words were written in 1976, certain of the plants mentioned will no longer be found in commerce. The selections of *Achillea* seedlings which Miss Pole made, mainly 'Lye End Lemon', 'Lye End Ivory', 'Lye End Pink' and 'Canary' were unfortunately not of sufficiently strong constitution to last. When my wife took over the Nursery after Miss Pole's death, we strove to reproduce the seedlings by vegetative means rather than selecting further colour forms that looked close to the original. This proved impossible, and with one or two messy winters, these finally put paid to this obviously weak strain of seedlings. Having said that, however, if there is anyone still with any of these plants in their gardens, we would be interested to hear.

Originally published in 1976. Volume 5, number 2

The Maligning of Magenta

by George R. Kingbourn

IN June, 1859, at the north Italian town of Magenta, a combined force of Sardinian and French troops defeated a larger force of Austrians. This was one step towards a unified Italian kingdom, and in Britain was a cause of some rejoicing.

At about this time the English chemist William Perkin had discovered a new series of dyes based on aniline, one of which, a brilliant red, was given the honourable name—Magenta.

We are by now quite used to this colour name, and all H.P.S. members will know that it describes the typical hue of the mallows, the cranesbill geraniums, herbaceous phloxes, some lychnis and peony species, and that of very many other herbaceous plants. Many shrubs and annual and biennial plants also share this honourable colour.

I stress this honourable, approving, aspect particularly because later this colour was to have for certain English gardeners a distasteful quality. My researchers seem to point to two very eminent gardeners as the chief source of this prejudice—Reginald Farrer and Augustus Bowles.

These two men were close friends who had made plant hunting expeditions together in the Alps. Both had written important scholarly books on plants and gardening. The gardening world, in fact, 'hung on their words'.

Earlier the Victorians had been conditioned to revere the judgement of such men as Ruskin and Carlyle who pontificated loftily on all matters. I think this attitude persisted later among the gardening fraternity who wished to be told definitely what they should like, and what to reject as persons of good taste.

Let us now turn to the words of those who vilified magenta.

Bowles writes of *Geranium psilostemon*: 'An awful form of original sin, but its black eye saves it from being one of the worst astringents of the vision in the garden. This colour reacts on my retina as alum does on my tongue.' Sir A. Hort writing later says of the same geranium: 'Perhaps the most furious floral example of colour, which in full sun is painful to most eyes.'

Geranium psilostemon

Of the related *Geranium sanguineum*, bloody cranesbill, Farrer says: 'It has too fiery a terribleness', and Bowles calls it 'vicious crimson'.

Of *Geranium sylvaticum* Bowles writes: 'some forms come perilously near magenta.'

Geoffrey Grigson writes of *Geranium pratense:* 'Showy and pretentious its flowers have the unpleasant tone of cheap poorly dyed, badly designed fabrics.'

Lychnis coronaria also comes in for some rough handling from

Farrer who declares: 'It sickens the mind's eye.' He also has some very intemperate words for the purple loosestrife: 'They bring not so much peace but war of battling horrible colour and in the end an Armageddon of the spade in an attempt to be finally quit of them.'

Bowles and Farrer then join forces to trample upon another relation of the battered geranium family—*Erodium manescavi*. Farrer writes: 'It is a large coarse rankness universally known in gardens, with flowers of a heavy flaring magenta-rose.' Bowles writes: 'The flowers are sinfully near magenta.'

Sacheverall Sitwell joins in the foolish fussing describing a double mauve pink, 'Napoléon III' as 'a violent uncompromising colour belonging to the era of magenta and heliotrope.'

Jason Hill writes of aubrieta hybrids—'They have broken out into fierce aniline tones of violet and magenta and can hardly be restrained from spreading into streams and puddles of flat blinding colour.'

Gertrude Jekyll, of herbaceous border colour scheme fame, generally avoids all mention of plants of magenta colouring, but gives a solemn warning about the use of petunias—'They should be avoided by all those who dislike strong crimson or magenta.'

One effect of the 'character assassination' of magenta has been that nurserymen and seedsmen generally avoid the word, substituting: purple-red, rosy red, crimson, carmine, cerise, etc.

However, Mr le Grice actually named a rose of his raising—'Magenta'. One wonders if it affected its sales adversely (I must ask).

In the Horticultural Society's colour-chart magenta is not mentioned and the word purple is regularly substituted; we have instead: fuchsia purple, roseine purple, rhodamine p., peony p., mallow p., cyclamen p., magnolia p., dianthus p., beetroot p., orchid p., phlox p., and petunia p. The many colour plates show the full range of magenta from the more reddish hues, shades and tints to those of a type approaching violet.

It would be wrong of me to suggest that all those who have written on plants and colour have denigrated magenta. The adjectives Tyrian, imperial, royal and handsome have been used by other writers with stronger nerves and more temperate language. If within the H.P.S. anyone wants to form a 'Friends of Magenta' group I will join, and then there will be two of us at least.

Originally published in 1977. Volume 5, number 3

Rodgersia

by Kenneth A. Beckett

HARDY perennials which combine handsome leafage with attractive flowers are not too common. In this category, *Hosta* and *Bergenia* are now well known, but *Rogersia* is still too seldom seen. This eastern Asian genus contains but six species and every one has garden merit. There are two main reasons for their lack of popularity; reputation for needing boggy soil and their large size. Although it is true that all species grow well by the waterside, it is equally true to say that any garden soil will do if suitably enriched with garden compost, rotted manure, peat, hop manure or any other source of humus. It may also be necessary to dispense a bucket of water now and then during dry spells though it should not be essential on a humus-rich soil and in the partial shade they prefer.

Rodgersias produce thick rhizomes which eventually form clumps or colonies, but in the smaller garden, they are easily kept in check with a spade should this be necessary. From these rhizomes spring long-stalked leaves bearing, in all but one species, several large, boldly veined and sometimes bronze or reddish-tinted leaflets. These may be digitate, all springing from the top of the stalk like the leaves of a horse chestnut, or pinnate like ash, i.e. several pairs growing from a common midrib, in this case with a larger, solitary terminal one as well, though see also *R. tabularis* below. The flowers are much like those of the more familiar and closely allied *Astilbe*, but are arranged in spumy, tiered panicles above the leaves.

The rhizomes may be planted any time from autumn to spring, preferably as early as possible so that they can get established before any spell of drought in spring. Propagation by division at the same time is easy. Seeds also provide an interesting, if rather more long winded means of increase. They should be sown on the surface of a peaty compost, covered with glass or a polythene bag and placed in a shady, cold frame in spring. The tiny seedlings must be acclimatised gently to partial shade or dappled light and be pricked off into boxes when large enough to handle. Subsequently the young plants should be set out in a nursery bed for a year, by which time they will be ready for permanent planting. Flowering starts in the second or third year.

The genus *Rodgersia* which is primarily Chinese, was founded by the great American botanist Asa Gray. He described the first species as *Astilbe podophylla*, a plant collected in Japan during the far ranging American Pacific Expedition of 1852–56 led by Rear-Admiral John Rodgers (1812–1882). As botanists will, and in this case justly so, Asa Gray changed his mind, removing *podophylla* from *Astilbe* and placing it in a new genus named for the Rear-Admiral. No subsequent botanist has seen fit to dispute this decision except in the case of *R. tabularis* (see below).

Five of the six species of *Rodgersia* are commercially available and the sixth—*R. henricii* from north Burma—is occasionally encountered in collectors' gardens. The following notes are arranged according to the plants' relationships not in the usual alphabetical sequence. All are summer flowering.

Rodgersia podophylla has the distinction not only of being the first species described, but of being the only one from Japan as well as China. Also formerly known as *R. japonica*, it attains 3 ft (90cm) in height. The digitate leaves are composed of five leaflets, each one up to 14 in (35cm) long, bearing three to five prominently toothed triangular lobes. These are bronze as they unfold, changing to green then back to a more reddish-bronze tint at maturity. The flowers are white, in 8–16 in (20–40cm) long panicles, but though pleasing, they are the least effective in the genus. *R. aesculifolia* has the same leaf formation, but the leaflets number seven to ten, lack the pointed lobes, and are, as the name suggests like those of horse chestnut, (*Aesculus*). They also have a bronzy hue but with a somewhat metallic lustre. The flowers are creamy white or pink flushed, carried in panicles up to 60cm long on stems to 3.3 ft (1m) tall. A well-grown, solitary clump can make a most strikingly beautiful focal point.

The same comment could also be applied to *R. pinnata*, a slightly less tall plant with pinnate leaves composed of 5–9 leaflets. Although the leaves are truly pinnate, the large burnished leaflets—up to 8 in (20cm) long—are borne close together and their formation can look digitate from a distance. The flowers are red in bud, opening white, but the haze of tiny petals creates an overall pink effect. In *R. p.* 'Superba', the flowers are truly bright pink and the leaves more coppery. A white flowered form is known and others in varying shades of pink, but they are seldom seen today.

R. sambucifolia has much more decidedly pinnate leaves though not really like the elder (*Sambucus*) as its name suggests. The several pairs of leaflets are a lively green and the flowers white. Further points of difference from *R. pinnata* are its smaller stature, about 1m, and its generally neater, more elegant appearance.

Rodgersia aesculifolia

The odd man out among rodgersias is undoubtedly *R. tabularis* and one cannot help having some sympathy for the botanist who has tried (without much success) to place it in a genus of its own as *Astilboides tabularis*. Also a native of Korea, this species has circular leaves borne in peltate fashion, i.e. the stalk joining the blade in the middle underneath. Each pale green blade can be up to 2 ft (60cm) or more wide with a shallowly lobed or notched margin. Well above these massive leaves are carried creamy-white, astilbe-like floral plumes creating the sort of contrast rarely seen in hardy perennials. For me this is the most garden worthy of all.

As stated at the beginning, six species of *Rodgersia* are allowed for in literature (See *A Dictionary of the Flowering Plants and Ferns* by Willis, eighth edition, the standard reference work in Britain for such facts). There is however a seventh name, *R. purdomii*, about which I can find no descriptive reference and, unlike all the species described so far here, I have not seen. If any H.P.S. member grows or has seen this plant, I shall be very pleased to hear from them. Until more information comes my way, I shall assume that the plant William Purdom collected is no more than a form of either a digitate or pinnate leaved species and has in effect been covered in this brief survey of the genus.

Originally published in 1978. Volume 5, number 4.

A Plantsman in the Caucasus

by Roy Lancaster

WHENEVER asked by the tour operators in which direction I should like to travel next I reply without hesitation East! Of course I am well aware of the floral wealth of the Americas and all points south but it is invariably the magical East to which my heart and mind responds whenever the subject of plant hunting arises. During the last decade I have been fortunate in being given the opportunity to visit several of the most exciting plant habitats east of the English Channel. The Swiss Alps and the Spanish Pyrenees provided me with my first happy hours in Europe and since then I have progressed to Greece and the Mediterranean, Turkey, Kashmir, Nepal and China. Many of those who only know of me regard me as a tree and shrub man whilst those who know me well are aware of my love for the whole galaxy of plant-life, not surprising, since my introduction to plants was by way of wild flowers and heaven knows how many years I have revelled in the delights of the British flora. I was pleased therefore when Ken Beckett enquired if I would like to write an article for the journal. Good! I thought, at last a chance to prove to those who don't know me that my interests extend far beyond those of the woody plant fraternity. Anyone who has accompanied me on my tours will of course need no confirmation of this fact.

One of the most important centres of hardy perennial plants in the wild must be the Caucasus Mountains of the Southern USSR and their associated hills and plains. If one was to make a list of well known garden perennials which have originated in the above mentioned region I am confident that it would be long and spectacular.

When therefore, the opportunity to visit the Caucasus was presented to me, I required no persuasion to accept. The idea germinated in 1978 after I had spoken to Martyn Rix then of the R.H.S. Garden, Wisley. Martyn had been in the Caucasus earlier that year and described it enthusiastically. Ken Lister of Cox and Kings did the rest and on a bright sunny afternoon in July 1979 our party of 12 plus myself (who's superstitious?) flew into Moscow on the first stage of our journey. The next day we arrived in Tbilisi, the capital of Georgia and sweated our way to our hotel for the beginning of what we hoped would be the experience of a lifetime. It is not my intention here nor is it the occasion to describe the domestic 'adventures' of our tour, suffice to say that, despite certain annoying and recurrent difficulties we managed in two weeks to see enough of the wild places to give us at least a taste of the floral wealth of that vast region.

Rather than repeat our itinerary in each hot, soggy, exciting, frustrating detail I shall simply extract the exciting parts and present them as a series of isolated experiences. If I make sparse mention of woody plants it is purely in deference to the supposed predominantly perennial interests of the Hardy Plant Society. Forgive and bear with me if I am wrong.

Georgian Military Highway

For all those visitors to Tbilisi professing an interest in wild flowers an excursion along this famous road is a must and if it isn't suggested by the tour guide then one must insist on it. The road runs northwards from the city first passing through dry (in summer) valleys where an abundance of scrub and aromatic herbs flourish. It is worthwhile spending at least a half day in such regions where many 'everlasting' flowers may be found. At the time of our visit there were shimmering seas of the tiny silvery pink *Xeranthemum annum* whilst a few steps from the road revealed two sea hollies in great profusion. The pale grey-green *Eryngium campestre* and the steely blue *E. caeruleum* formed a lively background for the fig-leaved *Althaea rugosa* whose 5–6 ft (1.5–1.8m) stems carried large saucer shaped flowers of the most exquisite satiny primrose I have ever seen. At the time of writing (late June) I am patiently awaiting the flowering of two of these hollyhocks in my garden grown from seed collected on one such hillside. Gradually the highway ascends a valley entering a zone of beech forest on the margins of which we found the tall pink-flowered *Lavatera thuringiaca*, a plant I first saw 17 years ago in a border in Hilliers' old Winchester Nursery now alas a sorry sight. The real purpose of the day however begins much higher, first in the subalpine pastures around 2000m where the colour and mixture is reminiscent of a Swiss or Austrian pasture at its best.

Amongst the gems we saw on that day two plants stand out in my mind's eye. The first *Betonica grandiflora* because its rich rose-purple flower heads brought me happy memories of my first job on leaving school when I spent an idyllic year in the Old English Garden of a public park in Bolton. There I first encountered the betony and I could never pass the border in which it flowered without stopping to admire its bold appearance. The second plant was *Astrantia maxima* (*helleborifolia*) with its charming button-like flower heads of rich pink. Like so many other perennials brought into cultivation from the wild this first rate plant develops a multi-stemmed clump in the isolation of a bed or border quite unlike the single stemmed individuals of the meadow where grasses and herbs present strong competition.

The banks above the road at this point support low patches of a superb cornflower *Centaurea cheiranthifolia*, the likes of which I have not seen in cultivation. It resembles the ubiquitous *C. montana* but with flowers of a rare sulphur yellow and is well worth introducing into cultivation if it is not already here.

The highway crosses the first ridge at 2,400m or thereabouts and the slopes above this point—Cross Pass—are full of alpines and small bulbs which are at their best early in the year as the snows are melting and before the grazing animals arrive. In late July we found *Daphne glomerata* hiding in the close-cropped turf whilst odd flowering plants of *Primula auriculata* and *Gentiana angulosa* survived in steep gullies. The two most abundant plants here, conspicuous by their bold clumps and avoided by the sheep because of their unpleasant nature were *Veratrum lobelianum* and *Euphorbia oblongifolia*. The first was not in flower but the handsome ribbed leaves typical of the genus were much in evidence. The spurge had finished flowering yet I remembered its attractive flowers from the Pontic Alps of N.E. Turkey where it grew above the Zigana Pass. It is a most desirable species and I am pleased to have a plant now established in a pot.*

On our way down from the pass I nearly caused our coach driver to have a coronary when I suddenly shouted for him to stop. The reason was that I had spotted a deep rocky ravine below the road ahead and something about the look of it set lights flashing and bells ringing in my head. Time was short, the ravine was dangerously steep but it contained a selection of the loveliest flowers of the whole tour. *Cicerbita racemosa*, with nodding spikes and chicory blue flowers, *Aster alpinus, Polygonum carneum*, the breathtaking blue pea *Lathyrus cyaneus, Sedum caucasicum*, the gorgeous orange daisies of *Inula orientalis*, the large leaved, tall stemmed *Doronicum macrophyllum*, the true Russian comfrey *Symphytum asperum*, wickedly rough to the touch and with gentian blue flowers and *Tanacetum* (*Pyrethrum*) *coccineum*. There were many more and several alpines for good measure. Would anyone doubt that we slept happily that night?

*This I have since given to the R.B.G. Kew.

Lagodekhi Reserve

This large reserve covers 13,300 hectacres in the southern foothills of the eastern Caucasus some 80km east of Telavi. We were fortunate indeed to gain entry but our elation was gradually sapped as we trekked steeply uphill through vast beechwoods. Not until we broke through the tree line at 1,700m did we find perennials in quantity but for the few who survived the climb it was memorable. I was particularly excited to find colonies of a giant hogweed 5–6 ft (1.5–1.8m) high with cartwheel sized heads of white flowers. No, it wasn't *the* Russian hogweed but a related species *Heracleum sosnowskii*. Growing with it were equally bold clumps of the yellow-flowered *Telekia speciosa* one of several giant yellow composites, another being *Senecio latifolius*. Other 'giants' included the sulphur yellow *Cephalaria gigantea* and *Aruncus dioicus*. The willow gentian—*Gentiana asclepiadea* was plentiful and I was interested to find *Symphytum caucasicum*, half the size of *S. asperum* and with pale blue flowers. A bold leaved spurge along the woodland paths was later identified as *Euphorbia grandifolius* and a plant of this is now thriving in my garden.

The climb had taken us six hours and after an all too short stay we had to return at speed achieving the descent in three hours.

Novy Afon

A sun-soaked resort on the Black Sea west of Sukhumi. There is a limestone hill immediately above the town and the wooded upper slopes are well worth half a day. We found *Helleborus guttatus*, leaves and fruit only, and *Cyclamen abschasicum* is plentiful in season. As in other areas of the Caucasus the large heart-shaped leaves of *Trachystemon orientale* carpeted the ground in places and only marginally less common were *Epimedium colchicum* and *Omphalodes cappadocica*. Like so many other plants of this region the last named was regarded locally as a distinct species *O. caucasicum*. The white-bells of *Campanula alliariifolia* always charm me, carried as they are in one-side racemes. It was frequent here and often associated with the evergreen clumps of two butcher's brooms—*Ruscus ponticus* and *R. colchicus*. The first is merely a narrow leaved *R. aculeatus* but the second is a distinct and localised species now represented though rarely in cultivation.

A plant which caught my attention in these woods was *Dioscorea caucasica*, a relative of our native black bryony—*Tamus* but with paler boldly ribbed leaves lacking the high gloss of the other. The fruits too differ in being winged capsules. It clambers into shrubs and surrounding vegetation and though hardly I have yet to see it in

British cultivation though I saw a well established plant on the rock garden in the University of Utrecht Botanic Garden, Holland some years ago.

Youzhni Preeyut

The above name was given to a small settlement in a wooded valley 1,100m in the mountains north of the so called Sukhumi Military Highway. We visited this place on the 1st August and arrived after a bone-shaking journey along a tortuous route, definitely not for the faint hearted. A track leads upwards beneath magnificent spruce and fir forest through dense thickets of cherry laurel and *Rhododendron ponticum*. Eventually it breaks through the cover and in the open areas lots of perennials are to be found. We almost trod on *Coronilla orientalis* which is a treasure of a creeping plant with crowns of yellow pea flowers. It grows like birds-foot trefoil but is quite different in looks. Lots of the plants we had seen previously appeared together with a fair sprinkling of new ones such as *Epilobium latifolium*, a splendid plant growing in rocky stream beds. This is much smaller than *E. angustifolium* much less invasive and very floriferous, resembling more *E. fleischeri*, which we at first took it to be. *Aconitum orientale* grew above the torrent its white helmeted flowers in tall branching racemes. This is a member of a widespread group represented in W. Europe by *A. vulparia* and its close associates and in the Himalaya by *A. laeve. Campanula lactiflora* also grew above the torrent forming bold erect clumps of leafy stems crowded with pale blue flowers. In a clearing we at last found our Russian hogweed—*Heracleum mantegazzianum* several plants up to 10 ft (3m) high with table-top flower heads. At one point the track wound its way between and beneath them and one had the feeling that Jonathan Swift was not such a story teller after all. We climbed the hillside to where the snow was in a state of disarray and retreat and here found the blue forget-me-not flowers of *Brunnera macrophylla* protruding from the wet soil. *Aquilegia olympica* was also present in the rocks close by, its blue and white long spurred lanterns hanging from erect stems. One of our number even found *Trollius patulus* with wide-open golden flowers on short stems thrusting through the melting snow.

It was an exciting and satisfactory end to our tour and for evermore when I walk through our gardens I shall not catch the gaze of a Caucasian flower without remembering this time.

Originally published in 1980. Volume 5, number 6

A History of The Hardy Plant Society

by Noël J. Prockter

THOSE members of the Hardy Plant Society who joined after the tenth anniversary in 1967 may not know of its origins.

The Hardy Plant Society as it is today was started in 1957 but long before this however, there was a National Hardy Plant Society. The following excerpt is taken from the weekly paper *The Garden* founded by Wm Robinson, (Price 1d. and dated September 3rd, 1910). In 'Notes of the Week' under the heading 'National Hardy Plant Society' we read that 'A meeting of growers and persons interested in hardy plants was held at the George Hotel, Shrewsbury on the 17th ult (August) most of the largest exhibitors being present. On the motion of Mr John Harkness (of Harkness & Sons, Bedale, Yorks.) seconded by Mr Frank Bouskell (of Loughborough), Mr A. J. Macself took the chair and opened the meeting by explaining the objects and aims of the Society. This was followed by speeches from Mr John Harkness, Mr Frank Bouskell and Mr W. Irving of Kew, who said 'I think however, that it is quite time such a Society was formed in the interest of hardy plants and I shall have much pleasure in supporting your objects and joining the Society when formed'. After a most interesting discussion, Mr George Gibson (Gibson & Co, The Nurseries, Leeming Bar, Bedale) moved, Mr R. West (Llandaff) seconded and it was resolved unanimously that a National Hardy Plant Society be formed . . .' Mr Frank Bouskell was appointed Secretary, Mr Macself Chairman of the Provisional Committee, Mr J. S. Brunton Treasurer and Mr R. T. Went, Vice Chairman'.

Among those also present at this inaugural meeting were such horticulturalists as Mr J. Artindale, Mr R. W. Hosier (Messrs Bakers, Wolverhampton); Mr G. C. Mudge (Messrs Barr, Covent Garden), Mr J. C. House (Westbury-on-Trim) and Mr A. J. Wommacott (Messrs Hewitt, Solihull.) It was also decided to hold the first meeting in Edinburgh at the Royal Caledonian Horticultural Society's show on Wednesday 7th September, 1910.

The first general meeting of the National Hardy Plant Society was held at the Hotel Windsor, London on Thursday November 3rd 1910, with Mr A. J. Macself in the chair. Among the business, rules and bye laws were adopted. An invitation was received from Sir

Frank Crisp for the Society to visit Friar Court (Henley on Thames) in 1911. I have no further record of what else happened that year but in 1912 the N.H.P.S. published its first Year Book with a list of 95 members. At the end is the Society's Annual Report and a balance sheet showing an income of £56.4.6. with a balance in hand of £3.0.8d. Also in the first year book there is a page of photographs of the Chairman, Hon. Treasurer and Hon. Secretary.

A second annual report and year book in 1913 was followed by a third annual report in 1914 in which the balance sheet shows a total income of £100.15.8d. with a balance at the bank of £39.15.11. The society was plainly flourishing.

In 1913 the N.H.P.S. was invited by Her Grace Adeline, Duchess of Bedford to visit Woodside House Gardens, Chenies, Rickmansworth, Herts. In 1913 they also had a trial of veronicas organised by Mr Frank Bouskell at Market Bosworth, Nuneaton. As the shrubby veronicas had not been segregated to *Hebe*, they were included in the trial. On June 4th, 1914 a show was held at the R.H.S. Hall, Vincent Square.

In 1915 the Society visited Aldenham House, the home of the Hon. Vicary Gibbs. A party of 30 members travelling from St Pancras, London to Elstree and then by waggonettes through the park to the gardens. This was undoubtedly the society's 'swan song', for from then on there appear to be no further records of the National Hardy Plant Society and presumably it ceased to exist.

A second Hardy Plant Society almost came into being in the early 1950s when the Delphinium Society found itself in difficulties. Several proposals were made that the Society should expand its scope to include all hardy plants, but these ideas were finally shelved, and the Delphinium Society continued and flourishes today.

In December 1956 a meeting took place at Alan Bloom's instigation at the home of A. G. L. Hellyer, with Will Ingwersen and John Sambrook, and it was this meeting that led to the founding of the present Hardy Plant Society.

According to a report in *The Horticultural Trade Journal*, March 14th 1957—'On Tuesday 5th March 1957 some 30 people met at the R.H.S. New Hall to discuss the forming of the Hardy Plant Society, the chair being taken by Mr A. G. L. Hellyer, Editor of *Amateur Gardening*.' The meeting was opened by Mr Will Ingwersen who said that there was room for an organisation to look after hardy plants, other than irises and delphiniums and he went on to say that such a society could also undertake the publication of literature on hardy plants which was at the time very sparse. The acting chairman then put the matter to the vote and it was unanimously decided that a Hardy Plant Society be formed.

The Society's first Chairman was Mr Alan Bloom of

Bressingham, Diss, Norfolk, Mr S. Miller Gault was elected Vice Chairman, Mrs F. E. Bloom, Hon. Treasurer, Mr Noël J. Prockter Hon. Secretary and Mr H. P. Champneys Hon. Editor.

The Annual subscription was to be 12/6 or 20/- for man and wife. Among those on the committee were Miss Wendy Carlile (now Mrs Bowie), Messrs Will Ingwersen, A. G. L. Hellyer, S. M. Gault and Ralph Gould (trial ground manager, Hurst & Son, Ltd.)

The new society's first outing was to Bressingham Hall, Diss, in July 1957 and the first exhibit was in July 1957 at Marlborough House, Pall Mall, London. By 1958 the Society had a new Hon. Treasurer, Mr J. S. Amos and in the same year Mrs K. Sanecki took over as Hon. Editor. In August 1958 our first exhibit was arranged at the Southport Show, while our first show at the R.H.S. New Hall was held on Tuesday and Wednesday 16th and 17th September. At this show the Thomas Carlile Cup for the best new or recently introduced plant was awarded to Miss R. B. Pole, from Lye End, St Johns, Woking, Surrey for her *Aster* 'Lye End Beauty'. (For further comments about 'Lye End Beauty' see the H.P.S. Bulletin Vol 1, No. 7, 1958). In July 1958 the Society visited Waterperry, Oxford.

The H.P.S.'s second A.G.M. was held at the R.H.S. New Hall Saturday 7th March 1959 when we had a Brains Trust, the brains being Mrs Margery Fish, Mrs Frances Perry, Messrs Alan Bloom and Will Ingwersen, with our Vice Chairman, Mr R. S. W. Pollard as Question Master. At this A.G.M. Mr Bloom retired as Chairman and Mr S. M. Gault was elected. At the same time, the Hon. Secretary Mr N. J. Prockter retired, being replaced by Mr R. G. Elms. Also in 1959 we visited the University Botanic Garden, Cambridge.

By the 4th A.G.M., held on Wednesday 30th March 1961, the future of the H.P.S. was in the balance. At this meeting the Vice Chairman, Mr R. S. W. Pollard suggested that an 'Extraordinary General Meeting' be called for Tuesday 30th May 1961 at the R.H.S. New Hall; there were then only 220 members. It was through the tenacity and determination of Miss R. B. Pole at that Extraordinary General Meeting that the Society did survive—I quote from *News Letter* No. 1, August 1961;

'Dear Members,

Had I anticipated that I should be called upon to take office as Chairman of the Society I doubt if I should have had the temerity to accept. As it was, the alternative seemed to be dissolution and I was not prepared to allow this if it could be prevented.'

What a staunch supporter and fighter the Society had in this dynamic and keen plantswoman. From that day on, the Society has never looked back and by 1981 the membership was 1,238.

So much has happened since Miss Pole became Chairman. In 1967 the Society produced a Tenth Anniversary Handbook edited by Kay N. Sanecki and in the *Bulletin* of 1967 Vol 3, No. 6, there is an article by Mrs Sanecki on 'The History of the Hardy Plant Society', but new members may not have seen this, or possess a copy.

Before going further it should be mentioned that from 1962 to 1971, Mr E. Michael Upward did ten faithful years as the Society's Hon. Treasurer until it was taken over by Mr Ron Noakes, a banking man who keeps our heads above water. When Mrs Sanecki retired as Hon. Editor in 1969, Mr Kenneth A. Beckett took over and continues to hold this position today.

By October 1970 Miss Pole had decided to retire from the office of Chairman and she wrote to me asking me to consider nomination, saying—'Of course you would find Miss White an excellent Secretary to work with'. And how right Miss Pole was. Without the help and guidance of Miss Barbara White the Society would not be where it is today. In fact, Miss White has served the Society most loyally ever since she took over as Secretary in 1963.

Suggestions that a Seed Exchange should be run by the Society were first made in 1964, but there is no further reference in the records until 1970 when Mrs D. Horne of Timberland, Lincoln, began its organisation. She gallantly continued the task until 1978 when Mrs Jane Smallwood of Hythe, Kent took over. Since the scheme started it has reached the stage when 10,000 packets of seeds need to be packed each year. Fortunately the Northern Home Counties Group are now helping with this onerous task which, in 1981, included approximately 1,150 different species and varieties, some from members overseas.

Since the H.P.S. started in 1957 no fewer than seven groups have been formed and are flourishing. Nottingham, Southern Counties, North Western, North Home Counties, South Western Region, Western Counties, and already a nucleus of Essex members are considering starting an Essex Group. In America a group has formed, 'The Pacific North West Hardy Plant Society' which says much for the interest in hardy plants across the Atlantic. In 1973 the Nottingham Group initiated the compilation of *The Hardy Plant Directory*. The leading lights behind this ambitious venture are Mr & Mrs R. Grout of Thurgarton, Notts., and in 1975 the First Edition of the *Hardy Plant Directory* was published and almost sold out before the print had had time to dry. A second edition was published in 1978–1979 and a third is in preparation, and I am sure all members will look forward to its publication.

In 1977 we celebrated our coming of age and it was fitting to hold this special event at Bressingham, the home of our President, Mr Alan Bloom and patriarch of the Hardy Plant Society. A full account of our Twenty-first celebrations appears in Vol. 5 No. 4, 1978 by John G. Scott Marshall, formerly editor of *Gardeners Chronicle*.

Further Society ventures include the formation of various plant groups: Geranium, Hosta, Euphorbia, Variegated Plants and the Propagation Scheme. There is also an advisory panel and a list for plants wanted. Most recently started is a group of enthusiasts who are dealing with the conservation of hardy plants. Members from England, Scotland, Wales and Belgium open their gardens annually for the enjoyment of other members and each year there are outings in the summer and autumn when we visit gardens of interest.

Publicity stands are staged at the R.H.S. Hall, London, also in Harrogate, Essex and Southport, and at a number of local shows.

Even if members are unable to attend the outings and meetings, they have plenty of good reading matter in the annual bulletin and in the three-yearly *News Letters* compiled by our Hon. Secretary Miss Barbara White.

This year marks our Silver Jubilee and we look forward with confidence to another twenty-five years of interest in hardy plants.

In the eight years since the above was written much has happened in the Society including, the death in 1987 of the Secretary and dedicatee of this volume, Miss Barbara White. The Society has gone from strength to strength, with membership topping the 6,000 mark and still rising. Local groups have grown considerably in number and have become the life-blood of the Society with some groups holding two or more well-attended events every month. The *Hardy Plant Directory* has become *The Plant Finder* and now sells over 15,000 copies annually bringing in welcome money and giving very good publicity. In keeping with its constitutional requirement to promulgate information about hardy plants the H.P.S. now publishes a series of monographs in conjunction with a major publisher. For a number of years the Society has exhibited at the Chelsea Flower Show.

The Society is alive and flourishing. (Ed.)

The main text originally published in 1981. Volume 6, number 1

Alas, Dear Friends

by Wendy Carlile

HAVING been brought up in the thick of the plant growing business I feel very fortunate that my memory can just go back before 1939.

Being involved ever since with the growing commercially of hardy plants, I have known many great plantsmen who were such characters and who freely saw one another through difficult times, of which there were many. For a lot of them, plants were their only love and I am afraid they often came before themselves or their families. Much of their time was taken up working amongst the plants which was most important to them, so that office duties like the paying of bills came very far down the list of priorities.

As I remember, my father was always out and about before 7.30 a.m. to see staff in on time, then to walk round looking at the plants to see for himself the jobs that needed doing. At this time, he occasionally had the good fortune to spot a novelty growing in the large batches of plants being grown. Those not sold retail were offered wholesale in the spring to the trade.

Of course, quite a few novelties were raised by keen amateurs, some by accident and some by planned breeding. Two good examples of this were Mr Frank Bishop with his delphiniums and Mr Russell with his lupins. These plants were promoted and distributed by the late Jimmy Baker of Bakers' Nurseries, Wolverhampton. Here indeed was a most delightful man, but quite unlike most nurserymen in that he was a very shrewd business man and also found time to be Chairman of Wolverhampton Football Club. Interestingly enough, being very lame in no way hindered him from moving amongst his plants, even if he was aided by his large American car.

At the same time as this there were many nurserymen raising their own new plants either by planned breeding or with the help of mother nature. I well remember the latter method giving us a marvellous double *Rudbeckia purpurea* which we kept going for several years before, alas, its lack of stamina finally caused it to disappear.

What a good thing it is that the memories of these plantsmen live on in the names of their plants. Ernest Ladhams of Elstead in Surrey still has *Hypericum* and *Cimicifuga* 'Elstead Variety' appearing in catalogues. Then there is *Campanula lactiflora* 'Prichards Variety', *Achillea prichardii, Geranium* 'Russell Prichard' to name just a few from that well-known nursery in Christchurch, Hampshire, now no longer in existence. Wm. Wood & Sons, of Taplow, Berks gave us *Aster amellus* 'Mrs Ralph Woods', while Mrs Margery Fish is remembered by *Artemisia* 'Lambrook Silver', named after the village in which she lived. From Perry's of Enfield came *Papaver* 'Perry's White', still in great demand; what a lot of plants they introduced. Who can remember George Phillips of *Thalictrum* 'Hewitts Double' fame? And of course there are so many more that will come to mind. My father would use 'Loddon' for the plants he raised, Waterers, 'Wargrave', Sunningdale their own name, and Blooms use either family Christian names, or Bressingham, the name of the village where the nursery is situated. They of course, have raised and introduced by far the most noteworthy plants in recent years. Before the last war we had regular visits from Dutch nursery firms who introduced many good plants. Since the war we have had some good plants raised in Germany, one of the best in my mind being *Aster novae-angliae* 'Almer Pötschke'.

As the plantsmen of the past have died, there seem alas, few coming along to replace them. The change in the style of nursery operation has a lot to do with this, many nurseries operating as Garden Centres where little growing is done. What plants are grown are in much fewer varieties. Because of this, young people do not get the chance to handle and see the range of good plants, and to evaluate one against another.

This restriction of variety does mean it is no longer worth growing plants with a poor constitution, which is probably not a bad thing. There are however, other very good plants which either do not propagate easily or do not take happily to the soil-less potting mediums much in use today when most sales are made in containers. These are the ones which are not really economic to grow commercially any more and will owe their survival, if indeed they do survive, largely to amateur growers.

Other plants sell themselves and it is very noticeable that most people today buy their plants from their appearance rather than for their names. This shortens the selling season for hardy plants considerably, but it does mean that those with a long flowering season sell best. My advice to people who enquire, is always to ask how long the plant is in flower. All this however, still means there are many good plants grown that the average man in the street knows nothing about.

Horticultural writers do a wonderful job in informing their readers of interesting and good plants and particularly of some of the less common plants. Many people are however, discouraged when they find that these plants are not readily available, but diligent searchings will often discover them being grown by a nurseryman somewhere.

One thing that saddens me greatly is that a number of plants come onto the market in a blaze of publicity, demand is created and large numbers bought by an unsuspecting public and who then find their new plant has poor constitution, or that it is no better than others already grown.

The emphasis on the types of plants grown has changed greatly in the last forty years. The large grand herbaceous borders have gone because time and labour is so costly. This has meant we no longer have the firms who showed groups of pyrethrums, helianthus, heleniums, echinops, eryngiums, chrysanthemums, asters, irises, delphiniums and subjects like these. The beginning of the end for such borders came with the introduction of the mixed border while the new idea of island beds directed interest to the smaller, sturdier sorts, especially as the average gardens of today are far smaller than those which were the home of the now old fashioned herbaceous border.

Today, it is not really possible to make a living from growing plants alone and many small nurseries survive only because usually all the family help out, virtually unpaid, or the wives have jobs outside horticulture. This is sad for the growing of those well-loved plants which are not good garden centre sellers.

What is the future, a wise man would not venture to say. Will love alone be enough to conquer for a few mad folk like ourselves, or will keen amateurs with their plant museums stand alone, perhaps with a barter system for rare plants? Who knows!

Originally published in 1981. Volume 6, number 1

Favourite Perennials in my Garden

by Christopher Lloyd

TO a large extent my favourite perennials are those that do best for me on a heavy, clay-based soil. Many of them are dirt common. Rarity has an appeal that's hard to deny, I admit, but I'm no snob about plants and those that flourish and look marvellous can be as common as they please; they are still for me.

Campanula persicifolia, for instance, which is uphill work on light, sandy soils, adores us and seeds all over the place. When it seeds into a low growing, colonising fern like the oak fern, *Gymnocarpium dryopteris*, or the maidenhair *Adiantum venustum*, it is a weed and has to be extracted with a sharp-pointed trowel as quickly as possible. But on many other occasions it seeds itself in dark places under bushes where you'd never have thought of planting anything, enjoys itself and contributes handsomely with its mauve or white bells (in roughly equal proportions) to the cottage garden medley of the late June garden.

Sometimes it achieves a really artistic effect—and I do think one should develop an eye for where a plant is growing as much as for how it is growing. White *C. persicifolia* coming out from underneath the daisy bush *Olearia macrodonta*, then likewise decorated with clusters of white blossom, its own slightly grey green foliage also contributing, was one such occasion. And blue *persicifolia* at the foot of my 'Zéphirine Drouhin' rose with shocking pink flowers, is another happy accident.

Campanula lactiflora behaves in the same self-sowing way, but makes a larger, tougher plant with deep thick roots. Again it will put itself in just the wrong place. I had one coming out of the centre of a *Skimmia* bush that looked too ridiculous. I hate throwing such seedlings away. Nowadays, as soon as I spot them I transfer them to rough turf. This, since I saw them flourishing in long grass in a Scottish garden. They looked beautiful. The owner told me that in autumn this same patch is thick with colchicums. All that's necessary is to cut the grass between the campanula's July flowering and the colchicum's appearance in late August.

Now every lactiflora seedling is a slightly different colour. The deeper shades look splendid in the company of the vivid rosy-purple *Penstemon* 'Garnet', especially if there is a back-up of purple foliage, as it might be *Cotinus*. The pale campanulas, which usually make the tallest plants, look super coming through the skirts of the silvery, willow-leaved pear, *Pyrus salicifolia*. You don't have just to think of hardy plants as units or groups in herbaceous reserves with others of their kind.

Japanese anemones seldom look wrong. They have the freshness of spring flowers and yet they bloom for us as persistently as bedding plants from early August to mid-October. I like both the pink kinds and the white, but not the doubles. I love many double flowers but doubling in anemones (and you notice this equally in the 'St Brigid' and *fulgens* of spring) gives rise to many narrow petals which are not nearly as beautifully shaped as the broad petals in the single bloom. The single white Japanese anemone, with its green button eye, and its circle of yellow stamens, is perfection.

Of course it does run and get into other plants, but that is not a serious defect. It is surprising how well white anemones look against a pale or white background. I noticed this in Hugh Johnson's Essex garden last August where they grew against the house in front of windows with white frames and bars. In another friend's garden they looked marvellous mixed up with the green and white foliage of the dogwood, *Cornus alba* 'Elegantissima'. The bush would never need to grow overwhelmingly big as you can cut it back as much as the situation demands each winter. In my own garden I reckon the anemone shows up nicely against the pale grey filigree of *Artemisia arborescens*.

Lots of plants thrive in moist shade and I have plenty of that. I only recently realised that the water forget-me-not, *Myosotis scorpiodes* (*M. palustris*) doesn't need to grow in water to be happy. In my first attempt to please it I hoiked a bit out of a local dyke and planted it at the pond edge near the lesser spearwort, *Ranunculus flammula*. I'd seen the two together at the water side in Sheffield Park gardens, in mid-Sussex, and thought how well they associated. Can there be non-flowering strains of the myosotis? At any rate mine proved to be one such. Then I was given a clone (which also comes as like from seed as peas in a pod) called 'Mermaid'. It is reasonably compact, as water forget-me-nots go, and it flowers non-stop from late May till autumn, just in a damp border with no special attention required. The blue-yellow syndrome is satisfying.

Ranunculus gramineus

Here you find it all in the one flower where a ring of yellow at the centre of pure blue petals looks so much like an eye.

I keep trying to find the right mates for a favourite buttercup, *Ranunculus gramineus*. Its leaves are of the spearwort persuasion, being lance shaped but distinctly glacous. The plant, which is tuber-rooted, is clumpy and throws up a foot-tall, branching inflorescence of larger than average buttercups in mid-May. They are not quite the deep butter yellow of our native buttercups but just a shade lighter. There are two blue flowered perennials that both go well with this. *Omphalodes cappadocica* is like a larger more intensely than average blue forget-me-not with evergreen foliage that looks extremely shabby in winter but by the time of its prolonged spring flowering most of this has been overtopped by young growth. It is only 9 in (23cm) tall and will, if required to, flower in deep shade, even among evergreen shrubs. However, the buttercup prefers an open site. Then there is *Ajuga pyramidalis* with spikes of very deep blue flowers on a clump-forming plant. This is barely 9 in (23cm) tall and it has none of the running, stoloniferous habit of bugle, *A. reptans*. *Pyramidalis* may sow itself a little; that's all. If you got these three species together and then planted a clump behind them of the exceptionally late flowering yellow jonquil, 'Tittle Tattle',

Veratrum album

you'd be delighted with the result, but I must confess I've not seen this jonquil in the bulb catalogues that come my way, of late.

This year I've also treated *R. gramineus* as a bedding plant and have plonked some hefty specimens of common borage behind them.

Veratrum album likes me, I am flattered to relate. It is a particularly effective species, since its proudly held, 5 ft (1.5m) candelabrums show up so well, with their white stars, at a distance. Even as they fade to green they continue to look good for many weeks. Furthermore the leaves continue fresh all through its flowering season, unlike *V. nigrum* where, after a fabulous start in spring, they quickly become torn to shreds, mainly by slugs.

V. album is a biennial flowerer with me. I had a spectacular display this year, not one spike last, a good showing the year before. I suspect that it also behaves like this in the wild. I saw it in the Carpathians in Slovakia and Romania last June, and it is there one of the commonest of all plants, yet practically all were blind. I saw no more than half a dozen flowering stems. This cannot be an annual non-event, else it would not be so widespread.

The only reason you do not see more of this top notch plant in British gardens is because it is so slow of increase. To be multiplied on any scale it must be raised from seed and it takes four or five years to reach flowering size.

Although it is perhaps a little less handsome, the same remarks apply to the tallest and stateliest of all the gentians, *Gentiana lutea*. Its ribbed leaves and bracts are magnificent, the axillary clusters of yellow flowers look fine, but it is again an every-other-yearer. So (while I'm on this intriguing subject) is *Eucomis bicolor*, a bulbous plant carrying solid 2 ft (60cm) spikes of whitish stars, edged in purple. Above the flowers is a pineapple-like tuft of foliage. Here is something different for the late summer and early autumn garden. Though it will not be hardy everywhere, a sunny, south-facing border will please it in most localities. You'll have kittens every year, waiting for its re-appearance, which is generally not till mid-June.

The flowering spikes are pollinated by bluebottles. I'm no expert on these insects but the ones attracted have bodies of a particularly alluring, metallic sheen. They are similarly drawn to the fluffy white spikes of cimicifugas. Here my favourite is the September-flowering *Cimicifuga ramosa*. It is an imposing plant rising to 7 ft (2.1m) on my heavy soil and the white flowers are set off by black-avised

Tricyrtis stolonifera

stems. These branch a little, the side spikes flowering later than the central one. The seed pods are ripe my mid-October and should be gathered quickly for long-lasting indoor arrangements.

Another late flowerer that yet manages to ripen its seeds in double quick time is the toad lily, *Tricyrtis stolonifera*. This (and its relations) is a plantsman's plant, one to stare at in wonderment at close quarters. Obviously liliaceous, rather like a martagon lily flower upturned, the segments mauve with large purple spots. A customer visiting my nursery asked me what it was. 'The toad lily', I told her, making things easy with an English name. 'I don't like toads', said she recoiling, and that was that. My strong sense of offence was caused by the aspersion on one of my favourite garden friends; toads are delightful creatures.

Toad lilies are easily raised from seed; I don't know about the cimicifuga. I keep meaning to try. *Eucomis bicolor* germinates quickly from a spring sowing. *Gentiana lutea* must be sown in autumn, the container exposed to frost, and will then come back like cress, in the spring. So too with the willow gentian, *G. asclepiadea*, which is a lovely plant, its blue trumpets so flatteringly displayed along the top sides of 2 ft arching stems. It has a way of seeding itself here into a damp lawn, and I often rescue its seedlings before the spring mowing season starts in earnest.

Dactylorrhizas are particularly satisfactory garden orchids, at home in many situations in sun or in shade but generally preferring moisture. They have been hived off by the botanists from *Orchis*, and from the gardener's point of view they have the practical advantage that a single root planted in a humus-rich border will quickly multiply so that you will soon be pulling the clumps to pieces (which can be done at almost any season with impunity) and moving them around to try in many other positions. *Orchis* tend to remain solitary and as their raising from seed is an exacting procedure, they are not likely to become popular.

Dactylorrhiza foliosa is undoubtedly the most dramatic species in my June garden with its solid, reddish purple spikes. They last a good month in condition. But *D. fuchsii* (*Orchis maculata*), the spotted orchid, is excellent in many ways, as a border plant where it makes clumps, in rough grass where it makes drifts and also when it seeds itself into paving cracks or into clumps of perennials like irises, that you seldom get around to disturbing. The colouring of its mauve spikes varies in different seedlings as do the leaf markings.

Of the rodgersias I am, I know, not being very original in saying that *Rodgersia pinnata* 'Superba' is the tops. From the moment its purple shoots first push through in spring to the last gasp of its long-lasting dusky reddish inflorescences in autumn, it always takes your eye whenever you are passing. The clone 'Superba' has the strongest dose of red pigment in it, but is far less vigorous than other clones and these are worthwhile too. I have an unnamed one given me years ago by Maurice Mason which is well enough pigmented with nice pink flowers, later darkening as they seed, and it grows about a foot taller than 'Superba', so it goes well behind it. Any batch raised from seed of a pigmented form (white flowered *pinnata* is a bit dull) should give worthwhile progeny. In front, copying Graham Thomas's recommendation, I have a dwarf hosta, 'Buckshaw Blue'. The contrast in leaf form and colour fairly jumps at you in spring, but the hosta doesn't stay the course like the rodgersia.

Originally published in 1981. Volume 6, number 1

Geranium kishtvariense: a new introduction

by David Sampson

TO some gardening folk winter can be a bit of a drag; the weather and the hours of daylight usually dictating the time spent in the garden. For me any unproductive periods are used in catching up with reading matter; preferably the accounts of the plant collectors. As I read I often wonder whether there are any plants left to collect, especially when one learns that, for example, Ludlow and Sheriff collected 25,000 specimens, not to mention those collected by Kingdom-Ward, Forrest, *et al.* But of course new species are being found and introduced all the time and we are all trying for the new good form or hardier form, and so it goes on.

One such plant came to me a few years ago which had been collected by Roy Lancaster during the Kashmir tour of 1978. Although on the tour, I was not present when a geranium was found in the woodland around the village of Gulmarg, 8,500 feet up in the Himalayas. When compared with known species its stoloniferous rootstock clearly separated it from its near relatives. It was subsequently named *Geranium kishtvariense* after the valley in which it was found.

From the original seed (Lancaster 159) Roy raised plants at his home near Winchester. It was from these plants that I received seed from which two young plants were subsequently planted out in light shade, where they grew slowly for two years, not flowering until the third. Although the plants are still quite young they are showing what I believe to be an exciting new plant for the garden.

The flower is a bright deep pink with an irridescent quality which does not lose its brightness on a dull day. They are about 1½ in (3cm) in diameter and arranged so that they are held well above the foliage on 9–12 in (23–30cm) stems. Flowering starts in May/June and goes through to October, with the occasional bloom in November. The leaves, deeply divided with a shining pale green surface and growing to a height of about 6 in (15cm), are produced from a slowly increasing root system, forming a loose clump. It dies right back in winter showing no sign of its existence.

At the moment I have planted it amongst woodlanders such as hostas and 'Wada' form of *Saxifraga fortunei*. One colour combination that goes well is the blue leaved *Hosta* 'Halcyon'. Nearby is the rare dwarf *Fothergilla alnifolia* which has sent a few suckers into the geranium, and the effect of the two together when the *Fothergilla* turns to its autumn colours is quite stunning.

As far as cultivation goes it doesn't seem to mind the alkaline soil of Winchester or the acid soil of East Sussex. I doubt if it will tolerate dry conditions and would recommend the usual well drained but moisture retentive soil. Full sun has yet to be tried, as early attempts at cultivation have bowed to the plant's woodland habitat, but like most geraniums it will probably grow well in the open where it would associate nicely with grey and silver plants.

As a garden plant it should be a winner. Plants and seed have already been circulated in this country and stocks are being built up to ensure its further distribution.

Originally published in 1983. Volume 6, number 3

Cosmos atrosanguineus

by Richard Bird

COSMOS *astrosanguineus* is one of those charismatic plants which one occasionally sees in established gardens such as Sissinghurst, and which immediately has one under its spell. Unfortunately falling under its charm is one thing, acquiring it is another. Until recently no nursery stocked it, and few gardeners had plants to give away—both due to the difficulties of propagation.

The plant was originally introduced from Mexico at the beginning of the nineteenth century, and it bears a resemblance to that other Mexican, the dahlia, both in the shape of its flower and in its tuberous rootstock. The flower is a dark maroon, almost chocolate brown in colour. The resemblance to chocolate does not end with the colour; it is blessed with a rich chocolate scent. The whole plant has simple elegance, with the flowers arching on 18 in (45cm) stems from a central clump. The flowering season is from late summer until the frosts. It prefers a sunny position in free draining but moisture-retentive soil.

Margery Fish knew of a white form. I am not certain whether I like the idea, the type being so beautiful, but I still have sufficient curiosity to wish to see it—perhaps it smells of milk chocolate!

It is a difficult plant with which to make associations because of its dark calm quality; too much colour or 'noise' around it can certainly detract from it. The most difficult time is when the plant is young, with only a few flowering stems; later, when it is mature it forms large clumps which are perfectly capable of holding their own. Being a late flowerer it is likely to find itself alone in the border, and certainly any dying or dead material should be removed. One of my plants is backed by a short, white form of *Anemone* × *hybrida*, which beautifully sets it off; one of those accidental associations that give so much delight in a garden.

Coming from Mexico it has long been considered tender, but many plants hitherto thought of as tender are now treated as being hardy. This may be through a bolder approach to gardening, through more knowledge of the tolerance of plants, or just the lack of paid gardeners to lift and replace plants each year. *Cosmos atrosanguineus* is now treated as hardy in much of the country. Some people still lift it late in the autumn and store it in a frost-free position away from mice. This is still probably sound advice in the colder, wetter parts of the country, but for most of us it is now considered sufficient to give it an insulating layer of bracken or leaves.

It is very difficult not to panic each spring, imagining that its non-appearance is due to the ravages of winter after all. This is because it is a very late riser, not usually showing above ground until the end of May. Last year one of my plants did not appear before July, by when I had long given it up. Therein perhaps lies one explanation for its reputation for not being hardy; gardeners have either deliberately dug it up believing it dead, or accidentally dug it up or overplanted it, not realising that it was still there. Being susceptible to frosts, it is a good thing that it keeps its head well down until they are over.

Propagation is usually given in books as being from seed, but I have never known it to set seed in this country. The normal way is by taking cuttings, and herein lies the reason for its rarity. Being late into growth it is difficult to get the rooted cuttings to develop sufficiently large tubers before they die back for the winter. Lack of stored material in the tubers means no plants the following year, however healthy the plants looked the previous autumn. One nursery, Washfield, has successfully had a large quantity propagated by giving the plants light and warmth through the winter, thus allowing for continuous growth. The plants subsequently overwintered perfectly the following year. With any luck this breakthrough will ensure that the plant will not be so rare in future; its charm certainly not depending on its rarity.

Originally published in 1983. Volume 6, number 3

Mertensia

by Paul Oliver-Smith

ONE of the perpetual mysteries of gardening is why some of the most beautiful plants that seem to have no vices or pests, just are not in everybody's garden. Surely nobody really enjoys spraying or dead heading or staking.

The borage family is not on the whole very spectacular, tending to be rather bristly and unpleasant to the touch, and preferring dry sandy soil; but one genus, the *Mertensia* surely has some species for everybody, some prefer moist shade and others sunny gravel. Of the 50 or so species which come mainly from North America and South-East Asia there are only four fairly easily obtainable from specialist nurseries, one of which is actually a British native.

The first to flower, *Mertensia virginica* pushes its bunch of soft blue green oval leaves through the bare earth in March to be followed by 2 ft (60cm) stems bearing on their arching ends sprays of mid-blue flowers. These are 1 in (2.5cm) long and are shaped like a Fifties ball gown: a smooth body with a curiously fluted bell in the purest of sax blue. They exude a sweet spicy scent, hence the name given to them, by the pilgrim fathers, of Virginian Cowslip. The plant goes on flowering for all of May if grown in its favourite site of moist shade, and if grown amongst low shrubs its scent is delightfully entrapped. The whole plant reverses itself and disappears below ground in July in a most tidy way.

This plant does seem to me to offer so many advantages of growing in a damp shady spot, having both attractive flowers and leaves, that to be provided with such a lovely smell as well, is truly gilding the lily. The only pests that seem to be of any significance are slugs and here a judicious layer of cinders or sharp gravel about the crown before the leaves appear does seem to be an effective deterent.

If they can be found there are two other forms, a pink 'Rubra' and a white 'Alba' form but they cannot eclipse the purity of the original, the colours somehow not really fitting the leaves but for the collector of white variants of everything, it is a must.

Mertensia virginica

While *M. virginica* is flowering prodigously a shorter version, *M. echoides* from the Himalayas, is putting up its foliage. This tends to break the soil in several individual bunches and is in flower in June. The blooms are a little smaller and unscented—but of a glorious deep rich blue and the bells, dangling from every curved stem sway gracefully in the summer breezes. It does not hurry underground and it is not uncommon for one to be spoilt by a second crop of flowers later in the year during September. The same conditions suit it well though it is not adverse to more sunshine but still with moist soil.

For the sunnier site *M. ciliata* from the Rocky Mountains is a treasure having distinct blue green leaves beautiful in themselves for a foliage effect. In late June the typical arched sprays, this time of sky blue flowers, appear but these start as pink buds giving an attractive gradation of colour, slowly changing as they become more open.

The three foregoing are relatively easy to locate and establish in almost any garden but if any of the following species can be obtained then they are well worth the hunt and the time spent in providing the right niche for them.

Of the tall species *M. paniculata* from Utah stands out with its profuse sprays of small flowers of a clear sky blue which are at least 2 ft (60cm) above the foliage. From the same state comes *M. brevistyla* which is less than half its height but again a good blue.

M. siberica confusingly also from the northern USA, and not the USSR, has a similar two-colour spray only 6 in (15cm) high of pink buds opening to mid blue not unlike lungwort.

Variations of the theme are *M. longiflora*, again from the USA which has grey-green leaves and the flowers occur much earlier in April being narrow tubes with only the last quarter bell shaped.

Breaking right away from the now familiar bell shaped flowers are the open five pointed blue stars in bunches at the ends of the stems which occur in one of the Himalayan species which would grace any rock garden that is not too arid. This is *M. coventryana* and should be much more frequently grown.

Found in the same mountainous region is *M. moltkoides* which is a spreading plant which has brilliant blue flowers on 6 in (15cm) stems. This does well in the front of a moist border as it keeps its colour for a long time.

Our own *M. maritima*—Northern Shorewort—is quite untypical. It spreads over the surface of gravelly soil in the full sun with its pointed fleshy glaucous leaves each with a scattering of large glands. These leaves earn it the name of Oyster Plant, delicious in salad. The familiar pink bud becomes mauve with a white throat when open. It has to be said that this is not an easy plant—its habitat is sharply draining sand but with the humidity maintained by sea mists and drizzle, a littoral alpine perhaps.

The nearest the mertensias get to the bristly leaf of the borage is *M. lanceolata* which comes from one of the more Southern state of Colorado. This has broad rather leathery leaves each with a fringe of hairs at the edges and the usual spray of dangling bells begins with the buds, clear pink which slowly turn to a pure turquoise as they open. From the other side of the Pacific in Japan there comes a very similar hairy leaved *M. pterocarpa* but this is doubtfully in cultivation.

So far as propagation is concerned, as with so many plants, seeds should be sown when fresh. This does mean trying to liaise with an overseas enthusiast as, excellent though the various seed schemes are, there is a long period between seed collection and delivery. However, established plants do respond to moving every five years or so, so that is the time to carry out root division of the thick fleshy fang like roots to provide multiplication, during the winter between October and March.

Perhaps through the efforts of someone reading this article some of the other species will become more readily available to the general public. Such a sadly neglected genus deserves to be better known.

Originally published in 1984. Volume 6, number 4

Introductions from Bressingham

by Alan Bloom

IT occurred to me recently to tot up the numbers of cultivars I'd raised and introduced since I began to dabble in 1926 and was surprised that it just topped a hundred. Naturally it pleases me when I see other nursery catalogues listing some of these and I suppose the majority are still in cultivation, but, sad to say, a few appear to be no more through lack of constitution or some other hazards along with a few more which have been superceded. I can make no claims as an expert hybridist, but have always had a fascination for raising from seed, hoping to find something good where breaks are liable to occur. In the early days, when my nursery was at Oakington near Cambridge, hopes included a find or two which would further my ambitions and improve my slender finances, but in recent years though with less time to dabble, my efforts have been directed more to introducing little known species and working up stocks of special selections.

The first seedling I named in 1927 and *Dianthus* 'Oakington' is still going strong. At that time my father's main efforts were on market flowers, and in taking up his interest in *Heuchera* for this purpose, *H.* × *brizoides* 'Bloom's Variety' emerged to gain an A.M.R.H.S., I think, in 1928. By 1931, the Oakington nursery was my sole responsibility and other heucheras came along, one being 'Coral Cloud' which superceded 'Bloom's Variety', and during the 30s several others were raised and named. From 1934 to 1965 I was wholesale only, which tended to restrict outlets of new plants although several were raised and introduced to the trade. Not all stood the test of time, and I want to mention a few of these in the hope that someone may still be successful in keeping them whereas I failed to do so.

Some of the 'ity' erigerons proved unreliably perennial, and I have lost the dwarfest of them—'Dimity', with its long display of pink flowers. So too has *Aubrieta* 'Mary Poppins', a double pink and at least four of a new range of *Pyrethrum* died out from a virus, just as stocks were large enough to offer. The best of them, the

× *Heucherella* 'Bridget Bloom'

double shell pink 'Venus' and the intense single salmon red 'Inferno', are I fear gone for ever, which is very sad, now that the disease seems to be overcome. These same remarks apply to some outstanding kniphofias, from a cross with *K. galpinii*. There were 'Bressingham Torch' and 'Bressingham Flame' but 'Bressingham Comet' is still with me, though reduced to a small but healthy nucleus. *K.* 'Jenny Bloom'—a very unusual colour has gone, along with some others, old and new, but a new batch of seedlings show great promise. × *Heucherella* 'Bridget Bloom' is not happy now, whereas it used to be so vigorous. Nor is *Aconitum* 'Blue Sceptre', but maybe this needs more fussing. It is certainly worth some kindness, for its stumpy spikes of blue and white are most attractive. Its stable mate, 'Bressingham Spire' continues to flourish but even the other blue and white *A. nepellus bicolor* has lost vigour with me—as has *Campanula latiloba* 'Percy Piper', and the dainty *Omphalodes* 'Anthea Bloom'. *Saponaria* 'Bressingham' was never vigorous, and remains a choice alpine plant, disinclined as it is, to provide much propagating material. I lost a natural hybrid *Mertensia*, which I named 'Blue Drop', because it resented my efforts to increase it. For a time, so did *Potentilla* 'Blazeaway', but lately it has decided to respond. Not so with *Veronica* 'Minuet', which I have lost, though I still have another of this original trio, in *P.* 'Barcarolle'. *Sidalcea* 'Puck' also lost its early vigour and I'm only just hanging on to its mate 'Oberon'—with some sickness beyond my curing so far.

I could make quite a list of cultivars others have raised which for one reason or another have failed to keep going at least with me. Some seem to suffer lack of vigour or become sick from intensive propagation—as happened with the named Russell Lupins. But happily, and by way of contrast, I'll end with a list of my cultivars which have maintained their vigour—and their popularity. *Achillea* 'Moonshine' I very nearly discarded, because it refused to flower. But it was then in shade and once removed into a sunny place it responded so well as to become a best seller. *Agapanthus* 'Bressingham Blue' is now a firm favourite with its deep blue flowers, as is the deep pink semi-double *Anemone* 'Bressingham Glow' and the already mentioned *Aconitum* 'Bressingham Spire'. *Aster novae-belgii* 'Royal Ruby' a dwarfish red keeps its reputation, as does *Astilbe* 'Bressingham Beauty', whilst the pearl pink simplicifolia-type 'Sprite' has become widely grown and loved. *Bergenia* 'Bressingham White' is indeed white, and no fault can be found with the little *Campanula lactiflora* 'Pouffe'. The fiery flowered *Gallardia* 'Mandarin' holds its place and top marks go to *Geranium cinereum* 'Ballerina', also to *Helenium* 'Coppelia'. *Heuchera* 'Scintillation' and 'Red Spangles'. *Phlox* 'Mary Fox' along with 'Eva Cullum', her one time colleague in our office, is much in demand as are most of the new *Crocosmia*—'Lucifer', 'Firebird' and others, and *Echinacea purpurea*, 'Robert Bloom'. *Scabiosa graminifolia* 'Pink Cushion' is always unequal to the demand, and sales for the mossy *Saxifraga* 'Dubarry' have been steady for forty years, as they have for *Thymus doefleri* 'Bressingham Seedling'.

I don't consider the above to be cause for pride, so much as for pleasure and a few have come as chance or even self-sown seedlings. What my fairly long experience has proved is that neither fanfares for a novelty, nor the R.H.S. Awards are the criteria by which a new cultivar becomes a firm or lasting favourite. Nor are the gardening public so very fickle, because in the long run, a plant stands or falls on its own merits, for beauty and reliablility.

Originally published in 1985. Volume 7, number 1

A White Litany

by Trevor Bath

SINCE I became interested in collecting white-flowered plants, and especially since I started doing a talk called 'Pale and Interesting', I've been struck by the banality of many of the cultivar names.

There is a definite surfeit of 'White Queens' and 'White Princesses'. I suppose the idea is to convey a feeling of cool authority, remote and inhuman. Perhaps the theme could be made more realistic and topical by naming a plant 'White Prime Minister' (. . . 'rank and overbearing growth. Difficult to eradicate once established. . .').

One of the more definite royal statements is made by *Primula* 'Queen of the Whites', to whom perhaps *Primula* 'Snow White' is a Lady-in-Waiting? 'Ice' and 'Snow' are also very over-worked sobriquets (*Iberis* 'Snowflake', *Physostegia* 'Summer Snow' etc.) sometimes still with royal connections as in *Monarda* 'Snow Queen' or is it 'Snow Princess'? In my experience this plant is very difficult to obtain, and impossible to grow to the flowering stage once you've got it. Maybe it should be renamed 'Snow Invalid'. 'Bride' is a name that tends to crop up quite a bit, too. But I can never understand why *Dianthus* 'Bridal Veil' has those red splashes on it—very sinister.

I have only lately come to realise how many beautiful white paeonies there are. I'm intrigued by the double variety called 'Laura Dessert'. Was it actually someone's name, or christened after a favourite pudding? It certainly looks good enough to eat, with its golden depths reminiscent of the best quality Cornish ice cream. It reminds me of a scene in a Betty Grable musical where all the chorus girls sported extravagant hats representing popular pudds. 'Lemon Meringue Pie' was especially memorable, and I long to see the film ('Diamond Horseshoe') again.

I've been racking my brains to think of original names for new white plants, preferably with 'edible connections' as they used to say on dear old 'Twenty Questions', as I'm an ardent foodie.

As far as dairy products are concerned, Margery Fish mentioned a violet called 'Skim Milk', so I'm surprised there aren't yet any called 'Yoghurt' or even 'Quark'. Or (back to the Arctic regions) how about 'Avalanche' and a digression into a favourite recipe ('Chicken Avalanche'—boiled chicken pieces on a mountain of rice, masked with an amusing sauce).

There are quite a few names from the bird world, such as *Tradescantia* 'Osprey', *Crocus* 'Snow Bunting' and *Rosa* 'White Wings'—confusingly, there is also a paeony with the same name. Another single white paeony, 'White Innocent' is my current ideal. One of the slides I use, shows the flowers and leaves making a perfect natural composition, worthy of William Morris. *Rosa* 'Iceberg' is a long-term favourite. Unfortunately, in my garden the pure white flowers are thrown into high relief by the black-spot on the leaves.

I must admit that some of the French names do give added glamour to white flowers—think of *Campanula* 'Fleur de Neige', *Philadelphus* 'Manteau d'Hermine' and *Rosa rugosa* 'Blanc Double de Coubert' but I still think *Rosa* 'Little White Pet' takes a lot of beating, both as a name and a plant. *Clematis* 'White Moth' is also an inspired choice, and I love the resounding ring of *Tulipa* 'White Triumphator'.

Pulmonaria 'White Wings'

I'm convinced that the success of *Pulmonaria* 'Sissinghurst White' owes as much to snob appeal as to its intrinsic beauty. My original white *Pulmonaria* came from Glazeley Gardens, years ago, as *P. saccharata alba*, and I can really see no difference between the two, but there is a difference in *P.* 'White Wings' (yes, another one!) which has a distinctive pale pink eye.

I dream of some yet-to-be-discovered plant with fragile, long, narrow petals fluttering and dancing in the breeze, which could be christened 'Paper Chase' (no doubt in the USA it would be renamed 'Ticker Tape Parade').

I really must settle down with Roget's *Thesaurus* one long winter evening and compile a list of suggestions for future use. In the meantime, if anyone has a white-flowered plant of distinction waiting for a name, what better way to honour the indispensable and indefatigable secretary of the Hardy Plant Society than by calling it 'Barbara White'!

Originally published in 1986. Volume 7, number 2

Meconopsis

by Peter Hainsworth

IT seems that gardeners in the south are taking an interest in growing *Meconopsis*—the Himalayan Blue Poppy. Normally that part of the country is too dry for best results, but Members may like to back the weather both ways by growing a few against a run of wet summers.

If permanently moist, gravelly soil alongside a stream can be found, or just a shady and easily watered corner, there is a good chance of success. Wet, slimey, boggy soil is not liked but rather that old gardening conundrum 'a moist, well-drained soil'. In effect, lots of rain. The plant is in full growth in June and July with copious thin leaves and a small root system of very fine roots. One can believe that it would have some difficulty in keeping turgid on an average summer day, so we have to do our best to reduce transpiration and keep the roots moist and well aerated so that they can work at maximum efficiency. Such conditions are the norm here in NW Scotland but those in the south will have problems . . . You have been warned—but like true gardeners you will have a go regardless. Besides there are dryish climates in the Himalayas so some species should work.

They are fairly tolerant of soil pH, the range 5.5 to 6.5 seems best. Mulched annually with plenty of organic matter (garden compost, dead leaves, etc.) as with many other things the range can be considerably extended. They are normally quite happy fully exposed to sun here in Scotland but full sun is normally well mottled by clouds. On clear dry days they do suffer, so shade during the middle of the day but light from at least half the sky is probably the best situation. The foot of a north facing wall is probably the best suggestion, if not too far from a tap and sheltered from wind. They would make marvellous silhouettes against such a background too. Tree shade might be too difficult to keep moist. Most members will by now surely have given up, but I continue for the sake of the odd one or two.

There are about a dozen species and variations available by

diligent searching of seed and plant lists, and that of the Scottish Rock Garden Club is probably the most rewarding. It seems likely that there are rather more specific names than species going around. G. Taylor in *The Genus Meconopsis* did much good work in reducing these, but that was in 1934, and since then a great deal of inadvertent hybridising has been going on especially between *M. betonicifolia* and *M. grandis* and between *M. napaulensis*, *M. regia* and their close friends. Best perhaps to treat these as two groups.

Nearly everybody knows the Himalayan Blue Poppy, nearly always *M. betonicifolia* (previously *baileyii*) or near hybrids, but rarely *M. grandis*. The two species are distinct in leaf; *betonicifolia* as its name implies has an oblong leaf 2–3 in (5–8cm) wide, truncate or cordate at the base and a margin of flattened lobes or serrations. *M. grandis* has a narrowly lanceolate leaf 1–1½ in (2.5–4cm) wide tapering at both ends and less obvious lobing. All other characteristics are so close and variable as to create confusion to all but the expert. In fact I have had plants from nine reputable sources purporting to be one or the other but were all as near as dammit *betonicifolia*. Safer to call them Himalayan Blue Poppies. One of the best strains I had from seed was called 'Crewdson Hybrids', good blue, strong plants and a few white ones thrown in. Also good were S600 and 'Branklyn'. But if you want something really special try the sterile hybrids *M.* × *sheldoni* and 'Prain's Variety' (also called 'Slieve Donard'). These have very large true blue flowers 4–5 in (10–12cm) across. Slow to propagate and expensive so dabble with seedlings first. Some say that this group is monocarpic unless the first year's flower stalk is cut down. There may be some truth in this but my own experience is that it depends on the strain of seed. Some from R.H.S. seed were decidedly monocarpic but most are good perennials. Some strains too give individuals with purplish flowers, which tendency seems to increase towards the end of the season and possibly under dry conditions. The answer is to raise plenty of plants and weed out what you don't like, if you have the strength of mind.

The largest group of names is covered by *M. regia, M. napaulensis* and their relations. These are always monocarpic, lasting one or two years before sending up a robust stalk 4–6 ft (1–2m), the top half of which is a branching panicle bearing several dozen blooms of red, yellow or white crinkly poppies 2–3 in (5–8cm) across. This is spectacular enough but they also have marvellous winter rosettes of beautifully scalloped leaves to 18 in (45cm) across

Meconopsis napaulensis

covered with gold or silver hairs. Worth putting on a hat and coat to see on a drizzly day or frosty day.

The original *M. regia* has probably been eroded away by hybridisation with *M. napaulensis* and would now have to be collected afresh in the Himalayas. The main difference between the two is again in the leaf. *M. regia* has an elliptic leaf tapering to each end and up to 16 in (40cm) long and 3½ in (9cm) wide, with small, sharp serrations. *M. napaulensis* and the rest of the group *MM. paniculata* (yellow), *wallichiana* (white) and *superba* (white) have very ornamental scalloped or even pinnately lobed leaves, and the colour of the hairs varies from plant to plant. (For those who wish to pursue the matter of identification in more detail I can thoroughly recommend the excellent article by Dr J. J. S. Cobb of Aberdeen in the Alpine Garden Society *Bulletin* for March 1984. It will soon cure them.) The R.H.S. Seed Distribution offer some fine plants in this group under collection numbers SSW 3996 and 8474 in wine and yellow. Some, like *M. superba* may do quite well in the south, it seems to like drier conditions than I can offer.

Relatively distinct is *M. horridula*, not as bad as it sounds, a three foot plant with a panicle of slaty blue flowers and bristly stems but easy to grow. The real 'weirdo' of the family is aptly named

M. dhwojii, a rather delicate looking plant 12–18 in (30–45cm) high with deeply cut leaves covered with black bristles, and bearing yellow flowers. Unfortunately everybody asks you to repeat the name. It is monocarpic and another worth trying in the south, but it is not very vigorous here.

M. quintuplinervia is a mat forming perennial with a dullish blue flower to each 12 in (30cm) stem. Mine has had to be shuffled about quite a bit, it is either too wet or too dry. Pale blue flowered *M. latifolia* did badly with me, its leaves covered with black fungal spots and eventually died out during the winter. It is said to grow 3–5 ft (1–1.5m) and might well do better in a drier climate.

I don't seem to have any record of *M. integrifolia*, yellow, monocarpic, to 18 in (45cm) high, but I have tried its hybrid with *M. betonicifolia* called *M.* × *sarsoni*. This grows about 18 in (45cm) with large creamy white flowers at the end of May, but its beauty is invariably spoiled by flopping with the first rain. Again you may do better.

There are several more names 'mentioned in the literature' but nothing notably distinct from the above, except *M. cambrica* which I felt I should not mention, has so far come my way. But then my experience only extends to about ten years so I am still trying new names.

Propagation for monocarpic species has to be from seed and just as easy for most of the others too. The sterile hybrids of *M. betonicifolia* have to be divided which is best done while soil temperatures are high enough for the plants to re-establish quickly, i.e. spring or late summer. Or split them in winter, pot them and keep them covered until spring. Remember the roots are delicate, no need to add insult to injury by too firm potting or planting.

Getting the seed you want is the first problem, getting it in a viable condition is the next. My best suggestion is to beg a pod from a friend, ripe or nearly so, leave it a week or so to air dry, then put it in an envelope in the fridge until spring. Good seed is small but not dustlike, about 1mm in diameter. Or if you have a cold frame try sowing it as soon as ripe and overwinter in the seed tray. They should come up like cress. My experience of buying from a seedsman, or getting it from a seed exchange is that you will be lucky to get half a dozen seedlings; perhaps none at all. The only time I had problems with my own seed was after a dry summer, which confirms my suspicion that the seed will not stand prolonged desiccation at room temperatures. And why should it—the plants are not adapted to that sort of climate. Some crosses are sterile anyway but straight species should be all right. We all have to start somewhere.

The seed is too small to be covered with compost so wet your filled containers well, sprinkle them with about ⅛in (4mm) of grit, and sow on this. A mist spray will snuggle the seeds in the crevices, then cover with clear plastic film. Leave in a light place but never in the sun and germination will take place in three weeks. Sometimes a second germination takes place a few weeks later—probably a dormancy effect. Ordinary cold greenhouse temperatures in March and April are sufficient. Seedlings and young transplants are very sensitive to overheating, usually showing it by turning yellow a week or so later and you wonder what hit them. I suspect that the fine roots get damaged if the compost gets warm. Some primulas are the same.

Two or three weeks after germination the plastic can be removed, but water gently, they have little root. Another three weeks, if you have nimble fingers and they have one true leaf, you can prick them out into a seed tray about 1 in (2.5cm) apart. I use a standard JIP potting compost but leave out the fertilizer base, it sometimes seems to damage the roots. Add instead, at about four trowelfuls to a bucket, some of your garden compost heap; they do better on it. When they reach 1–1½ in (2.5–4cm) high, which will be midsummer, mine go outside in a nursery bed—usually well rained upon and not too much sun—otherwise a few leafy prunings stuck in will carry them through for shade, and water at least once daily. Or you may find it safer to plant into 3½ in (9cm) pots, especially with final transplanting in mind, at least they can be moved around according to the weather.

By mid-August the leaves will be 4 in (10cm) long and you should be looking round for their final quarters, not too easy at a time of year when the garden is choc-a-bloc. Loosen them up with a garden fork so as to get good balls of soil, then puddle them in their new homes with a watering can rather than press them in, and carry on watering until you are rescued by rain.

Wishing you the best of luck and another wet summer.

Originally published in 1987. Volume 9, number 1

Eric B. Smith, 1917–1986

by Diana Grenfell

THE world of horticulture lost a rare figure in March last year. Eric Smith, who died peacefully in a Southampton nursing home after a severe bout of 'flu, has left a wealth of memories in the gardens of hardy plant growers and collectors, not only in Britain but in many other parts of the world.

He was a shy and private person—he never married—preferring to retire behind his plants rather than compete in the hassle of commerce and publicity. Totally shunning the limelight, he sometimes allowed others to reap the pleasures and benefits of the plants he raised—many of which he did not even name himself. Plants dominated his life and his only other interest seems to have been in astronomy.

Born in Southampton into a professional family, Eric attended Bannister Court School until the school closed down and he finished his education at home with a private tutor. He was articled to a quantity surveyor from 1935 until he joined the Army to fight in the Second World War in 1940. He served in the Royal Corps of Signals and took part in the North African Campaigns and in the Salerno and Normandy Landings (D plus 7).

At the end of the war he decided not to return to quantity surveying and took up architecture instead. He became an assistant with Dale & Tutte in Southampton. He abandoned this after four years and turned to plants. He became herbaceous plant propagator at Hilliers of Winchester and worked in the walled garden for four years. This was the time when he raised his famous hellebore crosses, some of which were still growing in the garden of his family home in Archers Road, Southampton until a few years ago. It was whilst he was at Hilliers that he spotted a particularly good blue form of *Hosta tokudama* and it was later named after Buckshaw Gardens, the nursery he started with Jim Archibald. During this time he also raised the first generation of the now-famed × *tardiana* hybrids some of which were distributed to friends in the Southampton area who often visited him when they bought plants from Hilliers.

Former employees of Hilliers who worked with him in the walled garden have praised his ability to spot a good new hybrid or an unusual variegated sport which he would diligently and patiently try to stabilise. He arrived for work at 7.15 a.m. each morning on his bicycle, a 15 mile ride.

However, he still could not settle down and returned to Dale & Tutte for a year whilst turning over in his mind the idea of starting a herbaceous nursery of his own.

Maurice Pritchard, the man he might have teamed up with, eventually took a job elsewhere and, after much correspondence and negotiation, he joined Jim Archibald in 1965 and they formed The Plantsmen nursery at Buckshaw Gardens, near Sherborne in Dorset which soon became a mecca for everyone seeking exciting new hybrids and rare plants not available anywhere else. The nursery was the first of the new breed of small specialist nurseries designed to cater for enthusiasts, both professional and amateur, who would willingly travel a hundred miles or so to pick up a single, much-wanted plant.

Eric's role at The Plantsmen was to raise new plants and propagate the stock whilst his partner, Jim Archibald, looked after the business and marketing side. Some of the best known of these plants were Eric's kniphofias, known as the Auburn Strain, the Buckshaw hybrids, the Lemon Cream Strain and the Strawberry Cream Strain, many of which were sent to the Royal Horticultural Society's trials. *kniphofia* 'Torch Bearer', a further selection of a single clone, gained an Award of Merit in June 1982.

Even more in demand were the hellebores. The best known raiser of hellebores is, undoubtedly Helen Ballard, but Eric excelled in the field of speckled and spotted *H. orientalis* seedlings with a pink ground-colour, known as the Zodiac Strain, the finest of which were named after the signs of the Zodiac. He raised a vigorous yellow hellebore 'Sirius' which was, at the time, outstanding. *HH.* 'Neptune', 'Miranda' and 'Pluto' are his best smaller seedlings from *H. torquatus* and very much sought-after by collectors.

Bergenias were another of Eric's interests and he used the slow-growing white *B. stracheyi* 'Alba' to produce a range of compact hybrids. Of these 'Bach', 'Brahms' and 'Beethoven' were selected and named and 'Brahms', considered the finest in Germany where they are better-known than in Britain, received an award in Munich in 1984.

Eric and Jim had a mutual interest in South African bulbs and they raised and put on the market the fiery orange-scarlet *Crocosmia masonorum* 'Flamenco' which was the result of several generations of selection, and *Schizostylus coccinea* 'Sunrise', which occurred in a first-generation batch of seedlings. This rich, soft pink seedling was another of his Award of Merit plants. His *Agapanthus* 'Blue Moon' received a Highly Commended certificate in the Wisley Trials.

The only truly hardy agapanthus with variegated leaves is Eric's 'Golden Rule'. Not a particularly vigorous, or eye-catching plant or one which I have ever seen flowering, but I have moved it to our garden at Lymington where the mild climate may encourage it to take on a new lease of life. Its leaves are 6–8 in (15–20cm) long, ¼ in (6mm) wide: they are faintly yellow-streaked and have a yellow pencil-thin marginal variegation.

The British Hosta & Hemerocallis Society is currently selecting one of Eric's, as yet un-named × *tardiana* to bear his name. Jim Archibald reports that Eric was reluctant to have anything named after him and Jim only managed this with a white-flowered *Crocus tommasinianus* which he simply had printed in their catalogue without asking Eric's permission.

Although Eric will be remembered best for his *Hosta* × *tardiana* hybrids, which have received extensive publicity in Britain and America and, latterly in West Germany, he was the forerunner of hosta breeders who saw the possibilities of gold-leafed varieties, and his Gold Leaf Strain were distributed from The Planstmen in the early 1970s. Eric used *H. fortunei* 'Aurea' and *H.* 'Kabitan' in an attempt to raise a hosta which retained the gold coloured leaves right through the summer. 'Gold Haze' and 'Pagoda', with good white flowers, are probably the best of these, although the harsh-hued, later named 'Hadspen Samphire' and 'Goldsmith' were very near to his aims.

One of the few hostas actually raised at Buckshaw Gardens was *H.* 'Snowden', a robust, greyish-leafed seedling, probably derived from *H. sieboldiana* 'Alba' and *H. fortunei*. Although a collector's item and a majestic plant, 'Snowden' has never quite attracted the attention that the similar-sized 'Krossa Regal', an American cultivar, has achieved. Undoubtedly Eric's best hosta is one of his first. *H.* 'Halcyon', one of the F1 generation of × *tardiana* hybrids which received an Award of Merit after trial at Wisley.

Eric's time at The Plantsmen was his most successful in

horticultural terms, but he was not an entrepreneur and had no genuine business aspirations. Indeed, his interest was the plants themselves, not their pecuniary value. Typically, when coerced into dumping valueless seedlings he would return to go over them in case some were worth saving.

He settled for safer things when The Plantsmen ceased trading. He went to work for Penelope Hobhouse as Hadspen House as head gardener and propagator for her small nursery. He lived in the Granary Cottage in the grounds of this hamstone manor house where plant collectors from all over the world came to buy his hostas or give him plant material in return for one of his 'treasures'. *Brunnera* 'Hadspen Cream' is one of the many plants bearing the Hadspen epithet which visitors could see growing in the gardens. *Rheum palmatum* 'Red Herald', *Camassia leitchlinii* 'Electra' and *Phormium tenax* 'Merlin' are still there as a reminder of his five years there.

Before his retirement to the family home in Southampton he gave pieces of most of his hosta hybrids to Savill Garden, Windsor Great Park, and to the Royal Horticultural Society's Garden at Wisley where they may now be seen as an important part of the National Hosta Reference Collection.

Originally published in 1987. Volume 9, number 2

Index

Page numbers in *italic* refer to the illustrations